What's Left?

What's Left?
A Political Memoir

TONY BOOTH

with Stephenie Booth

Weidenfeld & Nicolson
LONDON

First published in Great Britain in 2002 by Weidenfeld & Nicolson

A CIP catalogue record for this book is available
from the British Library

ISBN 0 297 82946 7

Weidenfeld & Nicolson

The Orion Publishing Group Ltd
Orion House
5 Upper Saint Martin's Lane
London
WC2H 9EA

Typeset by Selwood Systems, Midsomer Norton
Printed by Butler & Tanner Ltd, Frome and London

Contents

Illustrations

With Annette Crosbie and Rodney Bickerstaff outside Buckingham
    Palace, supporting the 'Pensioners Deserve Better' campaign[7]
With Leo Blair on election night, May 1997[3]
The soon-to-be prime minister and his wife on election night, May
    1997[7]
With Steph, June 2000[3]
At the wedding reception following my marriage to Steph, 2 October
    1998[1]
My daughter Lucy with her husband Stan and my grandson Peter[1]
As narrator in the *Rocky Horror Show*, Southampton December
    1999[6]
In the saddle for *The Duke*, an award winning film written and
    directed by John McArdle[1]
With Jim Cartwright in his play *Prize Night* at the Royal Exchange
    Theatre, Manchester[1]
With Sophie Dahl and Tony Dorrs in *Revengers Tragedy*, a film
    directed by Alex Cox[1]
Trying to organise a family group photograph at my 70th birthday
    party[8]
Me in June 2000[3]

The author and publishers thank the following for permission to use
    photographs:

1 Booth family
2 Mirrorpix
3 Camera Press
4 BFI Collections
5 Popperphoto
6 Topham
7 PA
8 Chris Adams

Family Tree

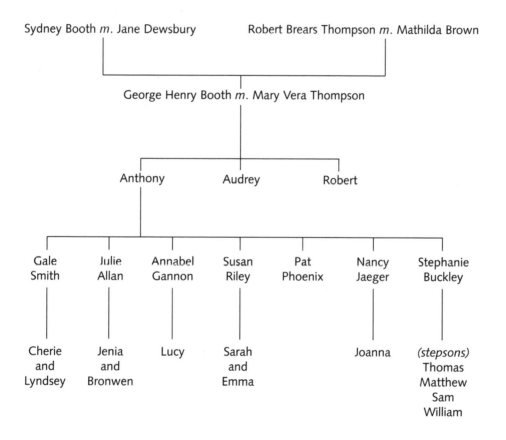

Sydney Booth *m.* Jane Dewsbury   Robert Brears Thompson *m.* Mathilda Brown

George Henry Booth *m.* Mary Vera Thompson

Anthony   Audrey   Robert

Gale Smith	Julie Allan	Annabel Gannon	Susan Riley	Pat Phoenix	Nancy Jaeger	Stephanie Buckley
Cherie and Lyndsey	Jenia and Bronwen	Lucy	Sarah and Emma		Joanna	*(stepsons)* Thomas Matthew Sam William

Acknowledgements

As with any book there is a team of people without whose support it would not have been possible to complete the project. Firstly, I want to thank our agent Jane Bradish-Ellames who initially persuaded me that writing this book was a good idea. She has continued to be a source of much encouragement and support. Through her husband, Ken, Jane has also proved a source of thriving rhododendron bushes for our garden. Jonathan Lloyd, who in the last few months has taken over from Jane as our agent, also furnished much-needed help, steadying wobbling, last-minute nerves. Thanks must also go to our editor, Ion Trewin. Not only the scourge of the split infinitive, his suggestions and advice have proved invaluable. Diane Taylor, the talented journalist and writer, was also a source of generous help and support in the early stages of this project. Finally, I want to acknowledge here my friend Syd Higgins and his generous work on my previous book.

Last, but not least, so much of the work has been done by my wife and comrade-in-arms, Steph. At first a reluctant volunteer – the project was not without its ups and downs and heated debate – she took the stream of consciousness that was my notes and shaped it into a coherent manuscript. She has persuaded, cajoled and when necessary forcefully demanded my honesty over occasionally painful truths. My greatest debt is to her, for she is a constant source of joy and the light of my life.

Tony Booth
May 2002

Prologue

1 May 1997

'The end is where we start from ...'

T. S. Eliot, 'Gerontion'

To avoid serious aggravation from Cherie, I decided to wear one of my son-in-law's suits and a tie to attend the election count at the local sports and leisure centre in his constituency. This actor in a suit always seems to evoke ribaldry and ribbing from family and friends and tonight was no exception, but the reaction from the huge crowd that thronged the roadway and footpaths leading to the count almost blew me away. Amidst the roar greeting the candidate and his wife a voice bellowed out, 'In court are we, Tony?' My son-in-law looked around, realized the miscreant was calling to me ... and laughed. Irked by his response I growled, 'If we lose this one, Tony, we'll deserve more than a bloody court appearance.' Turning, I yelled back to the wag, 'It's for the victory celebrations ... we're going to WIN!' The roar of the crowd's cheers swept us up the stairs and into the entrance. Every policeman in Durham seemed to be there, their usually stern and formidable faces wreathed in smiles. I thought, bloody hell, if the law's happy to see the back of John Major and the Tories, we are home and dry.

Invigorated by that thought as I waded through the backslapping, hugging, kissing members of the Sedgefield Labour Party, the long flight of stairs seemed like an escalator as we were passed from hand to hand. Special Branch officers struggled to get the candidate and his wife through. Almost throttled by the tie I'd been dragooned into wearing, I truly understood what the expression 'necking' meant. The tie was being used like a baton in a relay race as I was swung from one person to another to the top of the stairs. Finally, cheeks reddened and lips bruised, I was bundled into the observation gallery to be greeted by a sighing Cherie lamenting at 'the state of you' as she vigorously readjusted my tie, spat on a tissue and scrubbed the lipstick from my face. Then, running her fingers roughly through my hair, she pronounced there was nothing else she could do and departed for a more worthy cause.

Left to my own devices, I wandered over to join an old friend and constituency chairman, the lovely John Burton. Throughout the building there was a palpable air of expectancy as the early election results started to come in. On the floor of the count the Sedgefield result was a foregone conclusion. From behind the glass in the observation gallery we could see that there were so many votes for one candidate you wondered if there were any others.

'Whose votes are those, John?' I innocently inquired.

'You daft bugger, why man they're Tony's!' he shot back.

'No need for a re-count, eh then?' I answered and we both laughed and settled down to wait.

We'd both been there to see the start of Tony's parliamentary career in 1983 and were pondering if this was the beginning of the end or the end of the beginning, when suddenly my eldest grandson, Euan, bounded up to me. 'Grandad we've just won Crosby!' He yelped the words out like an eager puppy. Although only thirteen, he knew the significance of winning that particular Tory stronghold. I was born and raised in Crosby. My two older daughters, Cherie and Lyndsey, also grew up there in their grandparents' home, only leaving when they went to university. A Labour win in Crosby was almost beyond our wildest dreams. Not even the electoral landslide of 1945 had loosened the Conservative grip in that constituency. John and I struggled to our feet and looked at each other.

'Don't be daft,' I joked. 'If we've won Crosby my greatest fear will have come true – they've started the revolution and forgotten to tell me.'

Euan turned and beckoned me over to a television screen, 'Look at the screen, it's up there. Labour gain Crosby.'

I could hardly believe my eyes ... yes! Crosby a Labour gain. At that moment, Tony walked past. I grabbed him by the arm. 'Tony, we've won Crosby,' I yelled delightedly.

'Don't mess about at a time like this,' he replied.

'But look!' I pointed to the television screen. He looked up at the TV screen. A slow smile spread across his face. That smile remains preserved in my memory. It was a smile that acknowledged all the years of hard work. 'I'd better ...' '... start writing the speech', we finished off his sentence gleefully.

The speech was a great one. Tony was still writing most of his own speeches in those days. They were and are far better than the ones the spin doctors pen for him now. The vast room suddenly started to buzz with anticipation. A bevy of men with machine pistols and flak jackets had been stationed at various vantage points around the room. Not known for their leftish sympathies, they had remained aloof, and even slightly edgy, as the Labour Party members cheered each new result. Some of the security corps were tall, some short, some fair, some dark yet they all managed to look alike to the point where their features became indistinguishable from one another – a prerequisite of the job, I suppose. It seemed but a very short time after the Crosby result that they were reinforced by the real hard men, some in plain clothes, others tooled up. The heavy mob had arrived; even they now recognized the inevitability of a Labour win. Tony sat alone in a corner almost hidden by the phalanx of blue flak jackets and grey suits. Ignoring the celebrations in the rest of the room, he scribbled away at his acceptance speech. Afterwards, I remember joking to Euan that perhaps we had won this election because I had been safely exiled to the Isle of Man working on a film, *Owd Bob*, for most of this election. During previous campaigns I had pounded the streets with the candidates and other Party members calling on the faithful, the ditherers and the downright uncertain to put their cross in the right box. Unfortunately, most of my life I've been 'a trifle short of funds', to use the old thespian's excuse – broke to you and me. So, when offered any reasonable acting work I had to grab it.

I have always loved campaigning, keen to meet the voters on the street and trade jovial (or not) insults about and with the Tories. During previous elections, I had operated very successfully without the 'advice and assistance' of the Millbank machine. This time, however, when I accompanied John Prescott, soon to become Deputy Prime Minister, whom I had known for years, to a few of the northern constituencies we were surrounded by the Millbank 'wonks'. Prescott was keen to play down any sign of old Labour, but I didn't have the slightest urge or inclination to transform myself into an anodyne, grey figure presenting an image that New Labour believed could not possibly offend the sensibilities of the electorate, no matter what their political persuasion. Besides I wasn't that stupid – who in their right mind was going to believe that transformation?

It was April, the start of the campaign, but already Prescott was in a foul mood when I caught up with him in Oldham. He came barging over to me, incandescent.

Pop-eyed and purple with rage, he bellowed, 'You've got a bloody nerve turning up here after what you and that prick of a pal of yours, Ron frigging Rose have done!'[1]

Although somewhat surprised by his outburst, I stood my ground and said, 'What the bloody hell is up with you?'

'Don't come the innocent with me. He's saying that mates of mine are connected to that bloody mess he's created in Donny.'

'You mean that corrupt bunch that are going down the steps?' I countered, 'If they're corrupt they'll get what they bloody well deserve, mates of yours or not, pal!'

My partner Steph (now my wife) and the Oldham parliamentary candidate Phil Lomas were the bemused and stunned observers of this extraordinary performance. Suddenly, as one they performed a lightning pincer movement. Steph grabbed me firmly by the elbow and Phil bravely interposed his body between the two potential pugilists, leading Prescott swiftly away to canvass the opposite end of the market. This quick-thinking, nimble-footed action prevented a confrontation that would have strained the fabled abilities of the spinmeisters of Millbank. One of the local Party members said to me, 'It's the tension, Tony, it's getting to him'.

After about half an hour canvassing, one of Phil Lomas's assistants arrived and hustled us off to a photo opportunity with John Prescott. As soon as I saw the mob of cameras and journalists, I whispered to Steph, 'This'll be good, love.' Prescott saw us coming. He glowered briefly just to show me he hadn't forgotten, but then, politician to the last, he beamed a comrade's welcome and we put a brave New Labour face on things. The photo opportunity finished, we walked across the cobbled market square towards the campaign bus. A keyboard busker started an upbeat version of 'The Red Flag'. As I opened my mouth to accompany him, two of Prescott's minders, quickly alert to this danger, hustled me on to the campaign bus. As John and I sulked our way to the next date at Todmorden, the kind and ever-friendly Pauline Prescott gave Steph advice on how to stay cool and cope with the rigours of the campaign trail. We parted company after Todmorden and it was election night before we met up with the Prescotts again.

[1] Ron Rose, a television scriptwriter, has been at the forefront of the ongoing campaign to expose financial corruption and mismanagement on the Labour-run council in Doncaster. John Prescott is acquainted with several members of the council who have faced court proceedings as a result of this campaign. Knowing I am a friend of Ron Rose, Prescott decided to vent some of his spleen in my direction.

The campaign dragged on for six weeks. John Major's tactics were blatant. He was determined to bore us all into submission with his efforts to hold on to power when all the country just wanted to kiss him and his inept and despised government goodbye. Everywhere I went, everyone I spoke to, including the tax exiles on the Isle of Man (who, incidentally, were preparing to sell up and move to warmer climes at the prospect of a socialist victory), knew we were going to win. The only question was the size of the victory. I told everyone who would listen to bet on a 80–120 Labour majority. So, I guess on reflection I was cautiously optimistic and the bookies won again . . . damn!

At last, polling day dawned and there were queues in my village, Broadbottom. I had rushed back from my filming commitments to vote and to accompany Steph over to Hebden Bridge for her vote. At the polling stations the air was prickly with excitement and Labour Party supporters were gleefully hugging each other, certain in the knowledge that this time we were going to do it. That afternoon I caught a train to Tony's Sedgefield constituency while Steph went down to London, where we had arranged to meet at the Festival Hall later that evening. Boarding a Sprinter for a long journey like Manchester to Darlington is not to be recommended. Jammed in like sardines, with no trolley service owing to the usual 'broken boiler', I managed to find a seat opposite a couple and their luggage. They were perfect casting for a Les Dawson caricature of a northern couple returning from their Spanish holiday complete with sombreros, sunburn and vino. The woman was particularly chatty and boasted that her brother was an official of a northern health authority and that he had employed both her and her husband on considerable salaries to handle public relations. My mother always told me not to judge a book by its cover. Having said that, I have to admit that any talent this couple may have had was certainly well hidden from public view. When questioned on exactly what they did she proudly told me, '. . . not a lot'. Somewhat desperately persisting with this line of conversation, I asked her if she wrote the press releases, to which her husband replied, 'Don't be bloody thick man, she has trouble writing postcards!' They both seemed to find this very funny and fell about laughing. When she finally managed to get her breath back, she told me that her brother wrote them; she just handed them out. Her brother also insisted on fielding all the media calls himself. I made a mental note to tell Tony about this fraud at the National Health's expense. He had always been good at wading in and sorting out corruption, but I thought I would leave it for this evening.

Tony first got his foot on to the lowest rung of the political ladder when in 1984, after just over a year in Parliament, Neil Kinnock put him in charge of ferreting out financial scandals in the City. I tried to help Tony by reading the 'City Slicker' column in *Private Eye* and passing on anything I thought might be of use or interest to him. I was glad to see the back of the health authority couple. Their brash admissions about their sinecure made my blood boil, but this was not the night to be angry. No, tonight would be the turning point, even though I kept telling myself not to get too carried away. We had felt hopeful on three previous general election nights but I couldn't help feeling that tonight would prove to be the sea change the Labour Party so desperately needed and had worked so hard for.

A car was supposed to be picking me up at Darlington station when I arrived in the early evening, but as I stood forlornly on the deserted platform it was obvious that the car had been delayed. To pass the time, I spoke with the four taxi drivers waiting for the next train. We all agreed that tonight was going to be one to remember. The driver who eventually picked me up was a brawny, fleece-jacketed ex-miner in his mid-fifties. He was apologetic, but excited. He reminded me we had met before in 1982 when he had told me that he believed Tony was a future frontbencher. I, in turn, had told him I thought Tony would be Prime Minister before the end of the millennium. Now he was tensely awaiting the final result, as he stood to win ten thousand pounds – acting on my tip, he had put ten pounds on Tony. Would this be considered insider trading, I wondered as I cursed my luck for not taking my own advice? Declaring a vested interest in the result, he had offered his services as a driver and specifically asked that, if I was coming, he would drive me, as he wanted personally to thank me. I told him he was certain to collect and our laughter at my suggestion of a ten per cent commission carried us through to Trimdon.

Cherie's and Tony's house in the constituency lies at the end of a row of terraced miners' houses. To reach it you have to drive up a rutted track. The entrance along the ginnel between the houses had been blocked off by security, leaving only one way in. The road to the house stops halfway down the row of houses and any cars venturing further have to bounce down the track. As soon as we drove on to the road, I saw armed men and women accompanied by guard dogs slavering on their leads. At first I thought it must be some kind of Establishment joke and was nearly overwhelmed by the temptation to borrow Mae West's famous quip, 'Is that a gun in your pocket or are you just happy to see me?' One look at their suspicious faces made me decide it wasn't worth the risk. I had visions of being dragged from the car, bundled around the back of the house and unceremoniously shot. I got slowly out of the car with my hands up squinting into the beaming lights. Only then was I recognized.

A voice called out, 'It's OK, it's only Tony. Where have you been? Your Cherie was expecting you hours ago?'

I lowered my head and blinked as suddenly the lights were switched off. 'In for it?' I asked.

'And how,' a voice called back.

My eyes had now adjusted to the light. Miraculously, the hard, suspicious faces were replaced by beaming ones. Even the dogs had started to wag their tails. The thought that things must be getting better streaked across my mind as, hand-shaken and back-thumped, I made my way to the house.

Cherie and her mother Gale were soup- and sandwich-making for all the extended family, close friends and the security corps outside. They quickly pressed me into the role of a reluctant kitchen porter. The possibility of a government job at last? Still, you've got to start somewhere, as my mother was fond of saying. Dashing from room to room collecting and distributing crockery and food, I kept coming across items of furniture my late wife Pat Phoenix and I had given to Tony and Cherie when they were first starting out. Seeing them always brought memories of Pat flooding back. I had loved her deeply and she would have been so proud of them and their achievements, so excited and happy tonight.

It was the first time I had seen Tony in weeks and as ever we greeted each other with a big hug. 'I used to like that suit' he said, looking me up and down. He was dressed in his usual jeans and tee shirt. He only wore uniform on parade. He disappeared into the study with Alastair Campbell and Jonathan Powell, both of whom had a warm greeting for me. In fact, I was one of the people who suggested to Tony that he should hire the 'Burnley bruiser'. Campbell had previously been the political editor on the *Mirror*. After the media disasters the former Labour leader Neil Kinnock had lurched into – like the enduring image of his head in a lightbulb on the front of the *Sun* – a shrewd tabloid hack was just what Tony needed to fend off the Fleet Street rottweilers.

Cherie's half-sister, Sarah,[2] begged, 'Dad have you got a cigarette?

---

[2] Sarah and Emma are my daughters by Susan Riley. Sarah changed her name when she first joined the actors' union, Equity, as there was already a Sarah Booth on the membership list. She chose 'Lauren' as various friends remarked on her similarity to the young Lauren Bacall, Humphrey Bogart's widow.

I've run out.' Muttering, I suggested that we go outside in accordance with Cherie's non-smoking encyclical. We left by the back door, waved acknowledgements to the security on the gate and went round to the side of the house. We found a quiet spot and, as we were about to light our cigarettes, I noticed a red dot of light on Sarah's jacket. I nodded to her and she pointed at a similar one on mine. I had watched enough action movies to know what a red dot implied ... the night sight of a gun. We stood very still. Cautiously raising my hands, I reminded the two figures I could just make out in the bushes that we were family not foe. They advanced slowly, apologized, and I gave away another two cigarettes as we then all moved into the bushes and they joined us in a furtive smoke.

Back in the house, Cherie had changed into her smart election night suit. I looked at my daughter and felt proud. She had worked hard and grown into this new and demanding role. However, there was still no sign of Tony emerging from the powwow in the study. Cherie in her infinite wisdom – or was it desperation – delegated to me the job of making sure that Tony changed into a suit. I readily accepted this promotion from kitchen porter to valet, the first sure sign of New Labour's meritocracy in action. Whistling 'Things Can Only Get Better', I sauntered into the study and attempted to mime Cherie's instructions to Tony. Despite already being ten minutes late for the count, Tony remained unimpressed by my performance and continued his telephone conversation.

Knowing my daughter as I do, it was with a certain level of trepidation that I returned to the kitchen to report his lack of cooperation. Pushing me roughly aside, Cherie marched down the hall, flung open the study door and using her most authoritative voice instructed Tony to hang up NOW. Both Alastair and Jonathan suddenly found the ceiling extremely interesting. Her order was clearly non-negotiable and Tony sensibly terminated his telephone conversation. He gracefully shimmied around his irate wife, who was still in the doorway, and rushed upstairs. This vocal command that *all* women possess is truly awesome in its power to stop *all* men dead in their tracks. I believe it to be genetic. Using the bathroom after Tony, I noticed the tee shirt he'd been wearing discarded on the floor. It had the Labour election slogan emblazoned across the front. I quickly picked it up. I sensed that we might be about to enjoy an historic victory and I wanted to make sure I had my own personal memento of the day. I've still got that tee shirt, unwashed of course – the sweat is part of the history.

At the count Tony finished writing his speech. We were all – family, close friends and constituency officers – escorted down the stairs and on to the floor of the hall to await the announcement of the result. Tony's acceptance speech was funny, humbling and uplifting. I looked across at his father. Leo's face was a picture of tearful pride when Tony said that his only regret tonight was that his mother was not there to witness the moment. The tears and cheers carried us out in Tony and Cherie's wake. After a brief victory wave, they were ushered by the security men into their car and, sirens blaring, they were driven off into the night. It was now nearly one o'clock in the morning and they were on their way to London.

The rest of us remained standing at the back entrance to the hall. We were dazed and deafened by the noisy, north-eastern delight at impending victory. Suddenly, the security men moved in with well-practised ease, dividing us into groups and shepherding us into separate cars. The rest of the family were then also driven off at speed. I found myself seated in the rear of the vehicle jammed between my daughters, Sarah and Emma. The front passenger seat was occupied by a special patrol group officer, sweating under his body armour and trying not to sit on his automatic pistol. It had been such a long time since I had celebrated a Labour victory. I had almost forgotten what it sounded or smelt like or how much it made my brain sing. We drove out of town and into the darkened countryside.

It seemed we were in the car for a long time and, with no idea where we were being taken, I began to feel slightly nervous. Intimidated by the security men, the normally garrulous occupants of the back seat were silent. This silence started to unnerve me and I turned to Emma and hissed in her ear, 'Where in God's name are they taking us?' Clammy paranoia had kicked in. As the sad victim of too many spy stories, my imagination began to run riot. Maybe they were chauffeuring us to some disused quarry where a firing squad of hooded thugs awaited us. Memories of political gossip and rumours around in the seventies about the Labour Party and the stories of alleged plots by former SAS operatives to launch a *coup d'état* in the event of another Labour election victory contributed to my state of mind.[3] 'We're going to the airport where there's a plane waiting to take you to London', growled a voice from the front of the car. My dark fantasy slid silently away into the night.

[3] Chris Mullin's excellent novel, *A Very British Coup* (1982), later made into a television series, vividly illustrated the fear within certain sections of the Labour Party that the security services would seek deliberately to undermine a Labour government.

We arrived at Teesside airport, shrouded in darkness. Our man extricated himself from the front passenger seat and made his way over to the dimly lit security gate. An irate security guard began to remonstrate with him, finally declaring 'I don't care who you are this gate stays shut'. I got out of the car to stretch my legs and recognized the security guard as one of Tony's constituents whom I had known for years.

Hoping he had forgotten the losing tip I had given him, I called out, 'What's up Harry?'

Harry turned and called out, 'Bloody hell, it's Tony Booth. We did it, didn't we? We beat the bastards.'

Deserting his post, he hurried over and clasped me in a bear-hug. My arm around his shoulder, we opened the gates together. The car then drove onto the runway where a plane was waiting. On boarding I was delighted to see a euphoric Euan accompanied by a young couple from Tony's office. He wanted to go onto the flight deck. I had little difficulty in persuading the smiling pilot to let Euan join him after take-off so from here he could relay all the important election results. Nearly half an hour into the flight Euan's whoop of delight, accompanied by the pilot's dipping of his wings in a gesture of celebratory solidarity, heralded Portillo's loss of his north London seat at Enfield Southgate. He was not the only Tory Minister rejected by the electorate that night. It threw us all into a rumble and tumble of joy which continued until our arrival at Stansted airport.

As soon as we touched down, more security people were on hand to continue what was beginning to feel like a rather protracted busting exercise. I was, as usual, last off the plane, having chatted to and hugged the pilot and crew. On the tarmac I found that Euan, Sarah and Emma had been taken off by car, the exhausted Euan to be dropped off at home in Islington and Sarah and Emma on to the South Bank. The security guys laughed and invited me to join them on their bus for the ride over to the South Bank. Mission almost accomplished for them, they relaxed and we bantered our way through the journey. As we drove through the streets we could see revellers already celebrating Labour's victory. The nearer the South Bank, the bigger the celebrations. It was one of those perfect moments you know cannot last, like a particularly vivid rainbow – but while it arches across the sky everyone is affected by it.

I had arranged to meet Stephenie at the victory celebrations. Recklessly, we had not bothered to make contingency plans in the event of Labour losing. We had also failed to work out just how difficult it might be to find each other in a crowd of thousands. Fortunately for me, once she made herself known to the stewards who were running the event, they detained her in their office and only reluctantly released her once I arrived. We made our way into the celebrations. The atmosphere was electrifying. It made the hairs on the back of my neck stand up. As I hugged Steph to me we came across fellow actor Richard Attenborough and his wife, Sheila. Delighted to meet up with each other, we made our way together to the family and close friends' enclosure.

An excited buzz of anticipation swept through the Hall as word went round that Tony was about to appear to make his speech. People pushed and jostled for the best places. We had all waited so long for this moment. Giggling like teenagers, Steph and I managed to find a spot hidden by curtains on the stage directly behind where Tony was to speak. The roar that greeted Tony and Cherie's arrival seemed to vanquish the remains of the night and, miraculously, a new dawn rose. Tony seized the day and in his speech touched the edge of greatness. A new political life was beginning. The old one flashed by at top speed. Past Labour prime ministers and leaders paraded in front of me. Attlee's sad smile as I assisted him to his feet; Gaitskell's sneer as we stood on the pier at Llandudno and I berated him over Labour's policy on the bomb; Wilson's chuckle muffled by the stem of his pipe as we sneaked into the mayor's parlour and guzzled her best whisky; Tony Benn and Michael Foot, both old friends of mine and viewed by Millbank as being like me – out of date and out of touch with the ideas of New Labour. I remembered John Smith's giggles as he described himself as everyone's idea of the nice, wee bank manager. And the struggles of yesterday: to bring one member, one vote to the Party; the ever so polite public power struggle for the leadership of our party between Tony and Gordon Brown and the bitter private struggles witnessed off-stage.

But as the dawn rose, and the tears started to flow, most of all I remembered my parents and the rest of our family. Grandad, who taught me the fundamentals of socialism that have remained with me throughout my life along with his millions of jokes, tales and aphorisms. It had been a long, hard slog from Crosby to Downing Street, but we had made it. My last image of that historic and emotional night was the sight of my daughter and Tony surrounded by grey suits as they were led away to begin their ultimate political journey.

One

Bombs and Politics: a Liverpool Childhood

'There is always one moment in childhood when the door opens
and lets the future in.'

Graham Greene, *The Power and the Glory* (1940)

In the tiny backroom of my family home in Crosby we listened intently
to the King's abdication speech. I was perched on my grandfather,
Robert Thompson's lap as we sat in his favourite armchair, the one that
was in the farthest corner from the door and also the closest to the fire.
In my memory that room is forever shadowy from the branches of
the sycamore tree that filtered the light, and those shadows seemed to
enhance the reactions of the adults to what was clearly serious news.

My grandmother Mathilda, or Till, was the youngest of seventeen
children. Her family, MacNamara, had arrived in Liverpool from
County Mayo. At that time the drama queen of the family, this tiny,
bird-like woman was the complete opposite of my tall, well-built grandfather. Her once-beautiful red hair was now streaked with grey and her
famed sharpness of tongue made her more feared than admired. She sat
on the other side of the hearth clutching her tattered, lace-trimmed
handkerchief to her reddened eyes as she shook with theatrical sobs for
the King and his forbidden love. My mother, Vera, periodically appeared
in the doorway, tea towel in hand, her hair frizzed from the heat of the
kitchen. Like my grandmother, she too was deeply moved by the
romance of the unfolding drama. Grandad leaned across me to adjust
and tune the crackling wireless to listen to 'The Prince of Wails', as he
called him. I remember saying what a funny, squeaky voice he had
and Grandad growling something about the Windsors' lack of balls.
Grandma poured scorn on his manifest lack of empathy and understanding for the power of true love and then sobbed as my grandfather
turned off the wireless, pronouncing good riddance to bad rubbish.

In the free and frank discussion that ensued I received my first
political lesson in republicanism. From what I could gather, and I was

only five at the time, it seemed that kings and queens were a waste of time, space and money and that a republic was the only solution to this constitutional crisis. Till's response was that the only public, 're' or otherwise, that my grandfather was interested in was the nearest public bar. At this point Grandad gently lifted me down from his knee, heaved his frame out of the armchair and announced grandly that he was off to see a man about a dog. I remember thinking he's always going to see this man about a dog and we still haven't got one, but he was gone, his back broad enough to shrug off the barbed insults cascading after him.

Dogs were not the only animals that consistently engaged my grandfather's interest. He was also very fond of the horses, a pastime shared to a lesser degree by my father; and when he was home from sea he and my grandfather spent happy hours poring over the racing pages discussing form. The only blight to their peace of mind would be when my mother or grandmother decided to intervene. As their opinions would be based on little more than liking the name of a particular horse, levels of exasperation between the men at this completely unscientific approach would occasionally reach shouting point. Racing people are deeply superstitious and so my grandfather and father would feel obliged to back the horses picked by the women as they would surely win if they did not – even if the horse was three-legged, blind and an aged nag!

My grandfather liked nothing better than a day out at the races. On one occasion he had gone over to Chester. I was playing in the street – I cannot have been more than four – when a policeman approached me and asked where I lived. He had come to tell my grandmother that my grandfather celebrated his success at the races by getting roaring drunk. He was currently sobering up in Chester gaol. Did my grandmother want to bail him out? My grandmother's emphatic refusal meant my grandfather spent the night in a police cell.

The following day I was sent out to play burdened with watch duty – I was to report to my grandmother and mother immediately I saw my grandfather turn into our street. Eventually he staggered into view clearly the worse for wear and clearly monumentally fed up. I ran into the house to warn of his impending approach and was ordered to stand well back as my mother and grandmother readied themselves for his entrance. Our house had a small hallway that led into the kitchen. My grandmother took up her position on a chair behind the kitchen door as my mother handed her the heavy frying pan. With horrified fascination I watched as the women meted out primitive justice. As my grandfather crashed through the door demanding to know the whereabouts of his wife, he could not have known what hit him when she smacked him on the back of the head with the pan, completely pole-axing him. In the few minutes he lay spreadeagled and comatose on the floor my mother and grandmother quickly went through his pockets searching for the remainder of his winnings. Talking to me later my grandfather demonstrated the self-delusional and blustering tactics men often practise under the guise of self-knowledge or when seeking explanation for the inexplicable acts of women. My grandmother's actions were, he claimed, those of a woman deeply in love – why else would she be so powerfully moved?

I loved my grandfather. He was a man of strong opinions and much compassion who lived by his firm socialist beliefs. Like so many other decent people at the time of the Spanish Civil War he had been appalled by the bombing of Guernica and believed fascism to be an evil that, if not prevented, would be the cause of all-out war ... much as he hated agreeing with that charlatan Churchill! The opportunism of Churchill in his early political career as his loyalties wavered between Liberal and Conservative did little to endear him to the voting public, but it was his action in 1924, sending in troops against striking Welsh miners, that made him a hate figure for the working classes. For my grandfather, as with most left-wing activists, there was a profound irony in Churchill coming to embody the British determination and courage to stand off and ultimately defeat the fascist onslaught.

My grandfather was born in Ireland and as a child he had arrived in Liverpool with his parents and brothers and sisters. Their intention was to emigrate to America, but like so many they ran out of money and simply stayed put. He later worked as a docker, married my grandmother and had three children. The eldest was my mother Vera and there were two boys, Edgar and William. By the time I was born he was working as a barber and had his own shop on the corner of Denmark Street. This career choice had been forced upon him after his active involvement on the dockers' strike committee during the National Strike of 1926 resulted in his being blacklisted by the Mersey Docks and Harbour Board. My grandfather was a popular figure and his shop was always full with cronies as they discussed politics, racing and football. The 1930s were tough, with not much money around, and more than once he accepted payment in kind for his services. The monkey and the parrot were amongst my grandmother's least favourite exchanges.

At that time my grandparents were living with us in the house on Ferndale Road. Contrary to the legend spun by the fevered workings of the Labour Party machine about the ancestry and background of my daughter Cherie, Ferndale Road was not a slum in the backstreets of Liverpool – far from it. It was a quiet road of three-bedroomed terraced houses with bay windows and small front gardens. The twitching net curtains were an optional extra chosen by a small minority of our neighbours. Like the rest of the women in the road, my mother kept the house immaculate and our front step stood up to any competition with its daily applications of 'donkey stone', acquired in exchanges with the rag and bone man. Our house was different, though. We had a particularly distinctive front door. It was green with yellow trimmings. This was the nearest my grandfather could get to Republican colours from the man who sold him the paint in the local pub. Needless to say, my mother and grandmother were none too pleased at this arrangement, but as the house badly needed a coat of paint they were stoical in their acceptance.

As for any child born in the thirties, the Depression and the Second World War shaped my childhood. The other great threat to health and well-being was the ever-present menace of serious epidemics. In the winter of 1937 when I was just six years old my mother called the doctor to me. I was suffering from a high fever. When the doctor arrived he diagnosed diphtheria and I was rushed by ambulance to Fazakerley Isolation Hospital. He thought I was another victim of the diphtheria outbreak that gripped the country. The doctors who examined me at the hospital decided that in fact I did not have the disease, but as by now I had been exposed to infection I would have to be detained. I subsequently became ill not only with diphtheria, but also scarlet fever. I spent the Christmas of 1937 in hospital. Unusually, my parents were able to visit me and I remember they stood crying behind the glass partition separating us. Because diphtheria was a contagious disease it was the practice then not to allow visits to the patient, even to children. This meant children were isolated from their families for months at a time. It was only later I learned that my parents were given special permission to visit as the doctors did not expect me to survive into the new year.

A few days after their visit I was transferred on to the 'death watch' ward. This was a place of dread, beginning the inevitable progression up the ward from the bed nearest the hospital corridor to the top and the bed next to the curtains concealing the mortuary. I began this deadly game of musical chairs, reaching not the end bed, but the one before it – one stop from eternity. One night I woke disturbed by the boy in the top bed. He was very close to death. Earlier in the day a priest wearing a surgical mask had administered the last rites to him. Knowing I was also a Catholic, the nurse suggested – despite my gurgling, head-shaking protest – he do the same for me, to save time. I looked helplessly across at my fellow inmate and, powerless to speak, my throat tightened with fear and diphtheria as he slowly faded away. I watched as his spirit left him, rising gently through the dust motes. Managing a strangulated cry I attracted the attention of a nurse who rushed to pull the curtains around the corpse of the little boy before moving him through the final exit door. With a vacant space to be filled the nurses attempted to move me into it. With all my remaining strength I resisted and a compromise was reached. I was still moved to a bed at the top of the ward, but on the opposite side – this at least offered the hope of escaping oblivion. In probably the earliest example of my enduring refusal to meet all the expectations of the ruling hegemony, in less than a week I began my recovery and the progression back down the ward to the hospital corridor and eventually home.

Looking back it seems as if the 1930s were a time spent huddled around the wireless listening to reports and statements that would change not only our lives, but also the course of history. September 3 1939 was one of those times. We gathered round our wireless to listen to Neville Chamberlain – condemned by my grandfather as 'that appeaser' – make the announcement that Britain was at war with Germany. The silence that followed was finally broken by Till blessing herself and murmuring, 'God save us all', to which my grandfather replied, 'Says tiny Till'. Our nervous giggles broke the tension as the war goose-stepped into our lives. Within minutes of Chamberlain's broadcast the air raid siren began its heart-stopping wail. It was a sound we were to come to know intimately as, like so many others at that moment, we wondered if we would survive what lay ahead.

My father, George, had not been at home that day, but at the docks, 'working by'. This meant preparing a ship for its next voyage. Before the Depression he had worked as a ship's steward, but had been laid off and so had to take whatever work he could get. My father was dark-haired, of medium height and my mother claimed he looked like Gary Cooper. My parents' marriage was certainly a love match. My mother, who was slim and pretty with dark, wavy hair, had inherited Till's sharpness and temper, but not her bitterness. Her quick tongue was the perfect antidote to my father's sulks, which may have been partly the result of frustrated talent. As a young man he had won a piano scholarship to the Royal College of Music in London, but his parents had not allowed him to take it up. Instead he got no further than playing the piano in the lounges of ocean-going liners. With the outbreak of war, merchant seamen were desperately needed again. My father did not have the necessary five pounds to bribe the union officials to give him a ship out of Liverpool. Instead he was to join a vessel in Glasgow. The ship, the SS *Montrose*, was on the Clyde being converted into what the Admiralty described as an armed merchantman. My father came home on leave before the ship was to sail as an escort to the North Atlantic convoy. The night before he was due to go back to Glasgow my mother dreamed that the SS *Montrose* was sunk by enemy action with the loss of all hands. Waking my father, she spent the rest of the night playing on his sailor's superstitious nature in an effort to persuade him not to go. Joined by my grandmother at breakfast, the two women finally convinced him and my father went sick. On her maiden voyage the SS *Montrose* was the first armed merchantman to be sunk by the enemy with the loss of all hands.

My other grandparents, Sidney and Virginia Booth, my father's parents, lived in a semi-detached house on Sunnyside Road which looked out onto open fields and was in those days considered rather smart. My grandmother was the daughter of the notorious Dick Dewsbury who owned a small fishing fleet that sailed out of Formby. He had accumulated considerable wealth, not only from his smuggling activities but also from the protection racket he ran. His influence stretched from Ayr to Cornwall. My grandfather Sidney's family were Cumbrian farmers, but I never knew very much about that history. His parents considered that he had married beneath himself whilst Virginia's parents believed Sidney and his family to be too grand. Thus the couple had little contact with their families after their marriage.

My grandparents owned a Newfoundland retriever named Rover which we would take for walks in the park. As well as Franco's fascism in Spain, the government under Chamberlain had been forced to start a rearmament programme in the face of Hitler's threats. My grandfather would talk to me about the futility and madness of war. During the First World War he had been a pacifist and was imprisoned in Walton gaol. When he could stand the cells no longer he volunteered as a stretcher-bearer, but was badly gassed at Mons in 1916. His experiences left him, like so many others who survived that obscene slaughter, physically and emotionally frail. I remember sitting with him in the park early in 1939. He told me that he had a service revolver and if war was declared he intended to kill both his sons rather than let them go through the horrors he had experienced. Disturbed by the strength of my grandfather's feelings and frightened for my father and uncle Richard, I went home and told my mother. The response of the women was immediate and ruthless. They tried to get my grandfather Booth certified. Somehow, he managed to persuade the doctors otherwise. I do not know what happened to the revolver after that. I am sure it would never have been thrown away – no one would be so foolish in 1939. But that summer grandfather Booth suffered his first massive stroke. His third, on 24 December 1939, killed him.

My father was by now at sea, on a ship that was part of the North Atlantic convoy. My grandfather Thompson continued to rage against Chamberlain and Halifax. Their 'phoney war' approach and earlier disbelief about Hitler's intentions had left the country ill-prepared for the all-out conflict it now faced. Neither was he prepared to believe the false promise that it would all be over by Christmas. My grandfather had heard that story before. Although only a child of eight, I was old enough to realize what was happening and with my father away it was my grandfather Thompson I increasingly came to worship.

He was to prove the first – and major – influence on the development of my own political beliefs and attitudes. As we sat in the air raid shelters he would tell me the history of Britain to take my mind off what was happening in the skies above us. Through him I learned about the slavery inflicted upon us by the Romans; the fledgling democracy of the integrated society of Angles, Saxons and later the Vikings; the disastrous Norman invasion – those maniacs from 'beyond the Pale' who defeated our elected king and inflicted the hereditary system upon us. He took me step by step through the extraordinary story of the deliberately ill-educated majority and their struggle for universal suffrage. This was the history of the common people. Not the one in school textbooks, but the real story remembered in oral history of human suffering, of great determination and dignity and the strength of the human spirit to triumph and be free. My grandfather's stories were about Boadicea, Caradoc, Hereward the Wake, the Peasants' Revolt. He believed that the genocidal suppression of the Jacobite uprisings in 1715 and 1745 were primarily a ruthless imposition of Norman law on Scotland. What puzzled me then, and continues to puzzle me now, was how the heroes of pre-1066 and those who have since tried to follow their path to freedom are dismissed as mere legend or naive fools. Yet we are to make heroes of the deeply flawed promulgators and perpetrators of the Norman establishment. The continuing obsession with the status of royalty and the acceptance of their questionable and unearned privilege makes me despair that we will ever throw off those Norman shackles.

In the world outside the Anderson shelter the war was going badly. After Dunkirk we held our breath for the invasion. It never came, but as a vital seaport Liverpool was subjected to heavy bombing. On 20 June 1940 the air raid sirens were joined in their wailing by the first cries of my younger brother Robert. The whole family, my grandparents, my sister Audrey who was born in January 1934 and I, refused to leave my mother alone in her bedroom and my brother was born during the first daylight bombing raids on the city. I find it impossible to describe the sheer terror that the continuous bombing raids inflicted. Night and day they came, turning the city into a version of hell. As a child it was the smells I carried with me, that constant stench of burnt-out buildings. A pall of smoke seemed at times to blank out Liverpool. The council had built a brick street shelter almost outside our house, but my mother refused to use it. She was adamant that my sister and I were not going to pick our way through the broken bottles, French letters and other detritus of war that carpeted the way into that cold, dank and smelly shelter. I could not help noticing, however, a number of women guiding a cross-section of the Allied forces on short tours of its interior. But we were lucky enough to have our own Anderson shelter in our small back garden.

No family escaped some kind of suffering. The people who lived directly behind us had a lucky escape when an anti-aircraft shell passed over our house, but destroyed their back room. Fortunately, they were all in their Anderson shelter and survived unharmed. As we rushed to help them, the air raid warden was hammering on our front door as, unknown to us, an incendiary bomb had landed in our front garden. It was only after I was sent back into the house to make some tea that we realized what was happening. During one terrible week in May 1941 Liverpool was bombed for seven successive nights, destroying the city centre. A recently docked munitions ship received a direct hit, inflicting devastating damage on the docks and other shipping. One hundred and fifty people died when a school shelter was hit and over fifty people died in the Docks Road hospital. More than seventy thousand people in Liverpool were made homeless. There were few moments of relief from our tormentors, although I recall the cheers when the RAF Spitfires and Hurricanes brought German bombers crashing down into the Mersey or the Irish Sea.

Alongside the permanent fear of being killed by enemy bombs there was the ever-present feeling of hunger that never seemed to fade.

Christmas 1941 was approaching. I was ten and had never been so hungry in my life. All our hopes of short-term relief rested on my father's brother, Richard, being able to acquire something from his mother-in-law, Mrs Pick. Richard had married Hilda Pick in the smartest Protestant church in Blundellsands. My uncle Bernard, my mother's cousin and a priest, forbade us all to go under fear of excommunication. My grandfather Thompson expressed the view that the Pope surely had more important issues to be dealing with, such as halting the wholesale slaughter of civilian populations and bringing the war to an end. It would also take more than the threat of excommunication to stop my mother attending the wedding. We all marvelled at the grandeur of St Nicholas's, Blundellsands.

Thus it was that in the week before Christmas 1941 we set out for Mrs Pick's home in Green Lane, Tuebrook. I was immediately struck by her immense proportions and, having been cautioned by my mother before the visit not to stare at her moustache I was, of course, fixated by it. After making sure we had wiped our feet thoroughly on the brand new and thickly bristled doormat (where did she get that in wartime, we wondered? – we were soon to find out) she turned and waddled off, leaving us to follow in her sweaty wake to the back room. There my father's miscreant brother, Richard, was sleeping off his lunchtime excesses. His wife, Hilda, was also in the room sporting a bad perm and doused as usual in breath-stealing quantities of the cheap perfume 'Californian Poppy'. Nonetheless, she greeted us warmly and ushered us into the kitchen where we were served tea. We were given my favourite Spam sandwiches and also a custard cream cake.

My mother, sister and I ate a hearty meal. Then, wasting no further time on social niceties, Mrs Pick got down to business. She invited us into her back garden where there was the usual Anderson shelter. Unusually, this particular shelter not only had a substantial door, but was also heavily padlocked. Mrs Pick then produced a bunch of keys that would not have shamed a Walton gaoler. Pulling back the door she revealed a sight that left us open-mouthed – the interior resembled a pre-war butcher's shop. There was so much meat crammed into the shelter that access was almost impossible. Mrs Pick instructed me to scramble in and bring out a small shoulder of lamb. I climbed down into the shelter and, almost overcome by the stench of stale blood, followed Mrs Pick's urgent prompting and grabbed the nearest shoulder of lamb. My first choice did not meet with approval and, ordered not to be greedy, I was sent back to select a more suitable, smaller shoulder. Fearing that I would never escape from this abattoir I did as I was told and, with blood smeared all over my best jersey and trousers, I emerged back into daylight. I was greeted by my mother's rolling eyes as she sadly shook her head and hissed, 'Trust you to pick the smallest'.

Back in the kitchen the lamb was wrapped in newspaper and Mrs Pick then asked Audrey if she would like a sweetie. Audrey almost swooned at the offer. My mother used our sweet ration for sugar, so sweeties were a thing of the past in our house. As Mrs Pick rolled her way up the hall on her fat legs she complained bitterly about her feet. Her lisle stockings made a sound like sandpaper as they rubbed against each other. At the locked sitting room door she paused, hitched up her skirts to reveal voluminous brown bloomers and once more produced a large bunch of keys from the pocket. The blackout curtains were drawn and as she switched on the overhead light we were again left open-mouthed by the cornucopia of goods in the room. Alcohol of every description, boxes of chocolates, cigarettes, clothing and, to my mother's delight, boxes of nylons. Rooting through the nylons Mrs Pick found a pair she described as slightly substandard and, with the flourish of a Lady Bountiful giving alms to the poor, handed them to my mother, whose grovelling acceptance left me stunned. I had never before seen my mother behave like that, let alone to someone she disliked. Audrey was given a small bag of sweeties and then it was my turn. But, before I had a chance to savour the decision-making process, the choice was made for me as Mrs Pick grabbed a bar of chocolate and pushed it into my hands.

At that moment my uncle Richard appeared in the doorway. He staggered past us to help himself to a bottle of scotch. Suddenly, remembering the season and also that my grandfather liked a drink, he grabbed a bottle of brandy and offered it to us as his Christmas present. With a speed and dexterity surprising in a woman of her size, Mrs Pick crossed the room, snatched the full bottle of brandy and exchanged it for a half bottle. In retaliation, Richard then gave us a box of chocolates for my grandmother. Sensing the makings of a scene my mother hustled Audrey and me out of the room. As the front door slammed firmly and unceremoniously behind us nothing could deflate my mother. We were going to eat meat at Christmas.

Christmas that year turned out to be better than any of us might have anticipated. As well as Mrs Pick's munificence, the bombing of Pearl Harbor had brought the Americans into the war and it seemed finally that the tide would turn in favour of the Allies. Grandad sat in his armchair, a glass in one hand and the almost empty bottle of brandy in the other. He had already heavily censured his benefactor for stealing food from the mouths of children and was now on to another well-worn subject, Mrs Pick's patron Bessie Braddock, who had personally appointed Mrs Pick to her post as supervisor for school meals. The Braddocks, Bessie and her husband Tom, ran Liverpool as their own fiefdom and any challenge to the Braddock authority or their iron grip on the Liverpool Labour Party was ruthlessly dealt with. My grandfather's vocal and public accusations of their corruption during the General Strike had consigned him to the political wilderness of Crosby Labour Party. I sat at the table as my grandmother worked her way through her Christmas chocolates and my grandfather once again elaborated on the venal and fraudulent activities of the Braddocks. Bessie Braddock was a consummate performer whose shameless tactics would have made even that old rogue Horatio Bottomley blush. She revelled in her role as the 'Boadicea of the North' and yet nothing could have been further from the truth. With the explicit support of the unions, their vote-rigging activities were on a par with anything the Democratic Party in Chicago were to manage twenty years later, and like the Democrats their election slogan was an encouragement to vote and to vote often.

It is true that the hardship, fear and loss experienced during the war brought out the best in the vast majority of the British people. It is also true, unfortunately, that a number of people seized the opportunity to capitalize on shortages through profiteering and the black market. The Liverpool councillors, many of whom, said Grandad, were merely Braddock placemen, put Tammany Hall to shame with their violent and intimidating tactics. It was not only city councillors who owed their advancement or livelihoods to Mrs Braddock – she also held a number of police and magistrates in her sway. Her friends and relations, those she could rely on, had reserved occupations and were able to use the war to get fat and rich. Mrs Pick was just one example. My grandfather had written to the Labour Party in London outlining what was happening in Liverpool. His letter had been passed to Herbert Morrison (described by Nye Bevan as that archbishop of orthodoxy), then Minister of Supply in the wartime coalition government and later Chairman of the Labour Party. Nothing was done. The Bessie Braddock legend had been created and was allowed – and continues – to survive.

Although the war was for me a potent cocktail of bombing and politics, it was also the time for the usual rites of passage that are a part of childhood. My first school was St Edmund's Catholic Elementary School. My first teacher was Miss Bolger, who was stick thin, with buck teeth and hair dyed so black it looked like patent leather. Sadly for me, she lived in the next road to us and so all of my many alleged misdemeanours were reported to my mother whom she met in the local shops. Following these conversations, my mother would always feel the necessity to mete out further punishment.

In 1942, when I was ten, I won a scholarship to St Mary's College in Crosby, a Catholic independent school run by the Christian Brothers. However, I was too young and had to spend another year at St Edmund's where I was moved into the senior class with the thirteen- and fourteen-year-olds. This year group had their own air raid shelter. The headmaster, Mr McGowan, despite his reputation as a bully, had given up trying to control the senior shelter after turning up unexpectedly one break and finding Ullathorne, the biggest boy in the school, winning an erect penis competition. Like the rest of us, I think he found Ullathorne's dimensions and the obvious admiration of the girls intimidating and he beat a hasty retreat.

In the autumn of 1943 I started at St Mary's College, an institution I quickly came to loathe. The ironically named and now notorious Christian Brothers were exponents of wholesale bigotry and violence – yet it was many more decades before their sins finally found them out. They would make Attila the Hun look like a wishy-washy liberal and firmly believed that to spare the rod was to spoil the child. My grand-father's version of history, with which I regularly challenged the pre-vailing orthodoxy, earned me more than one beating. Imagination and a questioning mind were not well received by the majority of teachers in that establishment and yet, perhaps perversely, their antipathy served only to reinforce my own beliefs. Seated across the aisle from me was Kevin McNamara – no relation to my grandmother, Till – later a Member of Parliament for one of the Hull seats and Shadow Northern Ireland Secretary. John Birt, a future Director-General of the BBC, and Roger McGough the poet would later follow me through St Mary's.

At home the talk was not of winning the war – that was now taken for granted – but of what kind of revolution would follow it. My grand-father was convinced that despite Churchill's inspired wartime lead-ership, his clear expectation of continued power would be seen as arrogant and lead to a backlash in the armed forces. The Beveridge Report[1] began the debate on how we would create a more fair and just

---

[1] 'Social Insurance and Allied Services', more commonly known as the Beveridge Report and the work of William Beveridge, was published in 1942. This report was a crucial influence in shaping the post-1945 Labour government's policies and institutions.

society once the war was over. The Report did not go far enough, but it was a popular blueprint for action and Grandad was convinced that the Labour Party would win the post-war election with a huge majority. We were certain that we could rely on our hero Nye Bevan to ensure that the government kept its promises. We were also hopeful that the compromiser Herbert Morrison would be exposed as the fifth-rate politician we believed him to be and Bevan would become deputy leader of the Labour Party. However, even though our optimism was justified it was only 1943 and the war had still to be brought to an end. That year my father returned home. His ship had been torpedoed, the second time this had happened to him. He had been adrift in a lifeboat on the Atlantic for over three weeks before being picked up by a British destroyer. The experience left him gaunt and strained, his black hair heavily streaked with grey. Always a man of few words, he was now virtually monosyllabic. I gave up trying to persuade him to describe what it had been like as his reply was always the same – 'Water, water everywhere and not a drop to drink'. He would elaborate no further.

My mother, an avid reader, had introduced me to Daphne Du Maurier. I read *Frenchman's Creek* and bought my father the sheet music for 'Claire de Lune', used as the theme for the film. My father duly played to a packed front room one Sunday evening. These musical Sunday evenings were a regular feature when my father was at home. We each had to make a contribution and mine was the finale – 'Jerusalem', complete with a final family chorus. My father's piano-playing talent had come to the notice of Geraldo, who heard him playing on one of the troop ships. Geraldo and his Orchestra were famous at that time and he offered my father a permanent place in his orchestra. To my surprise my father turned down the offer. Here was an opportunity to do something he loved, see the world and get paid for it. I could not understand it. He was already away from home for long periods doing a job he hated. My parents, specifically my mother, reasoned there would always be work for my father at sea, but bands had a habit of breaking up. He put his loyalty and commitment to his family before any fulfilment of his own dreams and ambitions. Although I could only admire my father for his decision I knew, even as a child, that faced with a similar dilemma I would not be able to follow his example. When my time eventually came I went with my dreams. I am not the same man my father was.

With my father so often away at sea my mother was the disciplinarian of the family. A typical Liverpool matriarch, her word was law in our household and her sharp tongue and free use of the back of her hand were regular features of my childhood. My father only ever hit me once and that was on the urgent demand of my mother that he do something after I had been rude to her. Initially, he simply ordered me to my bedroom, but this did not pacify my mother, who knew I would seize the opportunity to lie on my bed and read. As I reached my bedroom I heard my father coming up the stairs behind me. As he came into my room and began to remonstrate with me I treated him to a copy of one of my grandmother's sneers. The force of the smack he gave me threw me over the bed and left me jammed down between the bed and the wall. Deeply chastened and humiliated I burst into tears, only to hear my mother reproaching my father for his excessive force. As she tried to help me extricate myself we both collapsed laughing at the farcical end to it all. My father never did understand the love–hate relationship between my mother and me.

The Catholic Church had an important role in our family life, certainly amongst the women. Their faith was devout and unquestioning. The men were much more sceptical and whilst the women observed the religious ritual the men, for the most part, refused to join in. As the eldest grandson I became the focus of hopes for a new generation of priests in the family. To this end, I was made to take Latin lessons and later forced into becoming an altar boy, a role I retained under pressure from home – to my everlasting shame and embarrassment – until 1949, when I was eighteen. So it was that at the age of six I was sent to Park House, a women's nursing home run by nuns, where the old priest who was the chaplain gave me Latin lessons three times a week. I was not allowed to disturb the sanctity of the nuns by using the front entrance; instead the priest would admit me by a side door. I had been having lessons for almost a year without ever catching sight of a nun when one evening the priest said to me, 'Reverend Mother has died. You and I will go to the chapel and say a prayer for her. You can practise your Latin.'

It was a chilly winter evening and my hyperactive imagination was already making my heart thump with fear as we made our way to the tiny chapel in the grounds. The creaking door opened to reveal the candlelit chapel. In my terror I was immediately fixated by the sight of an open coffin lying on a lace-covered table before the small altar. My feet remained firmly fixed at the entrance, but the priest insisted, 'Come with me, boy'. He knelt in front of the coffin and I knelt about a yard behind him. When I was that age small boys wore short trousers even in the depths of winter and as I recited the prayers I was shaking with a mixture of fear and the bitter cold of the stone floor as it penetrated my poor, unclothed knees. After an aeon, we finished. Struggling to stand on legs almost lifeless from the cold, nonetheless I was already planning how to make haste. But my nightmare was not finished. The priest turned and, sweeping me up towards the coffin, said, 'You have the privilege to kiss the Reverend Mother goodbye.'

I had never seen a dead body before and looking down on to the face of this old woman I saw the wizened and terrifying face of a witch from a story book. The experience was now beyond my endurance and I began to scream. In the ensuing struggle the priest dropped me and a candle was knocked over. Oblivious to anything but my own mortal fear, I ran for home. Later that evening the priest called at our house. He told my mother that the candle I had knocked over set fire to the altar cloth and only his quick thinking saved the chapel from going up in flames, causing the unwanted and premature cremation of the Reverend Mother. Needless to say my Latin lessons were abruptly terminated, but I had learned enough to become an altar boy and serve Mass.

I can vividly recall the day my grandfather was dragged, very much against his will, to our parish church, St Edmund's, to celebrate the Allied victory. Things went relatively smoothly up to the point when our parish priest, John Kieron, used his sermon to launch an attack on the Labour Party and outline the dire consequences that would follow from their victory in a general election. He specifically accused them of planning to nationalize Catholic schools. To my grandmother's shock and mortification my grandfather rose to his feet and began to berate the priest loudly and thoroughly for broadcasting Tory lies and propaganda. The church was in uproar as my grandfather half-dragged, half-carried my fainting grandmother out of the place. It was not that Robert Thompson did not believe in God. He did. But he did not believe in, and was implacably opposed to, organized religion and its corruption of one of the most beautiful creeds known to humanity. He argued that Christianity teaches love and peace and justice for all, but this social as well as spiritual search for truth and justice had been turned into a global business venture. It was, he argued, this emphasis on and concern with business considerations that had led the Pope, Pius XII, to refuse to speak out against the evils of Nazism.

I have leapt ahead. The first months of 1944 passed quickly as we waited for invasion news – only this time our invasion of France rather than a German invasion of Britain. The D-Day landings meant the

Germans were now fighting on two fronts, caught in a pincer movement between the Allies and the Soviet Army. Our only feeling was one of enormous and heartfelt relief. We felt no sorrow for or empathy with the German population. We wanted them to suffer as they had made us suffer. So, every time a German city endured a thousand bomber raid, we celebrated. Dresden? – remember Coventry. Hamburg? – remember Liverpool. Berlin? – remember London. Now, as our air raid shelters were obsolete, the German ones overflowed.

From the safe distance of the twenty-first century it has become fashionable and even acceptable to berate the Allied bombing action. This is, in my opinion, an arrogant misunderstanding of the feelings of the British population at that time. The misery and fear we went through are incomprehensible to a generation that did not endure them. We did not have emotional therapists on hand to talk us through our trauma so, although allegedly primitive and unsophisticated, revenge was satisfying and therapeutic. It is offensive to the memory of those who did not survive and to those who fought to bring us through to argue that we failed in any way by not showing more pity towards a genocidal dictatorship. One final thought on those terrible days and nights of the Blitz: any bonfire or firework display since the war has always seemed very tame. Once you have watched a city centre burn, seen rockets and anti-aircraft fire light up the night sky or seen the effects of mines, all else is a faint imitation. We had witnessed not just the Bonfire of the Vanities, but the Bonfire of the Insanities. On 8 May 1945 the war in Europe was over and we partied.

By the end of the war my brother Robert was almost five years old and more space was needed, so my grandparents moved out of Ferndale Road and into a flat over one of my uncle Bill's grocer's shops. My grandfather's barber shop was on the next corner to their flat and so everything became much more convenient. One morning, just as I finished my paper round and was about to go off to school, my uncle Bill pulled up in his car outside our house. I could see from the look on his face that something was seriously wrong. He motioned me back into the house. He told us that as my grandfather got out of bed that morning he had fallen to the floor suffering a massive heart attack. The doctor said later, he was probably dead before he hit the floor. It was my first experience of the wrenching pain of grief – although upset, I had been too young to understand my grandfather Booth's death some six years earlier. I looked at my mother and knew her devastation; putting my arms around her, we clung to each other in our loss. On the day of my grandfather's funeral the streets were lined with people who had come to pay their last respects. So many people had loved and would miss him. I had lost my guide, my mentor and my best friend. It would be years before I found anyone his equal. He died the day before St Patrick's Day, 1946.

That year, life dealt my family another in a succession of brutal blows. My father's ship was in dock being prepared for fumigation and he was supervising the final clearing of one of the ship's holds. As he leaned forward to check progress, a derrick broke loose knocking my father eighty feet down into the steel-bottomed hold. Sustaining horrific injuries from which he never really recovered, he was rushed to the Docks Road hospital. Unaware of his accident, I returned home from school to be greeted by my wailing grandmother, who had returned to live in our house, and a stony-faced uncle Richard. The shipping company immediately stopped my father's wage and we became a family where the money had run out. Clearly my paper round and any money my mother could earn from cleaning would not support us. In an effort to prevent me from having to leave school my mother sought help from her youngest brother, Bill. He had progressed from selling tea from his bicycle and sidecar to be the owner of three small but lucrative grocer's shops, one on Jubilee Road where I was born and the other two close to St Edmund's, the primary school I attended. Bill, however, would not offer my mother a job in one of his shops as it would mean making another woman redundant. Neither would he contemplate loaning her money as he did not believe that was right. My mother also approached my uncle Bernard, the priest, who wrung his hands and said there was little the parish could do. Besides which his parishioners might accuse him of favouring his own family. Our only hope of an income rested with me, so I left school and started work earning seventeen shillings and sixpence a week as an office boy in a bonded warehouse on the Upper Dock Road.

The new year brought with it a change of luck. George Huston, chief clerk at the American Consulate in Liverpool, was a member of the same Masonic lodge as my uncle Richard. Through him I got a job in the immigration section of the consulate in the Cunard Building on the pier head; I was paid four guineas. There I remained until February 1950, when I was called up for national service and my reluctant sojourn in the Royal Corps of Signals began.

Two
Daydream Believer

'There is love of course. And then there's life, its enemy.'
Jean Anouilh, *Ardèle* (1949)

Having survived the war, I was not persuaded by the political logic arguing that conscription was vital if the armed forces were to be maintained in a state of permanent preparation for further conflict. I had no desire to kill or be killed and I tried every ruse I could think of to get out of national service. As an asthma sufferer I believed I should be exempt from call-up and I consulted fellow asthmatics on the best way to induce an attack at the appropriate moment. One of them told me eating Lifebuoy soap worked successfully for him at his medical inspection. Not only did he have great difficulties breathing, but also the doctors were tremendously impressed by the foaming at his mouth and declared him unfit for military service. Desperation made me willing to try anything.

On the morning of my medical I forced almost a full bar of Lifebuoy soap down my unwilling throat. Unfortunately, I showed no signs of frothing at the mouth – the soap served only as a powerful laxative. My mother, unaware of my cunning plan, put it down to fear. Arriving for the examination, I had to make an immediate and undignified dash to the lavatory and whilst in there also consumed the last of the bar of soap. I then drank what seemed like gallons of water to make the soap in my stomach froth. Nothing happened, but looking at my green face in the mirror I was hopeful that this would help persuade the doctor to reject me. The *coup de grâce* of my somewhat deranged strategy was to smoke a cigarette. As a non-smoker this helped to increase my sweating, trembling nausea. But, sick as I felt then, it was nothing compared to how I felt when I was deemed fit for military service. My despair deepened when, on the train going home, I began to froth at the mouth, much to the horror of my fellow passengers. By the time I reached my destination my chin was sore from the seemingly endless volcano of lather that finally, and too late for me, erupted from my stomach.

So it was that in the second week of February 1950, I left Liverpool for Catterick. What a hell-hole! Situated in arguably the only grim area of the beautiful county of North Yorkshire, the place was under several feet of snow when I arrived. The journey to Catterick had been a nightmare. It took almost a day and a half because of heavy snow on the railway lines, which became covered again almost as soon as they were cleared. The journey was made bearable by the company of another eighteen-year-old from Liverpool, Ken Stevenson. We were to join the same training regiment, 4 TR. After changing trains at York and again at Darlington, where it seemed hundreds of other conscripts were gathered, we joined a local Richmond train. At Richmond we lined up under signs telling us which regiment was which. Snarling sergeants and screaming corporals harangued and insulted us into line and then on to the backs of lorries that slithered and swerved their way along snow-ploughed roads. The snow was piled so high on the sides of the roads it was level with the canvas sides of the lorries. Clambering out of the lorries in front of the guard room at 4 TR, we were greeted by the mustachioed, ramrod figure of the Regimental Sergeant Major, who informed us that we were 'a shower of shit' as he brought us to a ragged attention. Before stalking majestically off to the guardroom he expressed his hatred and contempt for national servicemen in general and then turned us over to the comparative mercy of the Company Sergeant Major. We were then marched off to the Nissen huts that were to be our accommodation. As the last into our hut I was left with the worst bed, the one next to the door.

Conditions for the national servicemen were bad and the treatment brutal. The strong were actively encouraged to bully, browbeat and assault the weak. The grinning corporals would only intervene when hospitalization, and thus explanation of the violence, looked inevitable. We awoke on the second morning to an early casualty of this officially sanctioned cruelty – one of our group was found hanging in the latrines. It was suicide. In those early days other men simply ran away, but this was a futile exercise. Catterick was under several feet of snow and the going difficult, if not impossible. They were soon brought back, locked in the guardroom and charged with desertion and after they were sentenced to military imprisonment we would never see them again.

It seemed to me that the war had prepared those of us from the city to cope better with the noise, explosions and scared screams than men from more rural areas. Whilst it was purgatory for us, it was hell on earth for them. But whatever our various backgrounds, the early fifties were not a good time to be a national serviceman. Britain was involved in conflicts around the world and it was mainly national servicemen who were committed to the fighting. It was clear that the War Office viewed the conscripts as little more than cannon fodder. Not only were the regular servicemen posted to softer options such as the Army on the Rhine, they were also paid more than double our one pound eight shillings a week.

I was still at that time the main financial support in my family. My father had only recently been discharged from hospital and his convalescence was to be slow and painful. Out of my wages I kept three shillings a week and the rest went home to my mother. It was around this time that the Labour government extended the period of national service from eighteen months to two years. Ironically, a senior member of the government, Emanuel Shinwell, was a former pacifist. How could a member of a Labour government, a self-professed pacifist, countenance, let alone sanction, such an action? Even as an ardent Labour supporter I soon gave up trying to justify the unjustifiable. I knew that I would have to find some strategy for surviving life in the army and fortunately I realized early on that the army had great respect for sporting prowess. At school I had played rugby for Merseyside, my cricket had been good enough for me to have a trial for Lancashire and my skill at football was also reasonable. I volunteered for all the teams and very quickly I was playing rugby and football for the regiment. Fear of fighting had given wings to my heels.

After a month of parade ground activity we were again divided up and assigned to different sections. Some of the men were posted for further combat training and then sent abroad to the war zones. Ken Stevenson and I were among those fortunate enough to be sent for training as teleprinter and cypher operators. These were supposed to be non-combative roles, but reports came through of the courage of teletype and printer operators that were frightening for the majority of us. The influence of both my grandfathers and my own experience of the terror and hardship that war brings had made me fervently anti-war. The government was sending young men still in their teens to the killing fields of Korea and Africa in defence of some incomprehensible and ideologically indefensible policy. I tried hard to persuade Ken not to volunteer. He would not listen and after only four months in the army he was posted to Korea. He was killed almost immediately, running across the runway from the aircraft. I will never forget reading of his death on the casualty noticeboard.

The sense of cold horror sent me stumbling to lie down on my bed. Was all the suffering of the Second World War to come to this? What had happened to our bright new dawn? Were we the generation of young men that Western governments had decided were expendable? Had we as children survived the bombings and dark days of the war only to die as young men in places far from home? I believed then as I believe now that politicians wage war, but it is always the people, mostly the young, who are sacrificed to the fight. Certainly, the government appeared to have learned nothing from the war – the world had become an even more dangerous place. The development, proliferation and constant threat from nuclear weaponry meant we now faced Armageddon. I have come to understand that governments, no matter how idealistic their promise, soon lose the 'vision thing'. It is we the people who have to keep the faith and remind our politicians of it.

The end of the war had brought such great hope. Glad to be alive, Grandad and I had worked energetically in Crosby for a Labour government. We had a campaign song for our candidate, Philip Voss:

> 'Vote for the Labour Party,
> Vote for Philip Voss,
> Go right to the polling station
> And mark your little cross.'

The Labour Party's landslide victory in 1945 did not include Crosby, where it was thoroughly beaten. The policies of the Labour government of 1945–50 were truly radical and groundbreaking, none more so than the establishment of the National Health Service. No one achieved more than the great Nye Bevan in delivering a service that is our treasured gift to each other. It was and should continue to be a commitment to the best of socialist principles.

Despite my well-known left-wing views and vocal opposition to war I was posted in the autumn of 1950 to work in the Signals Section in the War Office. I was based at Cambridge Barracks in Woolwich and I very quickly discovered that the brutality and mindless humiliations inflicted as routine on national servicemen were endemic, not merely confined to the raw recruits herded into Catterick camp. I was unpacking when a sergeant marched in and snarled, 'Booth, you're from Liverpool?'

'Yes.'

'Red or blue?'

'Red of course.'

'That's you finished', he said and walked out.

His name was Jones, a regular with only a few months to serve before returning to Liverpool and his job in the docks. The next morning, when we went on parade Sergeant Jones put me on fatigues. Day after day it was guard duty, sentry duty – fatigues all the time. On my first day I was sent to clean the latrines. When I finished Jones marched in, threw things on the floor and ordered me to clean them again. I had been in the army for nine months by then and to some extent I had become hardened to this level of idiocy, so I simply did as I was told. After about ten days I finally snapped when, after I had cleaned the latrines yet again, Jones walked in and began to urinate on the floor. Grabbing him, I banged him against the wall. 'That's it! That is it! Just because you support Everton and I support Liverpool. Now listen carefully you bastard. You're going back to Liverpool. One night you're going to be found floating in the fucking dock. Now you get off my back because I'm not fucking about.' As I let go of him he said, 'You fucking Liverpudlians are all fucking mad.' Then he walked off. Next day on parade I was not put on fatigues.

For the first time I was sent to the War Office, where it was soon discovered I was a hopeless operator, to be used only in the direst emergency and so I spent most of my time working in the office at the barracks. I had been there a few months when we received a notice that a soldier, Frank Mitchell, was being posted back to us from the gaol at Colchester Barracks. Mitchell was later to become a notorious villain of the fifties and sixties. Known as the 'Mad Axeman', he was an enforcer for the infamous Kray brothers. I was in the office when Mitchell arrived. He ducked under the doorframe as he came in. This man was huge – well over six foot and solid muscle. There was not an ounce of fat on him. The institutionalized bullying of the army inevitably dictated the assumption that someone of Mitchell's physical stature would have to be contained before he could pose any threat – real or imagined. I soon discovered that, like so many really big men, he was, in fact, a gentle giant – at that time he just looked intimidating.

One morning on parade Mitchell was seconds late because he had been on fatigues, cleaning latrines. He was immediately charged by a major, the acting Commanding Officer. When a soldier is charged he has two soldiers as escorts to march him in. That morning there was sudden and noticeable absence of available escorts and, unaware of what was going on, I was summoned along with another clerk from the office to be Mitchell's escort. We marched him in. After his case was heard the major asked Mitchell, 'Are you prepared to accept my punishment or do you want to wait for the Commanding Officer?'

Mitchell's offence did not deserve more than forty-eight hours and he indicated he would take the punishment meted out by the major. 'Twenty-eight days', said the major. This meant Mitchell would have to return to Colchester. We were then ordered to march him out.

Mitchell did not move. 'Hang on. What did you just say?', he asked the major.

'Twenty-eight days.'

'You've given me twenty-eight days for being ninety seconds late?'

'Yes.'

'You can't do that. You're not the C.O.'

'Don't tell me what I can or cannot do. I am the acting C.O. Get out of here.' The major was clearly agitated. Handing down draconian punishment was one thing. Dealing with a very large, stubborn and now angry miscreant was quite another.

Mitchell persisted, 'You're only a major – you can't give me more than twenty-one days.'

Almost beside himself, the major yelled, 'Don't question me. Get out of here.'

At this point Mitchell sat down on the floor. The sergeant major, who thus far had been a silent observer to this farce, ordered me and the other clerk to pick up Mitchell and carry him out of the room. We tried, but there was no way we were going to be able to move this man. Mitchell just sat there and laughed at our puny efforts. In an attempt to regain the initiative the major ordered us all out into the corridor to discuss how to proceed. Re-entering the office, we found Mitchell now lying on the floor. At this point, six of the biggest soldiers in the barracks came in and picked up Mitchell bodily and carried him off to the guard-room. The instructions were that he was to remain there until the Commanding Officer returned. Then the major turned his attention to me and the other clerk who had acted as Mitchell's escort. He told us we were a disgrace to the uniform – we should have done something to resolve the situation with Mitchell. As punishment we were to do guard duty, a task from which, as a sportsman, I had been hitherto exempt.

In the many and varied pecking sub-orders that exist within the military framework the one that organized guard duty meant the smartest soldier in the guardroom automatically got the easiest tasks. Much to my amazement and relief, that accolade was accorded to me. I was made 'stick man', which meant I collected the food and the tea and read the paper. Nothing too onerous, or so I believed until the moment I was informed that a duty of 'stick man' was to exercise the prisoners. At that time there was only one prisoner – Frank

Mitchell. The time came for the half-hour exercise period and a handcuff was snapped onto my wrist. I was then escorted to Mitchell's cell by the whole guard armed with rifles loaded with live ammunition. I entered the cell to find Mitchell on the floor in his vest and underpants doing push-ups like a steam hammer.

'Hello Boothie,' he said. 'All right?' He was handcuffed to me and the armed guard escorted us out into the exercise yard. This was a small, grim place surrounded by a high wall that was topped with barbed wire and broken glass. The steel door was slammed shut behind us and I was out there alone with Frank Mitchell.

'Come on Boothie,' he said.

'What are we going to do?'

'We're going to exercise, aren't we?'

He started sprinting round the yard dragging me with him. Every so often he would drop to the ground to do push-ups and I had no option but to get on the ground with him. In the way of conversation he suddenly said to me, 'You know? I could break your back just like that. D'you know what I mean?'

Whilst nodding furiously in my attempt to make sure he was certain I knew what he was saying, I managed between breathless gasps to reply, 'I'm really grateful you're not going to break my back.'

He then asked, 'What do you think about me being in here then?'

'It's not fair.'

'You're all right you are Boothie.'

After about twenty minutes I was in grave danger of heart failure, despite believing myself reasonably fit. So he picked me up, put me under his arm and ran round carrying me. He continued chatting to me, 'I'm going to break out of here and you can tell them if you like.'

Of course, I swore I would not breathe a word.

'Just tell them that when I decide to go, if they get in my way I will kill them.'

Two days later, when the guards went to Mitchell's cell at exercise time, they found him fully dressed. He picked up one of the guards and, throwing him at the rest, they collapsed like dominoes. He then walked out, jogged past the gate and down the road to Woolwich station. The alarm bell was ringing and lots of people were dashing about, but no one actually set off in pursuit. At the station Mitchell jumped off the end of the platform and disappeared into the tunnel to re-emerge into London underworld mythology as the 'Mad Axeman'.

Years later I used to drink in a pub in Lisson Grove that was run by a friend of mine. At the end of the bar one Monday evening I found a little old man wearing a trilby with an overcoat that practically came to the ground. He was with a group of men and one of them came over to me and said, 'Hello Tone. How are you doing? The old man wants to buy you a drink.'

I went over. The old man insisted on buying me a drink and we stood chatting for a while. It was now my turn. 'What will you have?'

'No,' he said. 'That's all right.'

'Come on,' I said. 'You're an old age pensioner, for Christ's sake.'

I thought his companions were just looking after him. But one of them leaned over and whispered, 'Don't you know who this is?'

I shook my head.

'This is Ronnie and Reg's dad.'

'Mr Kray?' Well, well.

We went on talking, Mr Kray and I, until just before closing time, but before I could think of leaving, Mr Kray said, 'When they lock the doors we'll have a good drink, son.'

And we did. So much so that, emboldened by drink, I asked, 'What happened to Frank Mitchell? I was in the army with him.'

'Do you know what was wrong with Frank Mitchell?' he said.

'No. Tell me.'

'Well my boys wanted Mitchell to do a job. So, they sprung him from Dartmoor and fixed him up with a very nice place in Plumstead – over a shop. When my Ronnie went down to see him he said, "What do you want Frank?" Do you know the one thing he wanted?'

'After five years in prison? A bit of crumpet!'

'Clever boy! He wanted a girl. My Ronnie said, "Of course I'll arrange that for you. Don't worry about that Frank, but it's a bit dodgy at the moment because everybody's looking for you. We've got to be certain to find a brass who won't talk and will come and do the business." I mean my Ronnie said to him, "You've got the reputation for being a fucking animal. You're the Mad Axeman." Every time Ronnie or Reggie went down to see him Mitchell said, "Where's this woman you promised me?" Six days went by and Mitchell was getting more and more angry. He wasn't allowed to leave the premises and he was getting special attention. Someone was with him all the time because he was an animal. You should have seen the food that was going in that flat.'

'So what happened?' I asked.

'Well, my Ronnie went in there and Mitchell asked again about a girl. Ronnie said "It's a bit difficult." Then Mitchell laid hands on my Ronnie. Nobody lays hands on my boys. He lifted Ronnie up, held him against the wall and said, "Let's get this straight. If you don't bring me a woman tomorrow I'm going to come round and fuck your mother." '

'What!'

'He said he was going to fuck mummy.'

By now I could only squeak in astonishment, 'And you believed him?'

'He was a bloody lunatic. He would have come round and done anything.'

As a Whitehall warrior I was now an object of both contempt and envy amongst my colleagues. Catterick was a long way from Liverpool, but London was another planet. Although still bearing the scars of war, its theatre and nightlife thrilled and intrigued me. The Nuffield Centre behind St Martin-in-the-Fields overlooking Trafalgar Square, a club for members of the armed forces, became like a second home. There I could get cheap meals and free theatre tickets. I grabbed the opportunity to see great actors, singers, dancers, musicians. I persuaded my Commanding Officer's secretary to accompany me, but he was not entirely pleased to discover this. He informed me, the first posting that came into the War Office for a soldier of my grade was mine. I assume he hoped for a posting to Korea for me, but as luck would have it the first vacant posting was to the Supreme Headquarters, Allied Powers, Europe (SHAPE). I spent the final year of my national service in Paris.

My mother used to say I had the luck of the devil. On this occasion she was right. I arrived in Paris in early spring 1951 to find my accommodation was not a barracks, but a clean and pleasant hotel. The receptionist handed me my room key, informing me at the same time that I was sharing with Mr Atkins. I was nonplussed when she then enquired what time I would like breakfast next morning and if I would prefer to eat in my bedroom or the dining room. Flustered, I replied I would eat at eight o'clock in my room. There was no sign of Mr Atkins in the room. I was by now very hungry, but unsure what to do I waited a while and then went back downstairs. 'Excuse me, where do I get something to eat?' 'Dinner is served between seventeen hundred hours and midnight.' Quite unused to being in a hotel, let alone abroad, I anxiously asked about cost. 'Oh no, monsieur. Everything is paid for.'

My first meal in Paris was wonderful, a revelation to my tastebuds and a world away from the stodge at Cambridge Barracks. It was also my first experience of wine other than that served at Communion! Afterwards I thought I should return to my room and wait for Atkins. By eleven o'clock he had still not returned so, exhausted by the long journey and the strangeness of everything, I went to bed. About half an hour later a drunk fell through the door – the elusive Mr Atkins.

'What time do you get up in the morning?', I asked.

'When you feel like it. Why do you ask?'

'I said I would have breakfast at eight.'

There was an uncomprehending pause before he collected his thoughts and said, 'You bloody idiot! Nobody gets up before ten. Go down at once and tell them quarter to ten.' I did as I was told.

The next morning, despite a monumental hangover, Atkins took me to SHAPE. The Americans were organizing duties at that time and I was sent in to see one of their officers. A Confederate flag was draped across the wall behind his desk. 'Hi, Tony. How you doing?' he drawled. 'I'm Colonel Jackson.'

'Stonewall, of course,' I replied.

Evidently pleased by my response, he invited me to sit down and tell him about myself. I felt the interview was going well up to the point when he asked me where I was from. When I told him I was from Liverpool he asked me if I was north or south. Misunderstanding his drift, I replied I was a northerner. Big mistake.

Leaping to his feet, he ordered me out of his office. 'Get out of here. I won't have any of you goddamn Yankees in my office,' he yelled.

In vain I protested I was from the north of England. 'What do I do?'

'Find out!'

The clerk outside the office asked what had gone on. Shaking his head at my stupidity, he said no one told the Colonel they were from the north. He then asked, 'What's he put you on?'

'I don't know.'

'He must have told you something.'

'He told me to find out. So what should I do?'

'Come back later, it's lunchtime.'

When I returned to the office I was told the British soldiers were under the command of a Sergeant Major, but he was on leave for a month. Nobody had any idea what I was supposed to do. I was told to go back to the hotel and report in once a week. Paris in springtime, and I was free to wander the streets exploring that beautiful city. The army had kitted me out with a civilian uniform of grey flannels, white shirt, black shoes, a Royal Corps of Signals tie and a dark blazer. I pranced around Paris looking like the typical Englishman abroad. One day I was leaning on the first-floor balcony of the Eiffel Tower when a group of American girls arrived and stood behind me discussing where they should go next. One of them suggested Sacré Coeur, but none of them knew the way. I then enjoyed a short but lucrative career as a tourist guide.

My blissful state was rudely interrupted by a summons from SHAPE. The Combined Services rugby team were on tour and had suffered a lot of injuries. I was ordered to join them. The next morning I met the team outside their hotel in Fontainebleau and was told I would be playing centre. I had done no training since arriving in Paris and was far from match fit, and when I found out who our opponents were to be, the French Combined Services, I was convinced some sort of mistake must have been made. My strenuous protests fell on deaf ears and that afternoon I walked out before a vast crowd that included Field Marshal Montgomery, our Commander-in-Chief. The first half went well and it was a comfortable three points each at half-time when they brought on a bucket of tea. I dipped my cup into it and, unprepared, took a thirsty mouthful. I think the tea leaves must have been dipped briefly into what was essentially a bucket of hot brandy! Whilst we were knocking this back an officer approached us to say that Monty was enjoying the game and he promised us a weekend in Paris if we won. With the bucket emptied, we started the second half legless. Within minutes the atmosphere of the game had completely changed and the French team played like savages. Our full-back was taken off with a broken leg – we were roundly beaten in every sense of the word.

Later, at the dinner for the two sides, I asked the French soldier sitting next to me what had changed for the second half. He said, 'We saw an officer speak to your team at half-time. What did he say?'

'He promised us a weekend in Paris if we won.'

'And if you lost?'

'Nothing.'

'Well our Commander sent his aide on at half-time to tell us that if we won we would all get a month's leave. If we lost we would all be sent to Indo-China.'

'Why didn't you just tell us? There was no need to half kill us.'

He simply shrugged and said, 'We had to be sure.'

The injuries I sustained in the game meant I was left behind when the team tour continued. Unfortunately, my presence on the field brought me to the attention of the RSM, to whom I should have reported on my arrival in Paris. My punishment was to be posted to Fontainebleau, which he believed to be the equivalent of SHAPE's Siberia. It turned out to be a stop on the route to paradise. Once again hotel accommodation was provided and, whilst the French and Americans felt the need to play war games, the British treated the posting as an extended holiday. There was a sizeable Communist community in Fontainebleau and their bars were out of bounds to the Allied forces.

It was the height of the Cold War and paranoia was rampant, but I was able to sit in the bars undisturbed by the Military Police. I had bought jeans and a shirt at a flea market and so did not look like a soldier. But it was a chance meeting in the street that was to bring sex, politics and religion, my three favourite subjects, back into my life.

Covered head to toe in mud, I was returning to the hotel after a particularly fierce rugby kick-around with the French. Walking towards me was a very pretty young French woman. I could not let the opportunity pass and so rather lamely asked her the way to the French barracks. She laughed and in the most incredible accent I have ever heard – a Yorkshire/French hybrid – asked me if I was asking to take her courting. I conceded that was my real intention and she told me that, as she was from a respectable family, I would have to gain the permission of her mother. Monique gave me her address and I went to her home that evening. Her mother Nicole, a stunningly attractive woman in her late thirties, was one of the local doctors. She was very correct, even stern, and clearly looked with some disapproval on her daughter being picked up in the street by a passing British soldier. After some persuasion she finally agreed that I might take her daughter to the cinema with her son, a spotty youth, as chaperon. We went to see a film I had previously seen in London, *In a Lonely Place*, with Humphrey Bogart and Gloria Grahame. There appeared to be a problem with the dubbing. Bogart now had a high-pitched, squeaky voice and Gloria Grahame sounded like Paul Robeson. Back at the house her mother invited me to Sunday lunch after Mass. Keen to make a good impression I paraded my Catholic credentials, even though I had not voluntarily entered a church since I was conscripted.

Monique and I saw each other several times after that, each time chaperoned by the spotty brother. She then told me she had another suitor, a Dutch soldier who was very serious about their relationship and wanted to marry her, but we continued to see each other over the next few weeks. Monique then invited me to a dance. Her mother had taken a table at this dance and both the Dutchman and I were invited. It was decision time. If I wanted to marry her she would agree. If not, she would announce her engagement to the Dutch soldier at the dance. Monique spent most of the evening waltzing in the arms of my rival. At around ten-thirty, Nicole announced her intention to go home. I offered to walk with her and when we arrived she invited me in for a drink. I sat at her feet and she stroked my hair. Eventually, we kissed and she led me upstairs, locking the bedroom door behind us.

Living *en famille* with Nicole gave a new and exciting perspective to my life. I left a post-war Britain still enveloped in dull greyness and the daily grind of ration books to find France vibrant and awash with colour. Perhaps Britain was simply exhausted by war and the human and emotional effort it had cost, whilst France, particularly Paris, having survived the brutality of German occupation, was determined to live life to the full, to recover *joie de vivre*. Whatever, France excited my imagination. Nicole encouraged my interest in the theatre and French literature and her political connections opened many doors for me.

Nicole, the daughter of reasonably well-to-do Communist parents, had been brought up in Chantilly. After medical school she had made a disastrous marriage. Nicole's husband was a chief customs officer stationed on the Swiss border. His excessive philandering and penchant for domestic violence caused Nicole to return to her medical practice in Fontainebleau. Her husband had retained his frontier position during the Occupation. Six years after the war he was living openly with his mistress and their child, only returning to Fontainebleau in the summer to visit his other children. During the war Nicole had been a member of the Resistance. The Germans assumed that as a Vichy official both he and his family were trustworthy, thus providing Nicole's Resistance activities with an excellent cover. As a doctor she had been able to help the injured Allied pilots who bailed out of their aircraft in the area. This explained why her daughter spoke English with a Yorkshire accent. Monique had spent several summer holidays near Wakefield staying with the family of a pilot whose life had been saved by her mother. During the war, the Resistance had given Nicole the use of a one-bedroom apartment in Paris. This was both a surgery and a safe house. After the war a grateful Resistance presented the apartment to Nicole and we would spend three weekends out of four in Paris. During the first weekend at the apartment Nicole took me to see a concert by an old friend of hers, Edith Piaf.

Piaf had given us excellent seats in a box. I was transfixed by the tiny figure on the stage. She was magnificent. I also remember thinking how much more sophisticated the staging and lighting were compared to the shows I had seen in London. Afterwards, I stood in the great chanteuse's dressing room whilst she and Nicole discussed, from what I could make out, the most intimate details of our relationship. Bright red with embarrassment, I almost blew my cover – as someone who spoke little and understood even less French. A handsome young man sprawled on a sofa was obviously enjoying every moment of my discomfort. Yves Montand was, at that time, Piaf's protégé, an aspiring singer who went on to become one of the great French actors. I came to know him quite well as he was a Communist comrade of Nicole's, and I was to meet him again a few years later in London under different circumstances for both of us. Also in Piaf's dressing room that night was another much younger man, Charles Aznavour, waiting his turn.

At dinner, whilst Piaf and Nicole engaged in animated conversation, Montand and I tried desperately to communicate in a hybrid Franglais which was a source of great amusement to Aznavour. I noticed how ill Piaf looked and later Nicole told me that during the meal she had tried discussing Piaf's health with her. Nicole was very concerned, as years of self-abuse with drugs and alcohol were clearly taking their toll on Piaf. Nicole had harangued the startled Montand on the need to take more care of Piaf, but at that point Aznavour had appeared with more wine.

Our first weekend in Paris also included taking part in a demonstration in support of a guaranteed minimum wage. Although I had been on a march in London in support of striking dockers, I had never before had the French experience. The numbers and noise were overwhelming. Nicole and I marched with those people in the French Communist Party who had also been members of the Resistance – the Francs-Tireurs et Partisans, the FTP, who were also known by their nickname, 'parti des fusillés' (the party of the shot). The gendarmerie stood sullenly by, but hiding in side streets were the dreaded CRS, the infamous riot squad. I was to experience police brutality against anti-war demonstrators in London, but my first experience of this kind of violence was on the streets of Paris. The British police usually justified any injuries to their prisoners by describing how they fell down the steps to the cells. The French police had no such sensitivities or scruples. They would move in to break up demonstrations with enthusiastic use of their batons. On this march the CRS ran riot; no one, even women and children, was safe. As they charged into the crowd, breaking it up and forcing people to run, Nicole and I found ourselves cornered.

We cowered on a doorstep trying to fend off the blows from CRS batons when the door behind us suddenly opened and a pair of hands dragged Nicole inside to safety. As I started to fall, my arms taking the blows aimed at my head, I too was dragged to safety. The people who rescued us were probably not Communist, nor were they necessarily supporters of the demonstration. They were simply decent French people appalled by the police brutality. However, the demonstration successfully brought the centre of Paris to a standstill and was my first direct experience of people power. It was only years later that I reflected on what might have happened had I been arrested that day. I was a British soldier working for SHAPE, on an anti-war demonstration with my Communist lover. Any headlines I have generated since would have paled into insignificance compared to what that one might have been.

It was the first of many demonstrations that I took part in alongside Nicole. Afterwards we would retire to the Communist bistros with other activists and talk politics, politics and more politics. My political education and the development of a left-wing political ideology grounded by my grandfather was thoroughly developed and reinforced. These were powerful and articulate influences. The French seemed to be locked into permanent revolution as governments fell almost every few months. The Fourth Republic had a version of the Labour Party Clause Four which stated that: 'any property and undertaking which possesses and acquires the character of a public service or a monopoly must come under collective ownership'. It would be more than thirty years later before these provisions became the legal foundation for the programme of nationalization undertaken by the French government during the 1980s – ironically, just as the Thatcher government was privatizing those in Britain.

The Café Dôme in Montmartre, popular in the 1930s with, amongst others, Henry Miller and Ernest Hemingway, was our favourite meeting place. There we discussed America's Cold War policy and our mutual fear that General Douglas MacArthur would fabricate an excuse to use an atomic bomb in Korea. General de Gaulle was then an omnipresent factor of French politics. He had not taken his rejection by the French people at the end of the war with dignity. Instead he sulked at Colombey-les-deux-Églises whilst the Left mercilessly ridiculed his arrogance and pomposity. His hopes lay with the admiration of the powerful right wing, then trying desperately to retain the French grip on the world's second largest empire (just as in Britain the left wing were keen to see the colonies regain their independence). For the French, political tensions in Vietnam and Algeria were about to boil over, with the Right and Left polarized in their support for the different sides in the conflicts.

Living a life that seemed a million miles from Liverpool and a wartime childhood of fear and deprivation, I discovered what a heady and passionate mixture the arts, particularly the theatre, and politics could be. As Christmas 1952 approached Nicole and I shared so many hopes and dreams for the future. She fired my imagination with plans for me to stay on in France after completing my national service and to study history at the Sorbonne. I was young, life was wonderful, but cold and cruel reality was lurking just around the corner.

On one of my rare visits to the military headquarters I was told to prepare for demob and my return to Britain. I had played rugby alongside my Commanding Officer and we had a good relationship; it was to him that I turned for help in my desperation to remain in France. Unfortunately there was nothing he could do, despite his sympathy for my predicament. There was no way the army would discharge me in France. I had to return to Britain. Wonderful, youthful naivety persuaded me I simply had to return home to be demobbed and explain to my parents I would be studying in Paris before returning as quickly as possible to Nicole and our future together. I had no sense of what really lay ahead for me.

As I walked back through the front door of the house in Ferndale Road I knew for certain I could not return to my life as it had been or as my parents and family thought it should be. My father, although pleased to see me, stood in the hallway grinning awkwardly, only commenting that I had grown taller and filled out. I was shocked to discover he was still convalescing and would be for several more months. My grandmother, Till, peering out from around the living room door, startled everyone by announcing that I looked like a French gigolo – a statement far more accurate than she could have known. My mother, who had opened the front door to me, also immediately noticed the difference. I was no longer the boy she had sent away and it was my relationship with her that would alter the most dramatically. However, in the short term, because I was not yet twenty-one, she felt able forcefully to reassert her dominant parental role. She had no understanding of my experiences in Paris and anyway would have rejected them as irrelevant to the life she believed lay ahead of me.

At eight o'clock on my first Monday morning back at home I was woken and directed to the Labour Exchange. The shipping line had eventually and grudgingly agreed to pay my father five hundred pounds in compensation for his accident – for a broken back, pelvis, legs and a shattered left arm. The union, operating with the shipping lines rather than for their members, had done nothing to help or pursue my father's legitimate claim. Rather, they told him he was lucky to get what was offered and stood to lose even that paltry amount if he persisted any further. The union underlined their position by telling him he would also never be allowed to sail again if he did not accept the company's offer. Until the compensation came through my family needed me to continue in the role of main financial support.

My mother had always taken cleaning jobs to supplement our income and she would set off five mornings a week on her old bicycle for houses in Blundellsands. My mother was a proud woman, but a woman who was prepared to do what was necessary to keep her home together. I know from stories she told me that some of the people she cleaned for behaved atrociously towards her. My mother was a strong-willed and sometimes difficult woman – I certainly was to have my problems with her – but she was also a good and principled woman. I still ache when I think of her being treated in such a patronizing, arrogant and insensitive manner by those who thought her poverty and her status as a cleaning woman legitimated such behaviour.

I tried to get back my former job at the American Consulate; however, the legislation that allowed national servicemen to return to their former employment did not apply to the consulate. As I left the Cunard Building I bumped into a man whom I knew from the time before I was called up. We used to travel on the same tram to work each morning and through conversations had got to know each other quite well. He was pleased to see me and after I explained that the consulate would not allow me to return to my previous post, he offered me a job. He was the chief accountant for the Cunard Steamship Company and my new employment would be in the accounts department. Delighted, I accepted his offer with alacrity, forgetting that sums were not my strong point. My unsuitability became obvious fairly rapidly, but I needed to keep the job. One of the senior clerks informed me that if I wanted to keep the chief accountant on my side I should either join his golf club or, his other passion, the Crosby Amateur Dramatic Society. As I was unable to afford golf, acting it had to be. This was a major turning point. For the first time I knew beyond doubt what I wanted to do for the rest of my life.

I had reluctantly abandoned my plans to return to France, although Nicole and I maintained a regular correspondence. I now wrote to her of my new love for the theatre. She came to stay for a short time and we parted with sadness, but as friends. If ever I changed my mind, Nicole told me, I would always be welcome at Fontainebleau.

I had promised my parents I would not leave home until I was twenty-one and not before my father was fit enough to return to work. By the summer of 1952 my father was at last able to rejoin his ship, the MV *Britannic*. Bored and unhappy with my job, but in desperate need of funds to pursue my dreams of an acting career, I signed on the same ship as my father. In October 1952 – I had just celebrated my twenty-first birthday – we sailed for New York. My career at sea was short and fairly ignominious, but I enjoyed the opportunity to travel.

I particularly remember five glorious days in Venice. On the first evening I teamed up with Richard, the young pianist from the ship. We discovered an all-night jazz club. When, in the early hours of the morning, we were presented with our bill, it looked as if we were expected to settle the Italian national debt. We simply did not have the money to cover it. I pleaded with the proprietor and in desperation offered Richard's services to pay the bill. The manager somewhat reluctantly agreed and my far from happy friend then played to an appreciative audience for over two hours. I meanwhile disappeared with a very attractive singer from the club and spent the remaining four days of my shore leave with her. She was extremely agreeable company – so much so, I found myself tearing down the quayside as the *Britannic* headed out into the lagoon, my jeering friends waving their farewells. I eventually located the shipping agent's office and persuaded a particularly unco-operative clerk to fund my train fare to Naples. I rejoined the ship to be informed by the grim-faced skipper that my sea-going career was over.

I was not particularly distraught at this news. I had managed to save enough money to achieve my ambition of moving to London and in May 1953 I arrived at Euston station. I felt there would be more opportunities for a raw, young, would-be actor in London than in Liverpool and that Wednesday evening, alone, apprehensive but exhilarated, I noticed a copy of *The Stage* on a news-stand. Reading it in a run-down hotel near the station, two advertisements caught my eye and I wrote the applications that night. Saturday morning brought two offers of work. One as an unpaid student assistant stage manager at London's Richmond theatre, the other to join a touring repertory company based in north Yorkshire. I chose the second. On the Sunday evening I travelled to the village of Hutton Rudby to join the Earl Armstrong Touring Repertory Company. It was a small band of five – six with me. There were Mr and Mrs Armstrong, who played the leads and directed the plays; Fern, their daughter, who was then the juvenile lead, but planned to join another repertory company to be with her boyfriend; and the young character parts were taken by Christopher Lethbridge-Baker and Ruth Green.

On arrival I was handed a script and told to learn it for the next night. By the end of the first week I had appeared in three plays and three improvised curtain raisers. I loved it. At the end of the week the company moved south to Pocklington. At rehearsal on the Monday morning of my second week I met the new juvenile lead, eighteen-year-old Gale Howard, who was working a summer season before going on to the Royal Academy of Dramatic Art (RADA). Born and brought up in Ilkeston, Derbyshire, where her father had been a coal miner, she was, like me, short of funds. I was captivated by her pretty, gamine looks and I relished the love scenes we were to play. At the end of the week the company moved on to Harlech for a limited season followed by a tour of north and mid-Wales. As we were in Wales the management decided to do a season of plays by Emlyn Williams. To create interest and boost the box office, local amateurs played the minor roles in each place we visited. Arriving in Dolgellau we were met at the hall by a man who introduced himself as 'Jones, the grocer'. He was to play the Abbé in *The Marquis*. After informing us that not only had he toured Mesopotamia in *Chu Chin Chow*, but that he was also the leading light of the local players, he returned to his shop leaving us to put up the set.

Like every touring company, we had to carry around our own scenery. We used reversible flats to make the sets for the different plays we presented on stages of varying sizes. We also had to use a small rostrum. That meant that for the major staircase in *The Marquis*, down which the couple descended before their wedding, we had just a few steps up to the rostrum. In Dolgellau the stage was so small there was only a very narrow gap between the staircase and the back wall. On the night of the performance Jones the grocer arrived hours ahead of time. I asked him if he would like to go over his lines, but once again he reassured me he was an ex-professional.

'Well look,' I said. 'You have to carry a Bible and we've stuck the Abbé's lines inside just in case you go wrong.'

As usual the main roles were taken by Mr and Mrs Armstrong. Towards the end of the first act I was sent to bring the Abbé from upstairs so he could marry the couple. I went up the stairs and offstage to where Jones was waiting.

'Now?' he whispered.

'Yes, now.' I helped him onto the rostrum.

Our cue came up. I walked ahead of him and said, 'I've brought the Abbé'.

Jones the grocer then stepped for the first time into the full view of the audience. As he stood at the top of the staircase the whole house burst into enthusiastic applause. I looked up at him as he stood there acknowledging the adulation. He waved to the crowd, bowed, bowed again even deeper and stepped back.

'Look out,' I hissed.

Too late. Jones stepped back and fell straight down the gap. He was five foot ten and must have weighed fifteen stone. It was a spectacular fall.

Pandemonium broke out in the audience as I dashed back up the stairs to find Jones firmly jammed in the gap, only his head above the rostrum. The toupee no one realized he wore was hanging at a jaunty angle over his left ear. The leading lady, Kit Armstrong, was shouting at me, 'Get him out. For Christ's sake, get him out.'

Jones was far too heavy for me to pull up so I ran round the stairs and, by dint of hanging on to his legs, managed to release him from below.

His hairpiece having completely disappeared during the struggle, Jones decided he wanted to go back for it. 'Forget the wig,' once again I hissed, all too aware that Earl Armstrong and his wife were furious.

As I dragged Jones downstage the audience gave him a round of applause and he managed to pull himself together. Then, 'Oh my God!' he squeaked.

'What now?'

'The Bible. I've lost the Bible.'

'Never mind. Just get on with it,' I urged.

'But the lines are in the Bible.'

'Yes, but you know the part.'

'No. No I don't. The lines are in the Bible.'

'What!'

We all stared at him in utter disbelief – a demented actor who had lost his wig and forgotten his lines. Levels of hysteria both on and off the stage were threatening to boil over.

'Just declare them man and wife,' snarled Kit Armstrong.

'I declare you man and wife,' the grocer managed.

'Now, in the name of God go!' said Kit Armstrong.

Jones walked up to the double doors at the back of the stage. In his flustered desperation he forgot the doors opened out on to the stage. If pushed the opposite way they jammed. Pushing them the wrong way, Jones locked us all on the stage. By now almost crying with panic and humiliation, he turned and said, 'I can't get out!'

Kit Armstrong snapped and rushed towards Jones screaming, 'I'll kill him, I'll kill him!' as she chased him up the stairs. As the audience burst into delighted and thunderous applause I ran after them and pulled down the curtain.

All that season we worked from nine in the morning until eleven in the evening. We shared the work – everything from painting scenery to building sets, applying make-up to selling tickets at the box office. I had never worked so hard for so little money, but I loved it. We had really good fun. It was also during that summer that Gale and I became lovers. At first we were very discreet. Management, in the form of Mr and Mrs Earl Armstrong, frowned upon such things. Gradually we grew bolder and at Christmas I travelled to Ilkeston with Gale to spend the holiday with her father and stepmother. There we visited various friends, including the local doctor whose son, William Roache, would go on to be a lifer in *Coronation Street*. We also realized that Gale was pregnant.

To prevent embarrassment when we returned to Wales for the pantomime season we pretended we had married. As a couple we tried to get a wage increase from the Armstrongs, but they turned us down and we decided to leave the company at the end of the pantomime.

In early February we travelled to London to look for work. We found rooms in theatrical digs behind the Marylebone Road. Gale was by now suffering acute morning sickness. We knew what we must do and in the late spring of 1954 Gale and I were married at Marylebone registry office, with two friends of Gale's as witnesses. Marriage brought us a change of luck. I was offered a job with a repertory company in Bury, Lancashire – the Frank H. Fortesque Famous Players. At lunchtime on my first day another young actor in the company, Peter Adamson, later famous as Len Fairclough in *Coronation Street*, suggested we visit the local pub. As we walked in, Adamson strode purposefully to the bar calling out to the publican, 'Two pints of bitter my good man and show us your cock!' The angry recipient of this request vaulted over the bar and with one blow felled my surprised companion. He then banned both of us from his pub. I decided it would be wise to refrain from accepting any future invitations from Adamson.

Gale and I found a small flat in a large Victorian house in a pleasant part of Bury, which was a welcome relief after our experience in London. My parents, although surprised, were pleased at my marriage to Gale. They believed it would bring security and stability to my life. Ultimately, they hoped it would bring me to my senses and I would leave the theatre and get a proper job.

It was on 23 September 1954, in Bury General Hospital, that my first child, Cherie, was born. During our earlier tour of mid-Wales Gale and I stayed with a pleasant couple who had a delightful daughter named Cherie. Gale fell in love with the name and decided that if our baby was a girl she would call her Cherie. When Gale went into labour she telephoned me from the hospital. I immediately left rehearsals to join her. In those days expectant fathers were not allowed in the delivery rooms and I paced the corridors, nervously chain-smoking. Eventually, a midwife appeared to tell me I was the father of a baby girl. Overjoyed, I held this most precious and beautiful bundle in my arms. It was love at first sight, coupled with the fear every parent endures, that any harm may come to their perfect child.

I was to have this experience again in my life and I love all of my children deeply and unconditionally. That does not mean, however, that I now like all of them.

Three

Travelling Hopefully

'. . . think of the Future as a promised land which favoured heroes attain –'

C. S. Lewis, *The Screwtape Letters* (1942), no. 25

The Bury season ended in the spring of 1955 and Gale, Cherie and I returned to Liverpool, to Ferndale Road. Although my father went back to work for the Cunard Line once he had recovered sufficiently from his accident, as soon as the compensation was paid they felt their obligations towards him had finally been discharged and sacked him. Fortunately, he quickly managed to get a better job with more money making regular trips to West Africa with Elder Dempster, then considered to be a rival shipping line. My sister Audrey had married an assistant bank manager, William Grey, and they lived with his mother in Crosby. Even so, my mother's house was crowded as my brother Bob, the youngest member of our family, was still at home and my grandmother Till also occupied a bedroom. This meant that Gale and I had to share Bob's bedroom with him – not the most auspicious of circumstances for any newly married couple, but it was a roof over our heads and my mother doted on Cherie. When Gale and I decided that we would have to return to London to look for work, my mother offered to look after Cherie, keeping her in Liverpool. Only too aware of the economic and housing difficulties we would face in London, we were happy to agree.

In London, Gale and I found work in a short season of plays with a repertory company back in the north on the opposite side of the Pennines in Barnsley – Gale as the assistant stage manager and I in the juvenile character role. With Cherie happy and settled we decided she should remain at my mother's home, as the only accommodation we could find in Barnsley was over a public house. The demands of repertory theatre made it difficult for either of us to get back to Liverpool to see her, but at that time Gale was as determined as I to make a career in the theatre and we were happy together. Our life was a constant round of provincial theatres. This meant that when Cherie was a young baby my mother was essentially her main carer. It was not until after the birth of our second daughter, Lyndsey, in 1956 that Gale decided she wanted to give up acting and theatre work.

Barnsley was followed by a summer season on the pier at Llandudno and it was there that I had my first verbal confrontation with a party leader. The Welsh Labour Party was holding its annual conference in Llandudno. On the way to the theatre one evening I recognized the figure of Hugh Gaitskell, the future Party leader, walking towards me. His demeanour suggested that he was both pleased with himself and at peace with the world. I soon put an end to that. I walked purposefully towards him. Spotting me, Gaitskell smiled his politician's smile. At that time I had very strong opinions (as I still do) on the issue of nuclear weapons and that evening in Llandudno I seized the opportunity firmly and articulately to inform Gaitskell of my feelings. As the smile and the colour slid from his face he quickened his pace to escape from me, but I was not that easy to shake off. By now virtually zigzagging down the pier, he managed to brush past me and snapped, 'If you feel that strongly about it, join the Labour Party.' And he was gone.

Then as now, my overwhelming feeling about Gaitskell was that he seemed to be cold and calculating – a politician with patrician inclinations. For those reasons he was not popular with the rank and file membership of the Labour movement – he was always seen as an Establishment man. However, his final remark to me did strike home. I made enquiries about joining the Party, but I was already struggling to pay my union dues and further expenditure on Party membership was out of the question.

A few days later, leaving the theatre at lunchtime with Gale and other cast members I had an altogether more pleasant surprise encounter. One of the company asked Gale about Cherie and particularly what she looked like. Gale saw a child toddling towards her and said, 'Very like that little girl...' and stopped shocked for a moment. She then looked up into my parents' smiling faces. They had brought Cherie on a surprise visit for the day. Our little girl had made her first tentative steps without us being there to witness the transition from baby to toddler.

After a Christmas season at Bognor Regis, Gale and I returned to Liverpool. Gale, pregnant with Lyndsey, decided to stay on in Liv-

My parents George Henry Booth and Mary
Vera Thompson were married at St. Peter
and Paul's Church, Great Crosby on 7 July
1930. My father was a very good looking
man – my mother always insisted he was
Crosby's answer to Gary Cooper.

This is one of the first photographs of me.
I am intrigued by the anxious look on my
face. Perhaps it was the thought of being
recorded for posterity wearing a fluffy hat!

A photograph from the mid-sixties. Although I can't remember the event, it was obviously important enough for me to be forced into wearing a suit and tie.

Pat and me in *A Girl Called Sadie*.

My brother Robert and me giving Quintin Hogg a hard time at Friends House, Euston. It was 1964 and Hogg was campaigning on behalf of Geoffrey Johnson Smith the Conservative candidate for Holborn and St Pancras.

Warren Mitchell, Una Stubbs, Dandy Nichols and me at a film press reception in February 1968. We were just about to go into production on the first *'Til Death Do Us Do Part* film and were asked by the photographer to use the soda siphons. I was the only one to comply with the instruction!

Alan Simpson (of Galton and Simpson fame), Eric Sykes, Johnny Speight and me at Liverpool, Lime Street. We were on our way to watch Liverpool play in a European match. Tony Hancock was still asleep on the train and Ray Galton had gone to try and rouse him.

Signing autographs before the royal variety performance in 1972. It was not the first time that day – the dole office had required my signature that morning.

Kim Novak, Laurence Harvey and me in *Of Human Bondage*.

Confessions of a Window Cleaner – what
every well-dressed window cleaner wore!

Pat and me holding the old Football League Division One Trophy which had just been added to Liverpool's silverware. For some reason, I thought it appropriate to dress as a used car salesman!

Pat was always sure Tony was a winner despite the fact in
this particular campaign, the Beaconsfield by-election, he
crashed to inevitable defeat in the Tory stronghold.

Pat and me supporting the campaign of our old friend
and comrade Tony Benn, Chesterfield 1986.

erpool and I went to London. I was offered the role of the vicar in a tour of what I believed to be Somerset Maugham's 'Rain'. Reading the script on the train back to Manchester, I knew I had made a dreadful mistake. This was not Somerset Maugham. This was a terrible chimera of the original renamed *A Girl Called Sadie*. Incandescent with rage, I realized I was trapped. I had already signed a contract, but I still tried to hand in my notice immediately. However, Jack Gillan, a north-country impresario, would not release me, forcing me to work the full six weeks of the contract. Angry and affronted, I knew I had to make the best of the situation and I made a conscious decision to have a good time. Playing the role of Sadie was an exciting and exotic actress, Patricia Dean. She was married to a former actor, Peter Marsh, who now worked in advertising and was later, once he had become a millionaire, to be an acquaintance and ardent admirer of Margaret Thatcher. Despite Pat and I both suffering pangs of Catholic guilt, a short, torrid affair was only interrupted by my departure from the company and the remote possibility of a role in the West End. It was to be my destiny to meet her again. By then she had become known as Patricia Phoenix.

In London I was offered a part in a West End production, *No Time for Sergeants*, at Her Majesty's Theatre in the Haymarket. This meant that I could afford to pay for accommodation, and after finding a flat in Stoke Newington I was joined by a heavily pregnant Gale. The flat was fairly small and cramped and it made sense for my mother to continue to look after Cherie until after the new baby was born. Lyndsey was born in Hackney General Hospital in the early hours of 18 September 1956. I had recently read a book about the old Celtic kingdom of Lindsey and, liking the name and enchanted by the romance of the Celts, I wanted the name for our new daughter. Gale and I reached a compromise – the baby would be named Lyndsey.

When Gale brought her home we were joined by Cherie, who was by now an active and demanding toddler. Even at two years old she knew what she wanted and was more than capable of articulating her demands. She did not want to be in London, she wanted to be in Liverpool with her grandmother whom she clearly missed, but also where she would not have to compete with the demands of a new baby sister. Up to this point Cherie had spent most of her short life with my mother and in reality knew her better than she knew Gale and me. Eventually, a combination of small baby, cramped flat and loud, determinedly miserable toddler made us give way and Cherie returned to Liverpool.

Our situation was made more fraught as we were also, as ever, short of money. To subsidize the small wages I was receiving at the Haymarket I would finish at the theatre, rush home and grab five hours' sleep before rising at four o'clock to work in Covent Garden as a porter, finishing at ten o'clock in the morning. I was a porter for almost a year and it was hard physical work. Once I was so tired, I fell asleep on top of a wagon and my employer, after half an hour's search, found me and explained succinctly that he did not pay me to sleep. Although on that occasion I was not fired, a few weeks later he 'let me go'. After that I tried to sell brushes door-to-door. The venture was a complete disaster. I did not sell one brush in the month that I worked.

I had a bizarre experience on my way to the theatre for a matinée – one of my film idols, Errol Flynn, literally fell at my feet. The superstitious side to my nature demands I arrive for a performance at least an hour before the curtain goes up. That particular day my bus and tube connections dovetailed so neatly I was actually two hours ahead of time. As I ambled down the Haymarket a taxi drew up alongside me and a diminutive figure wearing a floppy hat and a very shabby camel-hair coat fell out of the door. It was Errol Flynn. Helping him to his feet, I propped him against a lamp-post.

He thrust a crumpled five-pound note into my hand and slurred, 'Give that to the cab, sport.'

I crossed to the cabbie and as I gave him the money excitedly said, 'That's Errol Flynn.'

'Yeh ... bleedin' drunk,' he responded. However, this statement was soon qualified by '... but a bleedin' toff,' when I gave him the five pounds.

As the taxi drove off I returned to Flynn, who was still clinging desperately to the lamp-post. I started to introduce myself, but Flynn interrupted, asking me to escort him to the nearest hostelry and join him for a drink. The pub was crowded with late lunchtime revellers and a cheer went up when Flynn was recognized. There was so much I wanted to talk to him about, but inevitably the great screen lover was quickly surrounded by a phalanx of adoring female fans and anyway I was on my way to the theatre. As I left, Flynn doffed his hat and yelled at me, 'You're OK, sport.' Amongst his many wonderful screen roles Flynn was without doubt the definitive Robin Hood in the 1938 film. He swashed and buckled magnificently under the suitably adoring eyes of Olivia de Havilland and in thrilling contempt for Basil Rathbone and the splendidly villainous Claude

Rains. I cannot have been the only small boy who fell off walls and out of trees trying to recreate his antics. It still makes me smile with pleasure to recall I once had a drink with Robin Hood.

No Time for Sergeants, a comedy about the American Air Force and the testing of a nuclear bomb, was my first appearance in a West End production. Despite our current financial strain, I began to feel that perhaps I could succeed as an actor. At the same time being married and the father of two small girls placed me under huge emotional pressure. Although Gale was supportive of my ambitions, my parents were still disapproving. They wanted and expected me to shoulder my responsibilities in a manner they believed was right, which meant returning to Liverpool and finding regular and secure employment. But then, as now, I have never wanted to be anything other than an actor. The constant search for perfection and the exultant adrenalin rush experienced in those rare moments when you believe that you may have achieved something fine is almost beyond description. In those moments, you really can believe it is possible to fly. I have done many things in my life I now regret, but my determination to pursue my life in acting is not one of them.

It was during the run of *No Time for Sergeants* in 1956 that the Suez Crisis broke out. As I was still a reservist I received notice that I should report at once to my unit. I decided that I would ignore the summons for as long as possible and instead campaign with those who were opposed to the British action over Suez. Anthony Eden, who had succeeded Winston Churchill as Conservative Prime Minister the previous year, had a reputation as a peacemaker, yet he was prepared to fling the country into armed conflict over a situation where the moral rights and wrongs were far from clear and where Britain did not have the support of either the United Nations or the United States. Gossip, particularly amongst anti-Suez campaigners, suggested Eden was dependent on a cocktail of uppers and downers and if this was the case then clearly his judgement would have been clouded. It was obvious from the messy example of the French problems just beginning in Algeria that the potential for disaster was high and yet, as with the Falklands Campaign in 1982, I was astonished by the wave of jingoism that swept through the country.

Western Europe and America were deeply locked into the Cold War against the Soviet Union, each side, by this time, armed with nuclear warheads; as Aneurin Bevan argued, 'the great Powers are stalemated by their own power'. Yet at the beginning of the crisis Gaitskell, who had succeeded Attlee as Labour leader earlier in the year, did not advocate negotiation; instead, to the dismay of the Labour Party, he actually supported the government line. The Cold War was a monumental and extremely perilous game of bluff with the possibility that one day the ridiculous posturing would end with the bluff called. 'That is the bankruptcy of statesmanship. The world has travelled that way in my own lifetime twice. We dare not travel that way again, because this time there will be no return.' With this statement Bevan demonstrated one of the many reasons he was an inspiration to so many of us on the political Left. He articulated the fears that spurred us into opposing the government's military action in Egypt. I went to the rally in Trafalgar Square to demonstrate against government intervention and listened to Bevan's speech. It was a huge demonstration and I vividly recall the awesome sight of Nye Bevan, with his shock of white hair, as he roared his speech and its condemnation of the government famously telling us that, 'Mr Eden is too stupid to be Prime Minister'. Fortunately for me, as the crisis was relatively short-lived I was not called up. I completed the run at the Haymarket and then once again it was back to Liverpool.

Both Gale and I were frustrated at having to leave London, but we could not afford to pay for the flat without an income. My parents' house was still overcrowded, which made the situation difficult for all of us, but it was made even more so by the domineering behaviour of my mother. To be fair to her, she never once turned us away, but on the other hand we were not allowed to forget that it was her home and her word was law. Quiet and gentle Gale had to cope with both my mother and my grandmother. I had a much easier time as in the spring of 1958 I played Lennox in *Macbeth* at the Library Theatre in Manchester. I was then offered a season at the Liverpool Playhouse. This meant not only that we were together as a family for almost eight months, but also we contributed financially to my mother's household.

To save money I would cycle each day to the theatre. As this was a time when many actors still turned up for work in a collar and tie, my sweaty arrival in jeans and donkey jacket was somewhat frowned upon. Also, the other members of the company had all been to drama school and the fact that I had not was another black mark against me. Although I would always claim to be indifferent to such snobbery and the thoughtless social cruelties that accompanied it, I could still be made to squirm. Not unreasonably, my family, who had never seen me act, decided they wanted to come and watch my performance in *Desperate Hours*. I am ashamed to admit now that, far from being pleased, I was desperately uneasy at the prospect – particularly at what I assumed would be the reaction of the other actors to my grandmother, who I believed would 'want to make a night of it' and have a few drinks before the theatre. I arranged what I thought would be a foolproof plan. I told my family they were to come to the theatre, take their seats immediately without talking to anyone, watch the performance and then go straight home. On no account whatsoever were they to come backstage to see me.

The director at the Playhouse was Willard Stoker, whose rich family put money into the theatre. On first nights he would stand out front in evening dress and welcome the playgoers. That evening the first two acts went well. I deliberately did not look at the tickets I gave my family so I had no idea where they were sitting.

During the second interval Bill Stoker came into my dressing room and said, 'My dear, you're doing wonderfully well.'

'Thanks Bill.'

'Your mother, your father and that delightful lady your grand-mother are really enjoying it. I took them for a drink at the interval and they met Maud.'

Maud Carpenter, a fearsome snob, ran the Playhouse as her own fiefdom and she did not like me. The thought of her meeting my family almost made me swoon with social embarrassment. Trying desperately not to go to pieces completely, I had a thoroughly miserable third act. Despite this the play was well received and afterwards the cast went for a celebratory drink. However, all I could think about was my family and I just wanted to go home and find out why and how my plans had gone so catastrophically awry.

Arriving home I barged past my sister, who had answered the door, and began shouting, 'What the hell do you think you were doing? I told you to go to the theatre, do nothing, talk to nobody.' When eventually I stopped yelling long enough for my mother to be able to say anything she told me what had happened. My father had arrived home from work, they had got ready for the theatre, caught the bus to Williamson Square and walked through the theatre doors, ignoring everyone as instructed. At the entrance to the circle my father put his hand into the breast pocket of his best suit and discovered, to his horror, that he had left the tickets in his other jacket. The assistant manager was called, then Willard Stoker. Still clearly thrilled by all this attention, my mother related how wonderful Stoker had been – personally showing them to their seats and at the interval taking them for a drink and up to Maud Carpenter's office. Even though somewhat mollified, I was still concerned about what they might have said, but apparently my grandmother had played to the occasion and had been thoroughly charming.

After *Desperate Hours* finished I was able to stay on in Liverpool when the Playhouse offered me the role of Gratiano in *The Merchant of Venice*. I had become friendly with another young actor in the company and on a Wednesday afternoon we used to go to the Royal Court Theatre in Liverpool to watch the matinée. At that time the Royal Court was the number one touring date and many big names played there. One afternoon we arrived to find it was a ballet company. Neither of us were great fans of this particular art form, but as we had free tickets we decided to stay. We sat at the front of the stalls in a not particularly full theatre. Suddenly I had what I thought was a clever idea and said to my friend, 'Why don't we get some opera glasses and have some fun looking up their tutus?' When the corps de ballet came on we examined each one in turn, nudging each other and comparing notes. Then we would follow one girl around the stage until she got into a terrible state. Of course, we thought this was hilarious.

The next day, Thursday, was our matinée performance. The night before I had washed my jockstrap and left it on the radiator to dry. As I was always short of money, this was the only jockstrap I possessed so I had to wash and dry it overnight, but arriving in the dressing room I discovered it was still soaking wet. I could not wear it. In those days tights were cotton and not elasticated. I pulled them on, tied them with string at the waist and hoped no one would notice the absence of a jockstrap. My friend was playing Bassanio and as we walked on stage during the first act there was a noise from the audience. Turning to look out, I saw the first two rows of the stalls were occupied by the entire corps de ballet from the Royal Court. Every one of them was looking through opera glasses and they had us in their sights. They followed our every movement. What a time to be *sans* jockstrap! Determinedly maintaining my equilibrium throughout the opening scene, I and my friend had a good laugh about it once we were off-stage. Impressed by their sense of humour, we decided to show them just how good we were. They would not rattle us!

Things went well until the trial scene. My character has nothing to say for some time and, waiting for my cue, I sat on a stool towards the front of the stage, acutely aware I was being observed through the corps de ballet's opera glasses. When it came to the point where I jumped up and said, 'A second Daniel, a Daniel, Jew', as I did so I threw my arms out and heard a terrible ripping sound. Turning to face the audience I folded my arms and tried to feel the seams on the back of my shirt. Nothing appeared to be amiss. Whispering to my friend I asked if my shirt was all right. Looking, he assured me it was fine. Returning to my seat, I sat down. There was instant pandemonium among the corps de ballet – all the glasses were fixed on me. I was not about to fall for that old stunt, but still, ... maybe, I should just check my tights? Casually, as if perhaps I might just have an itch around my waist area, I put my hand in front of myself and found a gaping hole in my tights. I had unwittingly exposed myself to the matinée audience at the Liverpool Playhouse! The corps de ballet broke into applause and I completed the scene with my back to the audience. This was not just revenge for the corps de ballet. It was a total and humiliating rout!

When this work finished the only possibility of further employment was in a return to London. This increased tension levels at home as my parents did not hide their disappointment with my decision, but my greatest source of strain was Gale's adamant refusal to come with me. I did not have a job to go to and the initial accommodation would be a camp bed in the Notting Hill home of Philip Anthony, an actor I met whilst working at the Liverpool Playhouse. Gale did not wish to leave the girls and was no longer interested in theatre work. Cherie had started school – another generation of the Booth family at the St Edmund's Catholic school. Lyndsey was also settled so I could understand how Gale felt whilst still wanting her to accompany me. Eventually, we agreed that I would go alone to London and as soon as I had a job and somewhere to live Gale and the girls would join me.

I managed little employment as an actor for almost a year, but I was able to hitch-hike back to Liverpool to see my family fairly regularly. It was in the days before most homes had a telephone, so contact and support were difficult. I took jobs washing-up in restaurants and working in soup kitchens, but this barely paid my way. On a visit home I discovered that Gale was working in a chip shop. Cross and upset, I could not understand, when she was obviously capable of so much more, why she would take such a job. At that time we both still believed that it would not be too long before she would join me in London and I suppose this was a job without commitment she could walk away from at any time. After several further visits home, I did persuade her to try for a better job and she began working in the travel department of Lewis's, a department store in Liverpool. I was not unhappy in my marriage to Gale. Our core problem was, as with so many other young couples, a lack of money. For us this translated into spending very little time together, and gradually my visits to Liverpool became less frequent as Gale and I drifted further apart and I began to establish a life for myself in London.

I stayed at Philip Anthony's home only for a matter of weeks, but during that time I renewed my acquaintance with another actor, Tom Bell, also a regular visitor at Philip's. We first met when I was working in *No Time for Sergeants* and Tom visited Gwillam Williams, another member of the cast. Tom was good-looking and clearly talented, but unfortunately he has a dark side to his personality which I was only later, and at some personal cost, to discover, and which has, I believe, ruined many of his relationships – both with friends and family. But in those early days we spent a lot of time together doing whatever menial jobs we could find whilst writing letters to anyone we could think of who might give us work as actors.

One of our jobs was in a cheap eating place, the Soup Kitchen, next to the *Express* building off Fleet Street, where actors could eke out their dole money by moonlighting as waiters and kitchen hands. Tom and I were taken on at a pound a night plus our taxi fare. We were also promised there would be tips. We worked from six in the evening until one o'clock the following morning. I had some experience of being a waiter from my time at sea so I did that job whilst Tom stood behind the bar handing out the food. Most of the customers were printers from Fleet Street who came in for a good, cheap meal, but they never, ever tipped. The place was popular and we were kept very busy. To relieve the tedium Tom and I devised a game where each evening we would act a different role. One night I would play Brando and Tom would be Steiger in *On the Waterfront*. The next night I would be Humphrey Bogart and he would be Cary Grant. The customers loved it because they never knew who would be serving at their table.

One evening, however, a customer walked in and I could see immediately that here was not a person to fool around with. This man had a definite presence and, going over to take his order, I decided not to bother with any of the character-playing. He sat quietly at his table minding his own business, but he was certainly hungry. He ate his way through the entire menu. Later he called for his bill, which came to just under five pounds – a lot of money then.

He reached into his inside pocket for his wallet and then started searching through his other pockets and said, 'Oh hell! I've got my car keys and half a crown. That's all. I was meeting a journalist, I changed my suit and I've left my wallet behind.'

I could tell this man was not trying to pull a stunt. He had genuinely forgotten his wallet.

'I tell you what,' he said, 'I'll bring it tomorrow.'

'It's not down to me,' I replied, 'I just work here. I'll have to ask the manager.'

The manager was sitting behind the cash desk and when I asked if the customer could settle his bill tomorrow he was not impressed and insisted I get the money from him. 'He says he will bring the money in tomorrow,' I argued.

'You don't believe that, do you?'

'Yes I do.'

'Well, I tell you what. If you don't get the money off him I'll stop it out of your wages starting tonight. Two quid.'

'Oh come on. How am I going to get home?'

The manager shrugged his shoulders and suggested the bus. Going back to the customer I sat down at his table and said, 'OK, I'll level with you. I'm an actor and I only work here because I need the money. I believe you, but the manager says if I don't get the money off you he's going to stop it out of my wages.'

'I'll have a word with him.'

'No please don't do that, but if you don't bring the money in tomorrow I will have to work three nights here for nothing to pay it back.'

He looked at me and said, 'What's your name, kid?'

'Tony Booth.'

He wrote my name on the back of the bill and then, pushing it across the table to me, he said, 'Put your address on.'

'Why?'

'I'll send you something.'

'There's no need. Just bring the money in tomorrow.'

'I will pay, but I also want your address. I'm grateful OK?' I wrote my address, we shook hands and he left.

The next evening when I arrived for work the manager said, 'Your friend hasn't been.'

'That's all right. He'll be here,' I replied. But as the hours went by I gradually grew less confident. Then at around half past nine, when the café was really crowded, the man walked in.

'You did me a favour Tony. I'll never forget it,' he said to me. Then he walked over to the manager and gave him a ten-pound note. When he was given the five pounds change he handed it to me.

'You don't have to give me that,' I protested.

'No, no. You did me a favour.' Then he turned and addressed the crowded restaurant. 'Here, listen to me.' Immediately all activity and conversation ceased. He put his hand on my shoulder. 'This guy is Tony Booth,' he said. 'I want you to know he's done me a great favour. So, he's all right, see!' Then off he went.

Two journalists were sitting at a table near me. One of them said, 'How long have you been in with the Richardsons then?'

'What!'

'Didn't you know that was Charlie Richardson the gangster?'

Stunned, I said, 'You're having me on.'

The journalist was obviously impressed, 'No. Didn't you notice how he shut everyone up? We'll have to keep an eye on you. You're not a guy to mess with!'

One morning about ten days later I was still in bed when I heard someone hammering on my front door. Staggering over to the window, I opened it and looked out. There was a man with a van outside and, seeing me, he called, 'Tony Booth?'

'Yes.'

'Come on down here quick.'

'What is it?'

'I've got something for you. Is there anyone who can give me a hand?'

I got Tom out of bed and we went downstairs and opened the door. The man unlocked the back of the van and, pointing to a cardboard packing case of Marlboro cigarettes, said, 'Here. Get hold of this.'

'What's this?'

'A present from the Richardsons,' he said hauling it out. 'Come on. Get it inside quick. I've got to be off.'

'What's the problem?' I asked, as we dragged it inside.

'Well it fell off the back of a wagon didn't it?'

So there we were, Tom and I, with thousands of stolen cigarettes. We were completely terrified. We chain-smoked them, gave them away, lit the fire with them – anything, until they had all gone. I have never smoked a Marlboro since!

I continued to work at the Soup Kitchen for some months after this. One night Tom had gone home early and so at the end of my shift I set off alone to catch the bus at Victoria. It was one-thirty in the morning and apart from an occasional taxi there was no one around as I walked down Pall Mall. Then I saw a man coming towards me, his coat slung over his shoulder and he was carrying an umbrella. I was a few feet away when he asked, 'Have you got a light?' On the small chance this was not a proposition I handed him my lighter. As I did so he touched my hand. With my worst suspicions confirmed, I just wanted to move on as quickly as possible. Then I saw his face and immediately recognized him.

I was speechless, but he said, 'I've got a nice place above Admiralty Arch. Would you like to come back with me for a drink?'

I could not believe this madness and, realizing he had been drinking, I told him to go home and just be thankful I was not a blackmailer.

'You know who I am,' he said. 'I'm flattered.'

'Of course I know who you are. You're Selwyn Lloyd, the Foreign Secretary.'

'And you still don't want to come back with me?'

'No, I bloody don't. Go home.'

'Please yourself,' he said and walked off.

It was around this time I joined the Labour Party – that is, when they finally let me. North Kensington was my local branch and I arrived at a meeting fully expecting to be greeted with open arms. I suspect it was the CND badge pinned to my lapel that was the problem, but my application was turned down out of hand. Having finally made the decision to join the Party I was not about to accept rejection. I wrote to my local Member of Parliament, George Rogers, who was also at that time a Party Whip. He replied that he could not and would not intervene. Undaunted, I wrote to Labour Party headquarters to be told membership was the decision of local parties. I had met Michael Foot at the Trafalgar Square rally and, as a *Tribune* reader, I now wrote to him for help.[1] He agreed, but it was still almost three months before I gained membership.

My first ward meeting was a memorable experience. The branch officers, predominantly male, were also quite clearly on the right wing of the Labour Party. I was by far the youngest person at the meeting and as such was not expected to contribute and certainly not to ask questions – attitudes and practices that have, unfortunately, survived in my current Labour Party branch, Longdendale, where

---

[1] Michael Foot was the editor of the *Tribune* newspaper 1948–52 and again 1955–60. Whilst I did not agree with all that was printed in the newspaper – at times I believed it to be too right-wing – it was a vehicle for interesting debate. As a recent subscriber I can only lament the loss of its radical edge and the descent into sniping which so often these days passes for reasoned political discussion.

misogynistic attitudes are pervasive. In 1959 we were still to begin to recognize misogyny. A general election was looming so I asked the branch officers why there had not been a recruitment drive for new and younger members to help in the campaign. My question surprised the meeting, as this was obviously not a strategy that had occurred to them. After some discussion my suggestion was adopted and the task delegated to me. I was to report my progress to the next meeting. To the astonishment of the branch officers, people wanted to join the Labour Party and within three months new membership was considerably greater than established membership. The new members were also more radical and more left-wing in their politics and our first campaign was an attempt to deselect George Rogers.

In much the same way that peasants were assumed to understand and tolerate absentee landlords, the North Kensington branch of the Labour Party was to accept Rogers' continued non-appearance at branch meetings. He excused this neglect by maintaining his duties as a Labour Whip were so demanding he had no time to attend branch or constituency meetings. Moreover, this official role also prevented him from any active campaigning on behalf of his constituents. Despite several votes of no confidence by the newly invigorated North Kensington branch, Rogers was to be the candidate in the forthcoming general election. One of the genuinely progressive developments in the Labour Party over the last few years has been the change in the rules making reselection for sitting MPs compulsory. In 1958, however, deselection was unheard of. A member of parliament, unless voted out in a general election, had a job for life. I tried to uncover the procedure for deselection, but the rule book was kept at constituency headquarters and as there was only one copy it was 'not generally available'.

The Hegelian intricacies of Labour Party bureaucracy were surely intended, back in the mists of time, to be of use and support to the membership. Now they were used to obfuscate and obstruct. I found it ironic that the right wing of the Party, so afraid of the Soviets that they were pro-nuclear, presided over a party system so labyrinthine that Stalin would surely have been impressed. Unfortunately, George Rogers remained the candidate for the 1959 election, but his majority was a mere 877, having been 2,943 in 1955. I succeeded only in provoking the wrath of the local Labour Party establishment for my presumption.

Like so many others I joined the Labour Party not only to be actively involved in political campaigning, but also to have a voice at

Party conference, which in those days was still an important forum for policy debate. By the 1950s the left wing of the Labour Party began to mount a strong and vocal anti-nuclear campaign. It was and remains a powerfully emotional as well as pragmatic and intellectual issue – one that has, at various times, split the Party from top to bottom and given rise to deep and often personal enmities, such as that between Gaitskell and Bevan. I met Tony Benn, then a young Member of Parliament and still known as Anthony Wedgwood-Benn. Over the years we have become good friends and comrades, sustained, amongst other things, by our mutual horror of these weapons of mass destruction. Benn was in the Royal Air Force when the Allies dropped the nuclear bombs on Japan and later saw for himself the terrible destruction of Hiroshima and Nagasaki. He was a founder member, alongside Donald Soper, Tony Greenwood and Fenner Brockway, of the H-Bomb National Campaign – the forerunner to the Campaign for Nuclear Disarmament.

In 1951 Nye Bevan resigned from the government over the Budget statement and the decision to increase defence spending. He was followed out of government by Harold Wilson and a junior minister at Supply, John Freeman (later a noted TV presenter). In his resignation speech Bevan argued that the Soviets could have no intention of invading Britain as they lacked the necessary military force. The only possible outcome of the pursuit of a British nuclear programme would be the gradual loss of our manufacturing base as resources and capital were diverted into the defence programme. These were not only prophetic, but also brave, words at the height of the Cold War, when any dissent from the Establishment pro-nuclear line tarnished the dissenter as a Soviet supporter. Bevan went on in the same speech to recognize this inevitability when he further argued that the nuclear programme would also allow, and probably create, a political witch-hunt against the Left. In a speech in 1955 to a mass rally in the Albert Hall, Tony Benn was passionate in his support of Bevan's position.

It is too easy to forget in these days of a slick, bland party machine, of Mondeo man and Worcester woman, that active membership of the Labour Party was once a statement of strongly held belief in social justice and equality of opportunity forcefully articulated by such giants of the Labour movement as Keir Hardie, Nye Bevan, Michael Foot and Tony Benn. So many people at the grassroots of the Party and in the unions have shared and believed in that vision and over the years worked tirelessly towards the realization of those dreams. It was a party created by those who had faced poverty and exploitation, who had seen children die, who knew all about the extremes of such poverty and deprivation that the Conservative Party felt able, even in the 1980s, to claim were 'a price worth paying'. It was not ever, is never and can never be a price worth paying.

I joined the Labour Party because I believed and still believe all human beings are entitled to freedom from poverty and the opportunity and dignity that are the result of that freedom. It is a measure of our society how far we have come in delivering these basic human rights. When I hear the present Labour Party talk of a stakeholder society my heart sinks. It sinks even further with the concept of Great Britain plc, or the even more offensive 'cool Britannia'. If that is the case, the political choice at each general election becomes little more than the regular decision taken over insurance renewals – which offers the best value? Selfish decisions taken for selfish reasons, not the common good. Conviction politics appear to have been removed from the equation. Whilst I recognize it is opinions such as these that condemn me in the court of New Labour as an unreconstructed old Leftie, I would also argue that these people have hijacked the Labour movement. How socially just has the distribution of profits made by large business corporations ever been? What moral certainty drives the conviction that these are appropriate values for those who claim they are now in the vanguard of a movement for social equality?

In 1959 Labour lost the general election to the Conservatives led by Harold Macmillan. Of course the right-wing troika of Gaitskell, Anthony Crosland and Roy Jenkins blamed everything and everyone but themselves for Labour's defeat. The truth then, as it is now, is that the British public, if they are minded to vote Conservative, want the real thing not some pale imitation. Fortunately, in 1959 a profound change of attitude and policy lay just around the corner in the shape of Harold Wilson and the Labour Party's political resurgence of the sixties. However, the death of Gaitskell would not bring an end to the domination of middle-class values within the Labour Party. These influences were not gone – just waiting, dormant, to re-emerge in the nineties. The personal irony was, of course, that this would be under a Labour government with my own son-in-law, Tony Blair, as Prime Minister. Does God have a wicked sense of humour?

It was not only politics that was to undergo a sea change at the end of the fifties. Long-established principles and methods of acting were also turned on their head. Just as Macmillan and his brief successor, Alec Douglas-Home, marked the end of the line for patrician politicians, so the barricades against the working-class actor with a regional accent also collapsed. I was writing a steady stream of letters to producers and directors in my search for work. Tom Bell and I realized that polite letters including a photograph were not particularly productive. We devised the challenging letter. As attitudes in the profession began to change we felt able to question casting choices, accusing the decision-makers of being anti-working-class or, worse, bourgeois. The skill was in making the letter just provocative enough for the secretary not to put it straight in the bin, but to make the decision to pass it on, thus bringing the application to the attention of our intended recipient. Of course, some people were offended by the letters and refused ever to consider me for any role. I have come latterly to recognize one of the ironies of my life – I have strong political views, but this has not always translated into a skill at personal politics. However, I did have a degree of success with this strategy. The BBC gave me a part in a costume drama, *The Infamous John Friend*. The Boulting brothers were also provoked enough to interview me and further provoked, by my preference for Len Hutton over W. G. Grace, into giving me a small role in one of their films. An interview with Lindsay Anderson, then at the Royal Court Theatre, for a role in *The Long, the Short and the Tall* by Willis Hall was also a result of this strategy.

A further success from the letter blitz was an interview with Stuart Lyons, the assistant casting director for *Ice Cold in Alex*, a World War II, North African thriller. Fortunately for me, we hit it off very quickly and he offered me a small speaking role in the film, despite instructions to deal firmly and swiftly with this person who had the nerve to write such rude letters. I played the military policeman who at the end of the film came on with an officer, played by Basil Henson, to arrest Anthony Quayle and take him off. The director was Jimmy Lee-Thompson, a short, dark-haired man whose innate intensity was further deepened by a recent decision to give up cigarettes and alcohol. As a consequence he spent an inordinate amount of time tearing paper into small pieces.

A long time had been spent on location and the film had run over. John Mills, the star of the film, had a penalty clause in his contract that meant he was being paid an additional daily rate. For an actor that is a rare and precious thing and Mills, not unnaturally, was not fretting about the delay. I was called to the studios at Borehamwood for my first ever day's filming. As the film was being shot in page order we did the first scene and then I had to sit around for four days until I was called back to deliver my solitary line to John Mills. I was very nervous. Mills was completely relaxed. The director, by this stage, was almost beside himself. Everywhere he walked he was constantly strewing bits of torn-up paper which the script girl busily retrieved.

We started the scene and it was my big moment. My line was: 'Sir, I've come to collect the prisoner.' John Mills then delivered his speech. After a rehearsal Lee-Thompson said, 'Let's shoot. We're wasting time.'

I said my line and John Mills had just started to speak when from somewhere came the sound of rapid, heavy breathing. The sound man shouted, 'Cut! Cut! There's something wrong.' We started a second time, but again when Mills was speaking I could hear the heavy breathing. Once more the sound man shouted, 'Cut!'

We did the scene again and again. After sixteen takes the director was almost out of his mind and I became the focus of his rage. 'What are you doing? Are you making that noise? What is going on?' he screamed at me.

I could only shrug. The tension on the set was now almost unbearable. On the next take I once again delivered my lines and once again as John Mills began to speak there was the sound of heavy breathing.

Throwing a massive tantrum, Lee-Thompson came storming over to me and demanded, 'You! Are you breathing?'

'Yes,' I admitted.

'Well they're picking it up on the sound. Don't you know anything about filming? It's your breathing that's causing the delay. I'm going to tell you this only once – I will not have breathing actors on my set!'

We began the scene again and I delivered my line. Then, pressing my mouth as tightly shut as I could, I held my breath, but despite these precautions the sound of heavy breathing filtered onto the set.

'Cut!' Lee-Thompson looked at me.

'It's not me,' I gasped.

'Then who is it? Who is breathing on my set?' Just at that moment John Mills's spaniel came panting out from under a table. 'Oh look,' Lee-Thompson cooed. 'It's the doggie. He wants a drink of water.'

When *Ice Cold in Alex* was edited this whole scene, including my solitary line, had been cut.

However, it was a letter to Joan Littlewood that was to have the most far-reaching results. Littlewood ran a theatre workshop in a former London music hall in Stratford East. She also had socialist pretensions – certainly at work, where she smoked Woodbines. At home on her houseboat she preferred the hand-rolled, monogrammed variety. I wrote to her suggesting that the working classes were not geographically limited to the East End of London and asking if she had a particular aversion to northern working-class actors, specifically those from Liverpool. She responded by calling me to an interview. I was asked to act various situations, including a private moment. I was convinced that Littlewood did not like me and the interview was not going well so, feeling I had nothing to lose, I urinated into a fire bucket. Littlewood was appalled, but she was lucky – my first inclination had been to masturbate. The audition was for *Sam, the Highest Jumper of Them All*, a play by the American writer William Saroyan. By a stroke of good fortune he was amused by my audition and offered me a part in the play. Later, walking into the theatre bar, I had an encounter that would change the course of my life.

Four
And the World Goes Round

'Acting is a masochistic form of exhibitionism. It is not quite the occupation of an adult.'

Laurence Olivier

Julie Allan was perched on a high stool at the bar in the Theatre Royal, Stratford East. Dressed in a black skirt and tight, black sweater, her legs elegantly tucked against the stool, she was laughing at something William Saroyan said to her. It was love at first sight and my life would never be the same again. Family, friends, everyone was forgotten in that extraordinary moment. Over the next few months, against fierce competition from her other admirers, I pursued, I persuaded, I persisted and ultimately I prevailed.

Julie shared a flat in St John's Wood, near Lord's Cricket Ground, with another actress, June Cunningham. June and I worked together in an episode of *Knight Errant* for Granada Television and we often talked about our marital problems. At the time her own marriage was going through a difficult patch and so she was a sympathetic ear for the emptiness and difficulties I was experiencing. She knew that Gale and I lived different lives, effectively separated. I was certain Julie would end our relationship if she knew I was married so from the start fear of losing her prevented me from telling her about Gale and my daughters. I cravenly hoped June would be the one to tell her. When eventually she did find out Julie was devastated by my duplicity and cried and raged, but matters had already gone too far. Julie was pregnant with our first daughter, Jenia.

Even now, from a distance of some forty years, I cannot begin to explain the emotional impact of Julie Allan on me. I was truly, madly, deeply in love with her – 'mad' being a crucial word. I was willing to do anything, sacrifice anything to be with her. My feelings overwhelmed me, but they also made me a coward and cowardice made my behaviour shameful. Not only did I trick Julie, lying by omission;

I also did not have the moral courage to face my family in Liverpool. As my parents had recently installed a telephone I decided to call and tell them of my changed circumstances from a public phone box; with only a limited amount of change the agony – for me – would be cut short. Gale was not at home when I telephoned, but my mother was and so I broke my news to her. In the white heat of her fury she told me she never wanted to see me again, she would no longer accept me as a member of her family. My mother was no fool. She knew why Gale and I had married, her overriding concern was for Cherie and Lyndsey – how could I do this to them? Of course, she did not want to talk to me, she was not able or willing to understand my actions and she slammed down the telephone.

It would be several years before I saw my parents again. I managed to speak to Gale on a number of occasions after the initial conversation with my mother, but it was a tense and distressing situation and my actions left no opening for meaningful communication or negotiation. There was a world of difference between a husband who was working away and a husband who abandoned his wife. I know my behaviour caused my family a great deal of pain, but what goes around comes around and I was ultimately to pay an enormous and almost fatal price for my actions.

In some ways the turmoil in my emotional life was paralleled by the social upheaval of the 1960s. The sixties were possibly the most contentious and certainly one of the most creative decades of the twentieth century. A decade that not only advocates, but carries through, the ideal of placing flowers into the barrel of a gun has a great deal to be proud of. Yet the decade began with much of the monochromatic uniformity that characterized the fifties, with no hint of what was to come. Politics and theatre still appeared to be entrenched in their own particular time warp, one rooted in the expectations and behaviour of a different, more aristocratic, less plebeian age – the government led by Harold Macmillan, the theatre by Laurence Olivier who, with some of his contemporaries, hardly encouraged the hastening emergence of working-class actors and kitchen sink drama.

In 1895 Henry Irving became the first actor to receive a knighthood. Up to that time actors were seen as rogues and vagabonds – a travelling band of people who might and often did say dangerous and radical things. Once Irving was knighted the acting profession began not only to aspire to be, but also to be perceived as, part of the Establishment. We were no longer simply rogues and vagabonds and

I believe the loss of that edge of danger was a significant loss to the acting profession. Olivier was a massive and progressive influence on English-speaking acting during the first half of the twentieth century. For this I admired him tremendously. However, in the fifties Marlon Brando exploded on to the world stage in the vanguard of a seismic shift in attitudes and performance. Brando was prepared to bare his soul and a new generation of actors and writers were eager to follow in his footsteps and embrace a new realism. Olivier made the classic mistake of many former revolutionaries: assuming their vision is somehow definitive, they are unwilling to accept new ideas. Thus the revolutionary becomes the reactionary.

I do not believe realism was a factor in Olivier's performance. I always felt he continued to hide behind his actor's mask. For example, his much acclaimed role as Archie Rice in John Osborne's *The Entertainer* in 1957 is often cited as evidence of his readiness to work in and with new drama. But it was a classic Olivier performance. We were not witnesses to the seedy tragedy of Archie Rice, we watched as Olivier *acted* this unpleasant, third-rate comedian. In 1961 Olivier married Joan Plowright, a formidably talented actress who in 1959, at the beginning of her career, gave a groundbreaking performance as Beattie in Arnold Wesker's *Roots*. I have heard it suggested his marriage to Plowright somehow conferred radical credentials on Olivier. This suggestion, whilst breathtaking in its arrogance and misogyny, is also an unambiguous manifestation of the endemic snobbishness that still survives in British theatre and for which Olivier must bear a considerable responsibility. To this day many actors still feel obliged to deliver Shakespeare in the clipped and half-strangled tones used by Olivier. This can only be to sustain some erroneous sense of elitism that serves ultimately to prevent most of the audience from understanding a word that is said and pushes Shakespeare ever further to the outer limits of popular enjoyment.

But I cannot be, nor would I want to be, totally critical of Olivier. In the early part of his career he was a hugely positive influence and after he was appointed Director of the National Theatre in 1962 he made some courageous decisions. In 1967 he faced a crisis over the production of Rolf Hochhuth's play *Soldiers*.[1] In the play Hochhuth implies Winston Churchill was involved in the assassination of the Polish Second World War leader, General Sikorski. Ken Tynan, who

[1] The controversial nature of Hochhuth's work was also reflected in his 1963 play *The Deputy*, which accused Pope Pius XII and the Vatican of supporting the Nazis.

at the time was Literary Manager at the National Theatre and a champion for Hochhuth, told me Olivier had to be convinced to stand his ground against fierce Establishment opposition. Tynan argued that the credibility and legitimacy of the theatre depended on the ability to resist such pressure. Olivier, to his great credit, was persuaded by this reasoning and the production went ahead – a decision that almost cost him his job. I feel it is a great shame this courage was not reflected in a wholehearted embrace of new and exciting perspectives and techniques of acting.

The time was ripe for revolution in both politics and the theatre as the children of the war came of age. When the revolution arrived it was an explosion of talent and creativity that shook the foundations of politics and art. Harold Wilson was the herald of the new political dawn as Tory patrician politics faded and in the theatre Albert Finney, Vanessa Redgrave, Billie Whitelaw, Tom Courtenay and Peter O'Toole were just some of the actors in the vanguard. Inspired by the work of Pinter, Osborne, Arden and Wesker and other young lions, the Director at the Royal Court Theatre, George Devine, swept aside Rattigan and Coward and other pre-war boulevardiers. That is not to claim of course that any work or any actor pre-dating the sixties was intrinsically worthless. Far from it, as J.B. Priestley demonstrated. Although his plays were, sadly, to be neglected for a time after his death, Priestley gleefully seized the opportunity to write powerful, thought-provoking essays and articles on the nuclear arms race. John Gielgud and Ralph Richardson proved it was triumphantly possible at any age to ride a new wave. Peggy Ashcroft and Thora Hird were brilliant exceptions to any rule.

At the same time as this new realism hit the theatre, television finally reached a mass audience. It was through the most far-seeing, enlightened and imaginative Director-General the BBC has ever had, Hugh Carleton Greene, that a flood of talent reached into the sitting rooms of Britain. Television represented the real possibility of a truly egalitarian art medium. Sydney Newman, the Canadian producer of Armchair Theatre for ABC Television, and those great showmen the Grades and the Bernsteins were enthusiastic participants and contributors to the rapid evolution of television. Musically, the rest of the world followed where Britain led when the creative possibilities of popular music were reshaped as, yet again, established rules were ignored or rewritten. The Beatles, the Stones, all that fantastic music of the sixties was part of the social, cultural and political upheaval that defined the war generation as they threw off the expectations

73

and uniform greyness of the 1950s. It was a generation determined to seek out and try the alternatives to traditional thinking.

Ironically, the sixties is a decade remembered for challenging the Establishment, yet current politicians seem not to have recognized that even hippies and revolutionaries grow old and many are now pensioners. Successive decades have proved more passive, but the activists of the sixties have not forgotten how to organize around a morally just cause. Small wonder, then, they are not as amenable as the current government would like.[2]

Julie's parents, Ted and Kate Allan, had a profound influence on me. At that time in my life I was like a sponge soaking up new experiences, eager for knowledge. My socialist values had been developed first by my grandfather Thompson and later by Nicole, but Ted and Kate extended the depth of my political knowledge and the vision of my political understanding. My education had been brutally curtailed by my father's accident, but under Ted's guidance I received a crash course not only in politics, but also art and literature.

When I first met Ted Allan he was living and working in London, part of a small enclave of writers blacklisted as a result of McCarthy's Communist 'witch hunts' in America. Originally from Canada, his parents escaping there from the pogroms in Russia, Ted was a good-looking man of medium height with dark hair now beginning to thin and go grey. He lived in a beautiful but chaotic flat overlooking the Thames at Putney. It was crammed with books and scripts, the walls lined with modern paintings, and it was here that I met friends of Ted's such as Yves Montand, Arthur Miller, Irwin Shaw and Linus Pauling – he knew so many people, all of whom were glad of his friendship and hospitality. Ted's marriage to Kate had broken down some time before I met him and he was involved with a beautiful and much younger Greek woman whom he had met through friends, Jules Dassin and his wife Melina Mercouri. Dassin was the superbly talented screenwriter and director of *Never on Sunday*, a hit film of the sixties, the vibrantly beautiful Mercouri its star. Mercouri was later to change career direction and become involved in Greek politics. She was active in the resistance to the Greek military junta and, following the overthrow of that regime, was appointed Minister of Culture.

---

[2] The National Pensioners' Convention campaign to restore the link between average earnings and the state pension – a link destroyed by the Thatcher government in the early eighties.

Ted held profoundly left-wing political opinions. His best friend was Norman Bethune, a doctor who took part in Mao's Long March in the thirties. Ted and Kate named their only son after Norman and it was through this friendship that Ted was able not only to visit China, but also to meet Mao Tse-tung; the Communist Chinese admired and respected Norman Bethune so much they erected a statue of him in Beijing. There is a story, perpetuated by Mao himself, that he did not speak English, but Ted told me that it was in fact a myth and he was able to have many conversations with Mao. During one of these conversations Mao asked Ted if there was anywhere he would particularly like to visit. 'Shanghai', said Ted'; he had heard there was a large Jewish community there. Ted told me that when he made this request, Mao smiled. He understood immediately what lay behind the request – the rumours that Jewish Chinese people had been persecuted and forced underground. Ted was stunned to find the synagogue in Shanghai full of Chinese people, all of whom had a considerably better grasp of the Torah than he did. His confusion was only resolved when the rabbi, also Chinese, explained to him that when they had arrived in China the Jews had not brought enough women with them and so had intermarried.

Another friend of Ted's was Donald Ogden Stewart, the American playwright who received an Oscar for *The Philadelphia Story*. Ogden Stewart was also a member of the group of blacklisted American writers seeking refuge in London. When I met him he was living in the Hampstead home that had once belonged to Ramsay MacDonald. Julie and I accompanied Ted for a Sunday lunch party. It was a beautiful summer's day and, sitting out on the lawn, the wine and conversation flowed. Eventually, I went inside looking for the bathroom. Locating it I noticed what I assumed to be copies of two beautiful paintings by Picasso and Pissarro hanging on the wall. As I went through the door leading back to the garden I commented to a man standing there how impressed I was to see these paintings, even if they were only reproductions.

'They're not reproductions. They're genuine,' he replied.

'No way!'

'Yes. Seriously, the whole house is full of masterpieces of modern art. Go and have a look. Start in the study.'

I went back into the house and began to look at the incredible paintings that covered the walls. As I was walking out of the study I bumped into Donald Ogden Stewart. 'I was just admiring your paintings,' I told him.

'Do you like them? If you're interested I'll tell you how I got them. Come into the study and have a drink.' Settling down, he began to tell me the most remarkable story.

After he was forced to leave America in the early fifties he received an invitation to spend some time in the USSR. First he and his wife flew to France, where his royalties had been mounting up. Due to tight post-war exchange controls he had been unable to transfer the money out of the country, so he and his wife went on a spending spree. She bought several thousand dollars' worth of fine French lingerie that was parcelled up and taken with them on their flight to the USSR. On arrival at Moscow airport they were greeted by the Culture Minister and his wife who escorted the Ogden Stewarts to their hotel. As the Minister was running through the proposed programme of receptions with Donald the two women retired to the bedroom. Suddenly there was a scream and both men leapt to their feet. The bedroom door was flung open to reveal the wife of the Minister standing there in some of the beautiful lingerie bought by Donald's wife. The woman was ecstatic when the Ogden Stewarts told her she could keep it as a gift – such finery was unknown at that time in the USSR.

At a reception later that evening Marshal Zhukov sidled up to Donald and said his girlfriend had been shown the fabulous under-wear worn by the Minister of Culture's wife; would it be possible for him to have a pair of knickers for his girlfriend? Knowing how much his wife had bought, Donald was happy to agree to the request. However, after a few days the situation had become deeply embar-rassing. Everywhere they went someone would be begging for an article from their cache of French lingerie. Talking to the Minister of Culture, Donald explained it was very difficult to say no to these requests, but shortly there would be nothing left for his wife. In reply the Minister said he understood the problem and offered a deal. If Donald gave him the remaining underwear, for each item he would give him in exchange a modern Western painting of his choice.

'How can you do that?' asked Donald incredulously.

'It's simple. Stalin hates modern Western art. He says it is decadent. We have whole storehouses full of such paintings, just locked away. I shall take you tomorrow and you can help yourself.'

The next day the Minister arrived and as they were being driven through Moscow he said to Donald, 'There is only one condition. You may select only two paintings by each artist. Apart from that you can take what you like. How many articles do you have left?'

'About fifty.'

'Then you must select fifty paintings.'

From the USSR the Ogden Stewarts flew to London. The paintings – by Picasso, Monet, Renoir, Gauguin and many others – arrived with their baggage and decorated the walls in their house in Hampstead. If they became desperately short of money the Ogden Stewarts sold one. I know that during the war American servicemen often brokered a good deal in exchange for a pair of silk stockings, but there cannot have been many who did better than Donald Ogden Stewart!

Again it was through Ted's friendship with the American playwright Arthur Miller that I was able to meet Marilyn Monroe. Miller's play *A View from the Bridge* was opening at the Comedy Theatre and he invited Ted, Julie and me to see it. Afterwards, as we stood backstage waiting for Miller to say his goodbyes to the cast, Julie and Ted chatted to friends and I found myself standing across the narrow passageway from the surprisingly tiny figure of Monroe. Leaning against the wall, her loneliness and vulnerability were obvious. Miller appeared, but we could not leave immediately. We had to wait for Marilyn. Outside the streets were jammed with television crews, press, photographers and screaming fans. Heaving herself off the wall, Monroe wet her lips, wriggled her shoulders and backside, adjusted her stole, smiled 'I'm ready' at Arthur and, now completely transformed, went straight into 'Gosh all these people here for little me!' It was a completely astounding performance. Miller, grimacing apologetically, stumbled myopically after her into the seething mêlée. As we all looked at each other, struggling desperately not to laugh Ted broke us up with, 'That's Hollywood!'

Poor Marilyn. So much has been written about her and she was in so many ways her own worst enemy. I met her on other occasions when she and Miller were visitors at Ted's flat and there was always something rather desperate, rather lonely about her. In her desire to be accepted she would dress up in what she felt were appropriate clothes for the occasion. She would arrive at Ted's flat wearing jeans, a black sweater and spectacles – clothes she thought right for an evening with her husband's intellectual friends. Desperate to impress, she was seemingly unaware of the correspondingly desperate efforts made by most of the men present to impress her.

I did not have as close a friendship with Kate Allan as I had with Ted. Julie and her mother had a history of a fraught relationship made worse by the breakdown of Ted and Kate's marriage. Kate had taken the collapse of her marriage badly. She believed with some justification that Julie had taken Ted's side in the matter and, though they were not estranged, things were difficult. Kate was from the east coast of America. Tall, striking and extremely intelligent, the ability to speak fluent Mandarin was only one of her many talents. Her home in Hampstead was full of books and paintings, but unlike Ted's chaos Kate's home was calm and ordered. She was also a good cook and it was always a treat to be invited to Sunday lunch. At these occasions political debate took a different turn from that with Ted and his friends. Here the newly emerging debates on feminism were high on the agenda. Like Ted, Kate had an impressive range of friends and contacts and at her home I met the American writer and critic Susan Sontag, who, though easily strident, was fascinating as she tried out and discussed her ideas with fellow lunch guests.

Kate also introduced me to a friend of hers, Dora. It was only after meeting Dora a few times I realized she was in fact Dora Russell, the writer and academic, also the former wife of Bertrand Russell. She would make outrageous comments about men in general and Bertrand in particular and I was reminded of her opinions some years later when I shared a police cell with him. In a stroke of immense good luck for me I also met Dora Russell's son from her first marriage, Roddy Barry, at a poker game at Kate's home. He had written a play, *Pay Day*, which had been accepted by the BBC and he urged me to contact Stuart Burge, who was to direct it.

Taking his advice, I wrote to Burge saying that I had heard the BBC was producing a north-country play and as I was from that area of the country perhaps he should interview me. Not getting a reply from Burge I wrote again. Still nothing so I sent an overnight telegram: YOU'RE LOOKING FOR NORTH COUNTRY ACTORS. I AM A NORTH COUNTRY ACTOR. I'VE WRITTEN TO YOU TWICE AND YOU HAVEN'T REPLIED. HOW DOES ANYONE GET THROUGH TO YOU? DON'T YOU PAY ANY ATTENTION TO ACTORS? I EXPECT TO HEAR FROM YOU BY RETURN. TONY BOOTH. I found telegrams to be a very effective way of getting attention as they always went straight through to the recipient – secretaries were far too scared to open a telegram addressed to their employer.

The next day I received a telegram: RING STUART BURGE IMMED-IATELY. I telephoned his office and the secretary gave me an appointment for twelve o'clock the next day. Arriving for the interview it was clear Stuart Burge was not particularly pleased to make my acquaintance. I sat, keeping quiet, whilst he raged about my rudeness – how dare I impugn his integrity? Eventually, as his temper subsided, I had the opportunity to point out how very difficult it was for people like me to get to see people like him. I also asked why north-country actors, with genuine accents, were not used in plays featuring the north country. Why was it considered necessary to employ actors with a standard English accent whose idea of north-country dialect and culture was to use the 'Ee by gum' and whippet strategy? To my great surprise, he then asked me about my attitude to trade unions and we began to discuss politics in general. We found ourselves getting on very well together. Earlier in the interview I had told him I had not read *Pay Day*, so when Burge suddenly asked me if I knew what the play was about I again said no. He then gave me a copy and told me to read it and come back at ten o'clock the next morning. He wanted me to read the part of John, specifically the big speech on page thirty-six.

As soon as I was out of the BBC building I began to read the play. It was extraordinary. It was almost as if the play was written about me. Everything I discussed with Stuart Burge that afternoon – every opinion, every attitude – was articulated by the character John. What is more, John featured on every page of this ninety-minute play. It was an excellent script and I could not believe the BBC would employ such an unknown actor. Part-time waiter becomes star was the stuff of Hollywood legend. Real life does not work like that, but I worked on the speech and the next day returned to the BBC. As I walked into his office Stuart Burge said, 'Well?'

'It's me isn't it?'

'Yes, I think it is.'

I read the speech – and then some more and some more until I had virtually read the entire play. Then Burge said, 'This is terrible.'

As my heart plummeted towards my boots with disappointment I braced myself for what I believed was the inevitable rejection.

'Oh yes, I know . . .' I stumbled out the words, any words, desperate to say something whilst not allowing my voice to betray my utter dejection.

'No, believe me. This role is on offer to Patrick McGoohan, but I'm going to be completely honest with you. It's now twelve-thirty. His agent has until three o'clock this afternoon to accept or reject it. Quite frankly he's asking more money than we can afford. We've already gone to our limit. If he turns it down you've got the part. Rehearsals start on Monday. Give me your phone number.'

Although Julie and I were now deeply involved with each other I was, at this time, still officially sharing a house in Pembridge Mews with Tom Bell and we did not have a telephone. I gave Burge the number of the public telephone box on the corner.

'I'll ring you before four o'clock to let you know one way or the other,' he said.

'It will definitely be before four, because I've an appointment later?' I asked, neglecting to mention my appointment was my job at the Soup Kitchen.

'Definitely. Before four, I promise,' he answered.

I walked out of his office, my stomach churning with anxiety. As I walked home I made all manner of promises to and pacts with God if He would just let me get this job. At three o'clock I was pacing nervously up and down outside the telephone box. The minutes crawled past. Four o'clock came. No call. My anxiety levels climbed as I fought to keep people from using the telephone. 'You can't go in there! It's out of order. A dog's just been sick on the floor!'

At five o'clock I forced myself to walk away from the telephone box. The call was not to be. Coming to terms with rejection is the most difficult and pain-inducing part of an actor's lot. It is something that utterly fails to become easier to bear and that night I dragged myself to the Soup Kitchen in a miasma of misery. To come so close and lose was unbearable. Working half my shift, I was paid a pound and left. Meeting up with a friend I got very drunk, and later I sought and was given consolation in the arms of Julie. The next day I did not go home. I stayed with Julie until it was time for my shift at the Soup Kitchen. It was two o'clock in the morning before I arrived back at Pembridge Mews. At ten o'clock there was a loud banging on the door. I was handed a telegram: RING STUART BURGE IMMED-IATELY.

Bloody-minded, with a biting disappointment, I decided the only possible reason Burge wanted me to call him was so he could tell me I did not have the part. My head throbbing with a vicious hangover, I decided to go back to bed and telephone him at lunchtime. A couple of hours later I went to the telephone box and called Burge's secretary. Almost squawking with relief, she said, 'It's you. Don't hang up. I'm putting you straight through.'

When Stuart Burge came on the line I tried to be gracious and magnanimous about my rejection and wished him well with the production.

'No. You don't understand. Patrick McGoohan turned it down. You've got the part. I've been trying to get you for two days. What sort of house do you live in? You've got some very odd people answering your phone!'

I was lamely trying to make some excuse about the telephone when the penny suddenly dropped and I said, 'What do you mean I've got the part?'

'I can't pay you much.'

'Never mind that! I'll take it!'

Still almost disbelieving, I went straight to his office to see him. I was told I would be paid a hundred guineas – a small fortune to me, but in those days actors did not receive their fee until production was finished. As the rehearsal period was three weeks I had to continue working at the Soup Kitchen to survive. I would arrive at around ten o'clock in the morning and work until Stuart Burge let us finish, usually six or seven in the evening. I would then take the bus to the Soup Kitchen and work there until two o'clock in the morning. Rehearsals went well. The play, based on Roddy Barry's experiences as a Bevan boy down the mines during the war, was terrific. In his last week at work there had been an accident at the pit – the first in fifty years – and it had left Barry paralysed from the waist down.

At the end of the play my character, John, leaves the pit and goes to London. In the last scene John burns his pit boots in the station waiting room. I did my speech and put the boots on the fire, but they would not burn. We tried five or six times without success. Then we ran out of time. I was the only actor involved in this scene and it was decided the only thing to do was book a studio on another day for fifteen minutes to film the scene again, a stroke of great good fortune for me as it meant I would be given a double fee. I went along to the studio, but once again the boots would not burn. In the end there was no alternative but to give up and book the studio for yet another try. At the third attempt the burning of the boots produced such a conflagration the studio fire brigade had to control the blaze. I was also given another fee. That meant I received three hundred guineas for playing the part.

In the week before the play was transmitted I wrote to the six most important and influential theatrical agents in London asking them to watch it. Four of them replied, promising they would. The play went out at nine o'clock on a Sunday evening and I set off in good time to Julie's flat so we could watch it together. Crossing London I could not understand why so many people were still out on the streets. I wanted to stop them and say, 'What are you doing? Go home. There's a really good play on the television tonight!' Playing the leading role of John in *Pay Day* was a turning point in my career. The play received critical acclaim and when I returned home the next morning telegrams had arrived from all four of the agents, all asking me to do nothing until I had spoken to them. I chose Roz Chatto who worked for Christopher Mann because I liked her, but unfortunately she was not particularly successful in finding work for me. One of the other agents who approached me at that time was Denis Salinger. The dislike was, on both sides, instant and inexplicable, but when he eventually became my agent it worked to my advantage – he kept me constantly employed, mainly I think to keep me out of his office.

As I began to get more work Julie and I were able to set up home together and we bought a house in Putney, Ted Allan acting as guarantor for the mortgage. We established a happy domesticity despite my painful estrangement from my family in Liverpool and Gale's continuing refusal to divorce me.

In November 1961 my union, Equity, called a strike after negotiations over pay with the independent television companies broke down. Although I was not then on the council of Equity I was an active member and fully supportive of strike action. Realizing a strike was imminent I had been in communication with other trade unions, mainly the ETU, the electricians' union. Through Ted Allan's contacts with the Communist leadership of the ETU I was able to approach them for help. It was generally agreed by the grassroots membership of Equity that if we could win the backing of the ETU then the strike would very quickly be successful. The ETU readily lent their support to Equity in a reciprocal deal. This offer should have posed no problem, as it was the case in those days that if the electricians quite literally pulled the plug on film, television, radio or theatre then there was nothing actors could do, but await a resolution of the dispute. The deal with the electricians' union was presented to a general meeting of the Equity council, who rejected the offer out of hand. The strike dragged on for five months before the obtuse and pusillanimous leadership caved in, leaving many members in a worse financial and contractual situation than before the strike.

At ten o'clock on the morning of the return to work, Granada Television offered me a role in *Coronation Street*. It was a role that I had played for a very short time before the industrial action. The difference this time was my fee. Granada now offered sixty per cent less. I clearly and succinctly suggested to them what they might do with their offer. Granada then offered the role to two other actors for even less money. The offer was again rejected, but they eventually found someone desperate enough to work for the Equity minimum.

During the strike Ted Allan encouraged me to try scriptwriting. My first script, a half-hour comedy set in a second-hand shop in Liverpool, was accepted by ATV. Unfortunately, whilst ATV procrastinated over production, Galton and Simpson developed the groundbreaking series *Steptoe and Son*. However, ATV did continue to renew their rights to my comedy for a further two years. Buoyed by this initial success, I called at Ted's flat one day to discuss another writing project with him. Our conversation was interrupted by a frantic telephone call from an actress friend of Ted's begging him to hurry over to her home. On his return Ted told me what had happened. His friend's lover was Anthony Quinn, the Hollywood film star most famous in *Zorba the Greek*. However, Quinn was not only famous as an actor; he also had a reputation as a legendary and skilful lover to maintain and unfortunately it transpired his ego was a little fragile in this area.

Following an afternoon in bed the actress was not as enthusiastic and profligate with her praise of Quinn's performance as he would have liked. Bored and irritated with his raging insecurities and insistence that no woman had ever before expressed dissatisfaction, the actress informed him she had known better lovers and retired to the bathroom. When she eventually returned to the bedroom it was to find Quinn sprawled unconscious on her bed. Unaware that Quinn had taken sleeping tablets, and fearing the shock of her remarks had caused a heart attack, she telephoned Ted. Ted had a rudimentary knowledge of first aid from his time fighting with the International Brigade during the Spanish Civil War and he set about trying to revive Quinn. Increasingly desperate, Ted tried mouth-to-mouth resuscitation. Coming round, the startled Quinn, already suffering the humiliation of having his virility called into question, now found himself kissed by a man. Roaring, he threw the hapless Ted across the room and had to be restrained by his mistress whilst the true circumstances were explained. Able then to see the funny side of the whole episode, Quinn insisted Ted stay and have a few drinks with him before finally the sleeping tablets again took hold and Quinn collapsed into sleep.

One of my ventures into writing for television produced a not entirely welcome or anticipated reaction. Watching television one evening I became incensed by an army recruitment advertisement. As video recorders were not available I had to watch ITV night after night, hoping the army advertisement would appear so I could laboriously copy it word for word, and frame by frame. I then revised the ending so that in my version of the advertisement the recruit was killed and his ghost appeared, urging viewers to 'join the army and take my place'.

I had one of the best script agents in London, Gareth Wigan, and I took this short script to him. He read it in total silence and then picked up the telephone and dialled a number. Anxiously, I asked what he thought. 'Hilarious', he responded and I remember thinking that I hoped an audience would respond with a slightly more overt enthusiasm. He sold the script on the spot to an excited Ned Sherrin and his *That Was The Week That Was* team. On the Saturday evening my sketch was part of the show and as I watched the credits at the end I was just able to see my name in the legion of writers listed. On Monday morning I received a telephone call from an actor friend, Mark Eden, who told me there was a highly critical article on page two of the *Daily Mail*. Amongst other things the article declared, 'you get killed in the Russian army too, Comrade Booth!' I was not too perturbed by this. I have always felt that if I was upsetting the *Daily Mail* then I must be getting something right. However, my smugness was shattered later that same evening.

In those days *Panorama* was the flagship current affairs programme for the BBC and we were regular viewers. Julie and I settled down to watch it unprepared for what was to follow Richard Dimbleby's introduction. He announced he was going to make a personal state-ment and then, direct to camera, he launched into a personal diatribe – not against the *That Was The Week That Was* programme, but specifically me, the thrust of which was that I was a subversive influence attempting to undermine the morale of the British Army. As I was reeling from this shock the Secretary of State for War, John Profumo, then appeared on the screen further to denounce me. At that moment the telephone began to ring. It was Ned Sherrin, thrilled the show had been attacked on such a prestigious programme as *Panorama* and asking, 'Would I write another sketch?' I have never worked out whether Profumo's action in criticizing me was sincerely motivated by the highest of personal principles or simply a staggering example of Establishment hypocrisy. On balance I would incline to the latter, as it was only a matter of months before he was required to resign from the government after lying to the House of Commons over his role in the Christine Keeler affair.

The Tory administration was rocked by the Profumo scandal. Shortly afterwards Harold Macmillan, citing ill health, resigned as Prime

Minister. Macmillan was one of the very few Conservative politicians I had any respect for. During the First World War he fought in the trenches and so knew at first hand the horror and dreadful hardship the ordinary soldier was experiencing. Later, as Member of Parliament for Stockton, a northern constituency, he was active in attempts to alleviate and solve the problems created by the economic slump of the thirties. He was not dismissive of the suffering he witnessed; he was a 'one nation' Tory.

I went several times to hear him speak in the House of Commons and he was a consummate performer. I also believe he was genuinely shocked and dismayed by the behaviour of John Profumo – not by the fact that he had a mistress, but that he would discredit the integrity of the government by lying to Parliament. Macmillan's resignation precipitated the kind of political manoeuvring in the Conservative Party more normally associated with the election of a pope. A leader was expected to 'emerge' – a gentleman was required to be discreet in his quest for power, nothing so vulgar as open campaigning was acceptable. Of course, the whole Machiavellian process provided rich entertainment for anyone not directly involved. Rab Butler at first appeared to be the most obvious choice, but he was roundly loathed by the Tories as the senior partner in the years of Butskellism.[3] Matters took a more gloriously extravagant turn with the entry of Quintin Hogg into the contest. Hogg followed the fine example of Tony Benn and renounced his peerage in order to fight a by-election in Marylebone, a safe Tory seat. I, of course, campaigned for his Labour opponent Peter Plouviez, who was also at the time assistant general secretary for Equity.

I have always believed there is no such thing as a 'no-go' area when canvassing and I have experienced a few quite odd and sometimes utterly bizarre moments in the supposed territory of political opponents. One evening, canvassing for Plouviez, I knocked on the door of a peer of the realm. I was shown into the house by the butler and was offered a drink whilst my host explained he could not vote, but made it clear he was a disillusioned Conservative. Turning to his butler he enquired if he would be voting. Drawing himself majestically to his full height, the butler responded, 'My lord I shall of course

---

[3] Butskellism was the name given to the hybrid political philosophy encompassing ideas from the right wing of the Labour Party and the left wing of the Conservative Party. Essentially, it was a device to grab the middle ground in British politics, but ultimately served only to alienate further both Butler and Gaitskell from the mainstream of their respective parties.

vote Conservative. Now, shall I show this socialist out?' 'Socialist' was enunciated through clenched teeth and in such a manner as to demonstrate the word scorched his tongue. No vote there, but a chat and a drink and on to the next doorstep.

It was the unlikely figure of Alec Douglas-Home who eventually emerged as the new Tory leader. Douglas-Home appeared to be 'other-worldly' to such an extent I could not bring myself to heckle him on the occasion I heard him address a public meeting in Putney during the 1964 general election campaign. Politics can often be a brutal business, but I believe sadism is not one of my failings.

I committed myself enthusiastically to the Labour campaign. I had continued to be an active member of the Putney Labour Party since moving from North Kensington a few years before. My first experience of a Labour Party conference had been in 1960 at Scarborough, where Gaitskell made his now infamous speech claiming, 'some of us ... will fight and fight and fight again to save the Party we love'. The political dishonesty of Gaitskell, his arrogance and moral self-righteousness were breathtaking. In echoing Winston Churchill's rallying call in 1940 to withstand the enemy ('... we will fight them on the beaches ...') Gaitskell was guilty of drawing disingenuous parallels out of political expediency. In 1940 the country had its back to the wall and was fighting for its life. In 1960 we were fighting to save lives.

My commitment to the anti-nuclear movement pre-dated my membership of the Labour Party and certainly informed my reaction to Gaitskell and his pro-nuclear acolytes. Julie and I had taken part in the Aldermaston marches and it was on these marches that I became friends with Michael Foot and Tony Benn, men whose clear and honest integrity has been one of the beacons of post-war politics. Gaitskell's speech finally demonstrated to the delegates at the conference what many of us on the left wing of the Party, particularly after the 1959 general election, had come to believe. It seemed to me that Gaitskell, Crosland and Jenkins were determined to recreate the Party in their own quasi-patrician self-image and thus ultimately engineer the loss of its radical edge. The bile of my contempt rises whenever I chance to see Jenkins, pomposity intact, moving serenely through life. However, it was Jenkins' later role as a founder member of the Social Democratic Party with those other eventual losers Shirley Williams, David Owen and William Rodgers that I found utterly unforgivable. Then as now, I interpret their action as nothing short of treachery at a time when Labour fortunes were at the bottom of a very deep trough. Briefly newsworthy, the SDP failed to blaze a trail through British politics and once again, thankfully, Jenkins with his pretensions and his claret was relegated to the political sidelines.

Ted Allan taught me a great deal about the infiltration methods of political enemies, then more relevant to the American situation than the British, perhaps; but even so, I think a healthy dose of paranoia has always been essential for political understanding and survival. Fortunately, by 1964 the Labour Party had the more inspiring and solid figure of Harold Wilson as leader and we hoped and believed he would be the next British Prime Minister.

During the 1964 general election campaign I spoke at rallies all over London, from dingy church halls to crowded town halls, as well as helping with the more mundane but essential tasks of canvassing and leafleting. I was now making fairly regular appearances on television. I had been in the popular BBC series *Catch Hand* with Mark Eden and was also often cast as the villain in programmes such as *Dixon of Dock Green, Z Cars, No Hiding Place* and *The Saint*. This television fame (or notoriety) sometimes led to requests for me to share a platform with parliamentary candidates. I also pursued my personal campaign against Quintin Hogg, whose style of speech-making with its frequent pauses meant he was a heckler's dream 'feed'. The London *Evening Standard* helpfully listed the venues for political meetings and rallies. Having looked to see what course Hogg plotted around the city for that evening I would follow him. Invariably I would be ejected from the meeting, giving me plenty of opportunity to be ready and waiting for him at his next venue. I believe Hogg represented all that is worst in Conservative Party expectation and politics. He was arrogant and self-serving, implacable in his belief in the right of his social caste to rule. I despised him.

During the election campaign the Labour Party held a mass rally at the Empire Pool, Wembley, where I met Harold Wilson for the first time. His speech, delivered unashamedly in his Yorkshire accent, was perfectly pitched to fire the faithful and he dealt wittily and effectively with hecklers. At this rally he appeared to be not only a confident and competent leader, but also a man at ease with himself; in fact, the complete antithesis of Hugh Gaitskell.

Along with other actors who were supporters of the Party, I was asked to read out messages and telegrams of support from socialist parties around the world. We were each passed three sheets of paper or telegrams. As the junior member – in theatrical status – of the quartet I was handed three short telegrams. Vanessa Redgrave, who was to stand centre stage left, was given what appeared to be scripts. Vanessa Redgrave was and is one of Europe's finest actors, but even she could not inject passion into the turgid and badly written prose and I felt truly sorry for her. Her travail gave me the opportunity to read quickly through my telegrams and I was considerably more lucky. The first one was short and to the point, and a relieved audience applauded at last. The second telegram was greeted with cheers, but it was with the third and longest one that I was able to bring the audience to its feet. A rallying call for Labour victory, I read it with a zealot's relish.

Afterwards we sat in our allocated seats on the platform listening to the deputy leader's speech. I was not an admirer of George Brown and when he boasted of securing a parliamentary seat for his brother my self-control collapsed and I blurted out, 'Nepotism – that's bloody nepotism!' Harold Wilson looked across to me and raised his eyes to heaven. Brown scowled as a section of the audience began to giggle and it was that giggle that signalled yet another major change in the course of my life.

Five

Love, Labour, Loss

'Inspiring bold John Barleycorn!
What dangers thou canst make us scorn!'

Robert Burns, 'Tam o'Shanter'

At the end of the rally the owner of the giggle crossed the reception area and introduced himself. 'I'm Johnny Speight,' he stuttered as we shook hands. It was 1964 and although I could not have known it then, this meeting was one of the most momentous of my life. Speight bought me a large whisky and told me about a script he had written for BBC Television's Comedy Playhouse. Speight added that in his new script the role of Mike was originally written with his friend Michael Caine in mind, but Caine had now become too big a star to be interested in a one-off, half-hour television comedy. Thus Speight now had me in mind. Much later, clutching the script, I staggered drunkenly home to Putney and to an icy reception.

The next morning as I read *Till Death Us Do Part* – as the script was called – I was able, despite a monumental hangover, to realize what a groundbreaking and exciting piece of work it was. Flattered beyond belief, I telephoned Johnny Speight to say how delighted I would be to work with him. Although I had quite considerable experience of performing theatre comedy I had never before been offered a role in a television comedy. The challenge excited me and I knew if it was ever shown the programme would generate enormous controversy. Speight immediately suggested lunch – liquid of course – and my rapid and wretched decline into a notorious drunk got seriously underway.

The trigger for my heavy drinking was the collapse of my relationship with Julie, but Johnny Speight demonstrated how to do it properly. I had only a limited capacity for alcohol and initially I turned to drink in an effort to ease the problems I was facing at home and to numb feelings of increasing desperation. My grandmother used to say that when poverty walks through the door, love flies out of the window; Julie and I were by no means poor, but no matter how much I was able to earn our bank account was always overdrawn. With the clarity that hindsight so often brings I can now understand, and to a certain extent have accepted, that Julie was, in so many ways, very young; she was just into her twenties when we first met. Any resolution of the conflict created by the demands of the lifestyle she expected and my ability to fulfil those expectations clearly called for a far greater maturity than either of us possessed. Yet, despite everything that was to happen later, in the beginning Julie and I were happy and very much in love.

On one occasion we travelled to Paris together, the first time I had been back since my national service days. Julie's father, Ted, was working over there as screenwriter on the film *Paris Blues* and he suggested we spend a weekend with him. The film was directed by Martin Ritt and starred Paul Newman, Joanne Woodward, Sidney Poitier and Diahann Carroll. When Julie and I visited the film set we were invited to a party to be held that evening at the producer's country home. At the party, Ted and Julie circulated and I found myself leaning on a grand piano listening to Paul Newman as he played. I glanced across the room and noticed a woman dancing in a rather strange fashion. Turning to Newman I remarked, 'Every aspiring young actress in France feels obliged to do "a Bardot" ...'. He looked at me in surprise, 'That is Bardot.'

So near yet so far away – I did not know the genuine from a copy!

Julie and I were able to enjoy a higher standard of living than I had ever experienced as my critically acclaimed lead role in *Pay Day* had led to many other offers of work. A telephone call from the London office of the Hollywood film company Seven Arts invited me to meet the American director Henry Hathaway, whose many films included *How The West Was Won*. He was about to direct a remake of Somerset Maugham's *Of Human Bondage* with Kim Novak and Laurence Harvey. Hathaway and I got on well at this meeting and he offered me quite a good role in the film as one of Kim Novak's boyfriends. The film was to be shot at Ardmore Studios in Ireland and I was guaranteed three weeks' work over three months. From the day shooting began I would be paid a weekly retainer of two hundred pounds. I would also be paid extra for each day I was filming. I was delighted with the contract – in the mid-sixties this was a considerable sum of money.

Each week a cheque for two hundred pounds, minus my agent's

fee, would drop onto my doormat. Without having to do a thing I was paid three hundred and sixty pounds, but during the third week I was called to fly to Ireland to meet Hathaway, discuss my role and start filming the following Monday. I was met at Dublin airport and taken by car to my hotel, a beautiful country house in the hills above Ardmore. The hotel could only be reached by a long winding road and as we climbed the views became increasingly spectacular. This was when my continuing love affair with the south of Ireland began. It is truly God's own country!

I had travelled in my only suit, of which I was inordinately proud. It had a high velvet collar and a long flowing jacket, the height of fashion in the mid-sixties! My battered holdall somewhat reduced the overall sartorial effect, but I was still taken aback as I entered the hotel lobby and met Hathaway, who said, 'That's great. You're wearing the costume. That's perfect.'

'No, no. It's mine.'

'OK so it's yours. We'll hire it. I'll pay you ten pounds a day for your suit!'

Uncertain if I should be insulted at the implied slander or pleased by the prospective financial gain, I nonetheless accepted his offer with alacrity. Later over dinner I had a long and at times animated conversation with Hathaway about the Oscars that were shortly to be awarded. I rehearsed my belief that the competition was far from fair. Hathaway, who was a member of the judging panel, did not take my criticism well, reacting angrily. I stood my ground and said to him, 'Come on. I bet you voted for a film made by the last studio you worked for, didn't you?'

'Maybe,' he said.

'Well, that's how it's carved up. That's why a great actor like Brando hasn't received an Oscar, whereas others get it for playing the game or just reaching a certain age.'

We talked well into the night and in no time it was two o'clock in the morning. We both retired for a few hours' sleep before getting up at the crack of dawn for what was to be my first day on the film.

However, on arriving at the studio I discovered I would not be needed until ten o'clock. In my first scene Kim Novak played the part of a Cockney waitress in a tearoom. I was introduced to her and she seemed to be a really pleasant woman. When Hathaway appeared he was nursing both a monumental hangover and a newly developed disillusionment with the Hollywood awards system. We began to rehearse, but Kim Novak was nervous. Hathaway, growling like a bear with a sore head, had a further detrimental effect on her already dire Cockney accent. In the scene Kim was standing by the table at which I was sitting. After four or five lines of dialogue, Hathaway turned to me and said in a voice suffused with a poisonous mixture of exasperation and contempt, 'Have you ever heard anything like that in your goddamn life?'

'What?'

'The accent. For Christ's sake, she's supposed to be a Cockney.'

Poor Kim just stood there frozen in an embarrassed agony. I said nothing, deciding at this point that discretion was the better part of valour. It was an extraordinary outburst. Then he said, 'Carry on.'

I delivered my line: 'I'll have crumpets and tea.'

Kim said, 'Anyfing else?' And at that point Hathaway exploded in perfect illustration of the phrase, 'he lost it'.

'Anyfing else? Anyfing else? Have you ever heard anything like it? Baby not only can you not do an accent you can't damn well act!'

The whole set froze as Hathaway demolished Kim, at one point informing everyone that she was not his choice for the role. He had wanted Elizabeth Taylor. His behaviour was atrocious. It was an utterly deplorable thing to do.

After a few minutes I plucked up enough courage to intervene. 'I think that's enough Henry. You're upsetting Miss Novak.'

But nothing would stop him now. At one point I had to restrain him when it looked as if he might actually hit her. The torrent of abuse only ended when Kim ran off the set in a torrent of tears. Suddenly exhausted by the force of his emotion, Hathaway flopped down into his chair and shouted, 'Get me a coffee!' Calling for the first assistant he told him: 'Get Novak back down here'. Turning to me he said, 'Am I glad to get that off my chest'. He then catalogued the problems he had encountered with the film and Kim Novak in particular. Eventually, the message came back that Miss Novak would not leave her dressing room. 'Fine,' said Hathaway. 'We'll just sit here and wait.' Hathaway's invective against the iniquities of the Hollywood system was only interrupted by the first assistant bringing the information that Kim Novak had telephoned the producer, Ray Stark. Stark had driven from Dublin and was now with her in her dressing room. He wanted to see Mr Hathaway in a few minutes. Stark walked onto the set and pointed to Hathaway. 'You're fired. Get off the set.'

Hathaway stood up and in true Hollywood style threw the script into the air and pronounced, 'You don't sack me. I quit!' He turned to me and said, 'Come on Tony. Let's go.' Then he stormed off the set.

I stayed where I was. Stark looked round and said, 'That's it. You can all go home. We'll be in touch when we're ready to start shooting.' Then he left.

There was a stunned silence, but gathering my wits I asked the first assistant, 'What now?'

'You heard the man. Go back to your hotel.'

Whilst I was being driven back I wondered anxiously what I should say to Hathaway. I need not have worried. He had already left. I was told that by the time he got to the hotel his bags were packed and standing on the drive. A waiting taxi then whisked him to the airport. During that same evening the first assistant arrived with my air ticket and the next day I flew back to London.

Weeks passed, but every Tuesday a cheque for one hundred and eighty pounds arrived from Seven Arts. One day some ten weeks later the telephone rang. It was Jenia Riesser, the casting director for the film. She asked what I was doing as she had a part in a film for me. In *Of Human Bondage*. I laughed and told her I was already working in it, but that I had been sent home after the Hathaway incident to await a fresh call.

'Great,' she said. 'I'll get straight on to your agent and talk money.'

'But I'm already under contract. I've been getting a cheque every Tuesday.'

'Oh my God! I'll ring you back later.' A little later she called back and told me my contract was cancelled. My first reaction was to think perhaps honesty had not been the best policy when she went on to say my new contract was in fact worth more money.

I returned to Dublin to discover there had been two more directors after Hathaway. Now the new director was Ken Hughes (who had recently made *The Trials of Oscar Wilde*) and who with Bryan Forbes had completely rewritten the script. I immediately liked Hughes, but as he told me at great length, he intensely disliked Laurence Harvey. Once again the atmosphere on the set was poisonous. Everyone was very unhappy and that unhappiness was clearly reflected in the final cut. The film was a mess and did not make any money. Each night over dinner Hughes would complain how difficult it was to work with Harvey. In the new script I had a fight scene with Harvey and Hughes told me how much he was looking forward to it. 'I'll give you twice your daily rate if you smack him in the mouth,' he begged. When eventually it came to the fight scene half the crew and Ken were urging me to floor Harvey and the other half wanted me to punch Ken. I had no particular feelings either way and just wanted to get the whole thing over. We rehearsed the scene without incident, but when it came to the take Harvey, instead of moving away from the punch, ducked into it and so by accident I hit him. He flew backwards, landing on his backside amongst a pile of dustbins. The crew cheered and burst into applause. Harvey was, however, gracious in his reaction to the incident – or so I thought.

We actually got along reasonably well and one day we were chatting when he suddenly asked if I was interested in clothes. A little unsure of his drift I replied I was not particularly bothered. 'Oh, I am. I love shoes. I've got hundreds of pairs. Last summer I was making a film in Spain and I had some beautiful shoes made for me. The only problem is that they were sent on to me after I'd left and they don't fit. Would you believe it? They made a special last, but I've got fifty pairs of shoes all different sizes. Only about a dozen of them fit me. How are you off for shoes?'

I told him that I had the pair I was wearing and another pair back at the hotel.

'I tell you what,' he said. 'Go to my dressing room, tell my dresser I sent you and pick out whatever you like.' Amazed at his generosity I went to his dressing room and tried on about half a dozen pairs. Harvey's feet were bigger than mine, but I thought I could stuff the toes with tissue and the shoes would be perfect for interviews, funerals and other formal occasions. Harvey came in and said to me, 'They look great don't they? Do you want them?' I indicated the four pairs I really liked and he said, 'Great. They're yours for fifty quid a pair. That's what they cost me.'

Stunned, I replied, 'You must be joking. I thought you were giving them to me.'

'OK. I tell you what. We're both actors. You can have them for thirty quid a pair.'

'Larry,' I managed to stutter, 'I wouldn't pay thirty quid for any of them. I've never paid thirty quid for a pair of shoes in my life!'

'Oh well, take them off and piss off!'

The happiness Julie and I initially shared was deepened by the birth of our daughter Jenia on 5 February 1963. Jenia was born in the London Clinic, a private hospital, but by the time Bronwen, our second daughter, was born on 21 February 1964 money was already running out and Julie gave birth to her in a National Health maternity ward. Julie's father was wealthy and doting, continuing to indulge her every whim, but eventually I was struggling to maintain a lifestyle that included an account at Harrods and an au pair to look after our children. Five years into our relationship I was spending more time out of the house drinking than at home.

During those five years I had not seen either Cherie or Lyndsey, partly under pressure from Julie who did not want anyone from my past, particularly my family, to encroach on our shared present and future; also, because my family were finding it hard to forgive me. Some progress towards reconciliation was made after Julie gave birth to Bronwen. Although my parents were still angry and hurt by my decision to leave Gale, two more beautiful – and innocent – grandchildren were the reason they gradually began to accept my new family, even visiting Julie and me. It was only then they told me that my grandmother Till had died three years earlier in July 1961. But increasingly, my dependency on alcohol and the resulting guilt-ridden rages increased as a combination of financial and emotional pressure finally began to tell.

The rationale behind the Comedy Playhouse programmes was to showcase twelve new and different comedies. Television viewers would then vote for their three favourites and their choices would be made into new comedy series. During the recording of the *Till Death Us Do Part* episode the reception we received from the live audience made us confident our programme would be one of the three selected. Later, when the cast and crew retired to the BBC bar, I met Tom Sloan, then Head of Light Entertainment, and his assistant Frank Muir. Both of them hated the programme and Muir in particular was at his acerbic best in expressing his distaste. They informed a dumbfounded Johnny Speight and me they had already decided, before a vote had been cast, which three programmes were to be made into series. This list did not include *Till Death Us Do Part*. Sloan and Muir could hardly have been more wrong. Our pilot episode won more votes from the viewers than all of the other eleven put together, but it still took over a year for the BBC to give way to continuing public demand and commission Speight to write a series.

I was offered the lead role in a pre-London tour of a Philip King farce, *I'll Get My Man*. It meant I would be away from home for about a month, but I hoped time apart might help Julie and me to think more clearly about the problems in our relationship and begin to work them out. During the first few weeks I was away we endured several difficult telephone calls, but when she failed to meet me in Edinburgh as we had arranged I began to understand that a reconciliation might be more difficult than I had imagined. At the end of the tour I was out of work again. I was deeper into debt. I returned home to find the house locked and my family gone. Without giving any indication of her intentions, Julie had taken our daughters to Boston to join her father who, with the end of McCarthy's purges, was able to return to America.

It was to be 1979, almost fifteen years, before I saw Julie again, but at that moment as I stood outside the house, initially uncomprehending, I experienced utter emotional devastation. I had given up everything for Julie – my marriage to Gale, the respect of my parents, but most of all Cherie and Lyndsey – and there was no way back. Rejecting many of the personal and moral values I was taught as a child, I gambled all I had and all I was on my love for Julie and I had lost ... and yet ... and yet, why did it have to end that way? Some residue of Catholic guilt meant that when I fell from the path I fell very hard. But Julie could not hurt me nearly as much as I could hurt myself. My thirteen-year exploration of the depths of drunkenness began as I sought oblivion at the bottom of a glass.

Thirteen years of Tory rule came to an end with Labour's triumph in the 1964 general election. Euphoria was only slightly tempered by the narrowness of the victory. This election was also notable as the first time actors were used to court voters. It was Hugh Jenkins, then assistant general secretary of Equity, standing in Putney, who deliberately deployed actors in his campaign in an attempt to raise his public profile. Harold Wilson had one of the best political brains of his generation and, combined with his ease in public speaking, it served to make him a formidable opponent to the aristocratic Alec Douglas-Home. From my first meeting with Wilson I believed him to be a man who tried, at least in the beginning, to maintain a level of political honesty and it was this that convinced not only the Party but also the country that he wanted change as much as we did. A key factor, I think, played well for him – that he was perceived by the electorate as 'an ordinary man', a man in touch with his roots and the reality of most people's lives. Whilst it was true that he had a double first in economics from Oxford it was also true that it was not privilege but ability that had taken him there. He was seen by many as the epitome of the hoped-for meritocracy. Some of the reforms made by the Wilson government were not only radical, but far-sighted: the introduction of the Race Relations Bill; the Trades Description Act, 1968 and later that same year new and liberal laws on abortion and homosexuality.

Nineteen sixty-six was again a general election year and I poured my energy into the campaign. After the narrow victory of 1964 we were determined to achieve a working majority for a Labour government. I appeared on platforms, giving speeches alongside Labour ministers and friends such as Michael Foot and also with Harold Wilson. It was following a campaign rally that Wilson and I shared the ignominy of ejection from a mayor's parlour. After the speeches a small but select band were invited to the parlour for drinks. As I stood chatting to Wilson a waiter approached us and in whispered tones informed us that the lady mayoress kept a very good scotch in her pantry. Discreetly removing ourselves from the party, Wilson and I followed the waiter. He was right: the mayoress was keeping the best stuff back. The waiter was just on the point of refilling Wilson's glass when a tornado in the shape of the small but perfectly formed mayoress crashed through the door. Needless to say, she was absolutely furious to find us partaking of her best whisky and in high dudgeon ordered us not only from her pantry, but also from the building. Of course, Wilson and I were objects of curiosity as we made our exit, red-faced and sheepish, through our fellow guests. It was only when we were outside the building, away from her mighty wrath, we felt it safe enough to start giggling.

Labour won the election, increasing its majority from four to ninety-six, making Wilson the first incumbent Prime Minister during the twentieth century to secure an increased majority. However, the authority of the government was immediately challenged by a number of strikes, most notably by the National Union of Seamen. John Prescott, later the Member of Parliament for Hull and Tony Blair's Deputy Prime Minister, was then both an active and prominent organizer in the seamen's strike – one of those tersely described by Wilson as a group of politically motivated men. I sided with the seamen, who needed financial help. I wondered what might be done and then an opportunity presented itself. Whilst believing, as I still do, that the best chance for positive social and political change lies with a Labour government, I also believed that a new, more radical approach was possible with the arts in the vanguard. I had the opportunity to explain this position to John Lennon when I met him at the mews home of a mutual friend. We had both gone to the house, not far from Paddington station, one late afternoon to buy marijuana. Within a few minutes of Lennon's arrival the mews was blocked with screaming, fainting teenagers who managed simultaneously to block the main access road to the station. An apologetic and embarrassed Lennon was now captive in the house as the only way out was through the blocked front entrance. As we settled down to wait for the frenzied fans to be dispersed, Lennon calmed our host's fears of a police raid and asked him to put together the large quantity of 'smoke' he had ordered.

Lennon and I started to discuss the problems of Liverpool – the endemic poverty and deprivation – and I suggested to him it would be a marvellous gesture for the Beatles to perform a concert in Liverpool, with the profits going to aid the unemployed and also to support various industrial actions such as the seamen's strike. He was interested in the idea. I believed the concert could be organized at Anfield football ground as I had contacts with Liverpool's manager, Bill Shankly and the secretary of the club, Peter Robinson. He told me he would speak to his management, but sadly nothing came of it.

Our reveries were interrupted by the telephone; it was a high-ranking police officer ordering Lennon to stand by for a further call. He would then be escorted through a cordon of police officers to a police van and taken to his destination. Our host was by then completely frantic, absolutely certain he was about to be the subject of a police raid. Lennon, however, told the police officer he was at the house for a sexual assignation and as he was then still married to his first wife Cynthia he asked the officer to be discreet. The police were concerned only to relieve the massive traffic jam around Paddington and a deal was quickly struck. The telephone rang again and the police ordered Lennon to hold himself in readiness for departure. This he did by clutching his genitals. The noise outside the house was deafening, but within a few minutes a phalanx of burly policemen assisted by two mounted policemen forced a passageway through the now hysterical and fighting teenage girls. As the police hammered on the door Lennon said his goodbyes and, concealing several ounces of marijuana about his person, dashed through the open door to be manhandled into the waiting police van and driven off pursued by a tidal wave of females.

Inside the house we waited for the mews to be cleared and for a telephone call from Lennon telling us he had reached his destination. Less than half an hour later he called to say he had arrived and the police had not queried his story of an assignation. It was now safe for the rest of us to leave and as I walked home through the twilight I was still giggling at the thought of Lennon and his dope having a police escort to safety. But that still did not help the seamen.

It is clearly because of incidents such as this that the Establishment, eagerly assisted by much of the media, has succeeded in generating the idea that the sixties were hedonistic and self-indulgent, just sex and drugs and rock and roll. Certainly, on the King's Road on any given day it was possible to get passively stoned under the clouds of marijuana drifting from the cafés. But of far greater importance and significance during this decade was that much of the Western world was in political turmoil. I do not know when the term 'global village' was first used, but for me it was during the sixties that I began really to understand its meaning and relevance. The world had become smaller and issues such as the genocidal activities of the United States Army in Vietnam had to be recognized as global. It was a matter of international conscience as a whole generation of people believed they could rewrite the rules of the political game, ultimately changing the world and making it a safe and just place. The old ideas, mores and political wheeler-dealing were seen as the province of mainly white, middle-class, middlebrow, self-seeking time-servers.

With my emotional life frozen under a permafrost of pain and rejection, exchanged for a continuum of forgotten one-night stands with forgotten but accommodating women, I gave my commitment to political activism. I was arrested on several occasions whilst taking part in demonstrations. I made a number of appearances before Mr Robey, a stipendiary magistrate and son of the famous comedian George Robey, known professionally as 'the prime minister of mirth'. Unfortunately his son had not inherited any of his father's wit and humour, seeming instead to harbour a deep antipathy to any member of the theatrical profession. Whenever I appeared before him he always handed down twice the fine imposed upon my fellow protestors. It might have been that he hated *Till Death Us Do Part*, but in the early sixties, in my pre-Speight years, I once appeared before him in the company of Bertrand Russell, John Osborne and John Arden.

We had all been arrested the day before whilst taking part in a CND demonstration in Trafalgar Square. When I arrived at Bow Street, Arden and Osborne were already the occupants of a cell. Police logic appeared to dictate that as thespians, and thus potentially dangerous subversives, it would be easier to monitor us if we were kept together. I had not met Arden or Osborne before, but we were getting on well until Bertrand Russell arrived in the early evening. Awestruck as he walked through the cell door, we watched in amazement as he dropped his trousers and unwound a dhoti. His only comment, as he settled down to sleep, was on the usefulness of always carrying a clean blanket when taking part in a demonstration. Of course, this immediately killed any conversation as we were concerned not to disturb the great man. Our good intentions were, however, not shared by the police who every hour throughout the night would rush into the cell determined to catch us in the unnatural practices they were certain all actors and writers enjoyed.

During Wilson's time in 10 Downing Street I was invited to a number of receptions. It was on one of these occasions that I recognized Clement Attlee. He was sitting alone and ignored as the crowd moved around him busily networking, constantly glancing around to check for 'important' people. I went across to Attlee and we chatted, about nothing in particular. I just wanted the opportunity to talk to this great man. When he was ready to leave I helped him to his feet. The sad smile he gave me acknowledged that politics had moved on and he no longer had a role to play. At that moment I understood there is nothing quite so 'ex' as an ex-prime minister – even the best.

Although I was invited a number of times to Downing Street, when I received what seemed to be an invitation to Harold Wilson's birthday party I was not immediately convinced of its authenticity as at the time I knew several notorious practical jokers. Determined not to be caught out, I filed it in my jacket pocket, planning, when asked by one of the jokers if I had received any good invitations lately, to produce it with a flourish, thus demonstrating complete sang-froid. Over the next two weeks I made tentative, but determinedly casual, enquiries of the other cast members on *Till Death Us Do Part* about invitations to Wilson's birthday party. However, none of them seemed to be aware that Wilson's birthday was imminent and made no mention of a party at Downing Street.

I was living at the time in north London in Chalk Farm and also maintaining a residential drinking-post up the hill at the 'Sir Richard Steele' pub, where I kept company with the journalists Peregrine Worsthorne and Hugh McIlvanney and the television writer Leo Griffiths, who later wrote the series *Minder*. There was also a constant and motley collection of thespians known collectively as the 'Hampstead Irregulars'. Another of my drinking companions was the terrific actor, the late Patrick Wymark, probably most famous for his role in *The Power Game*. I was by now completely mystified by the 'invitation'. I did not appear to be the victim of a practical joke – no one had mentioned it – but how could I know if it was genuine? One evening Wymark opened his briefcase and produced with a flourish an invitation to Wilson's birthday party. Delighted and relieved, I rooted through my breast pocket and compared it to mine. It was not, after all, a joke. Wilson's birthday party was held within a short time of the 1966 general election when the spate of industrial unrest was at its worst. The political problems faced by Wilson helped to fuel rumours of a 'palace revolt'. At the party I confided these fears to Wilson, whose response was sanguine; 'I know what's going on, I'm going on'. It was the first time I heard him use the phrase and he clearly liked it as he went on to repeat it to resounding cheers from delegates at the Party conference.

I was greatly saddened by Patrick Wymark's death in 1970 and I attended his funeral service with three of his drinking companions. Afterwards the four of us piled into my car to follow the cortège. I was forced to stop at traffic lights, but as we watched the funeral procession move up Haverstock Hill towards Hampstead we were sure we would soon catch up. Despite the traffic I was able to keep an eye on the cortège as it made its way in the direction of Golders Green crematorium. Bringing up the rear, we followed sedately. As we entered the chapel a man handed us black paper skull caps to wear. Somewhat puzzled, we did as requested. Turning to one of my companions, Peter Kinsley, I whispered, 'A Catholic service and a Jewish burial?' Peter muttered something about Patrick covering his options. The chapel was crowded, but we eventually managed to find seats not far from the front. It was only when the rabbi began the service we realized we were at the wrong funeral. Red-faced, we squeezed our way back through the crowd to the exit, all the while muttering a stream of embarrassed apology. Dashing back to my car we eventually found the right chapel and bravely faced the withering glances and suspicion of the other mourners that we had stopped off for a drink. I do, however, strongly suspect Patrick would have seen the funny side of it.

Despite my liking for Wilson I was aware that, like most men, he had his weaknesses. There was much speculation about his dalliances with the opposite sex. Several years later, in a state of financial desperation and with bankruptcy beckoning, I worked on a film with the soft-porn actress Mary Millington. I really liked Mary. Her vulnerable loneliness and fragility touched something in me and I felt protective towards her. We spent a lot of time talking and she told me of her liaison with Wilson. Her spluttering surprise when she thought I already knew her secret convinced me she was telling the truth. The story has been vigorously denied by Joe Haines, Wilson's former press officer. Several months after we finished the film Mary committed suicide. On the night she died Mary tried to telephone me, but I had already collapsed into a drunken stupor and was unaware of her call until the next day when, of course, it was far too late.

The Vietnam War loomed portentously over the sixties and galvanized anti-war demonstrations, not only in North America but also in Western

Europe. There was a very real fear that the American government would successfully pressurize Europe into supporting its action with troops as well as arms. At the now notorious Grosvenor Square demonstration mounted police deliberately and provocatively rode at defenceless women and children and I was not the only person who suffered a beating as we tried to protect them. Not surprisingly, when I next met Harold Wilson I was keen to raise the issue of any attempt to involve British military in Vietnam. There were half a million American troops in Vietnam and the American President, Lyndon Johnson, was attempting to persuade the British government to send a token force.

Johnny Speight and I had tickets for a European Cup match at Anfield in Liverpool. Leaving Johnny's suite in the Adelphi Hotel to conquer the bar, we met Harold Wilson in the corridor. He was in Liverpool to attend a meeting in his Huyton constituency. Delighted to meet us, Wilson invited us into his suite for a drink. Fortified by a stiff scotch I launched into a tirade against American involvement in Vietnam. Johnny was more concerned with the veracity of tales circulating that Lyndon Johnson was in the habit of exhibiting his allegedly large penis to visiting heads of government. Undeterred by his interruptions I persisted, growing ever more angry under the influence of the scotch. Poor Harold Wilson was by now using his pipe to try and create a protective smokescreen as Johnny and I hurled insults over his head. Wilson appeared greatly relieved to see us leave, though he was kind enough to say he had enjoyed our chat and looked forward to talking to us again.

After Julie left me I moved around London living in various flats and houses, never really settling anywhere for long. At one point I had a first-floor flat in Notting Hill Gate. This flat had the added bonus of a balcony on which I often used to sit, catching the sun. One afternoon in late October, during one of those mellow Indian summers, I was out there when the French windows of the flat next door but one to mine opened. Out walked a breathtakingly beautiful young woman. I could hardly believe that despite living in my flat for several months I had not seen her before. I smiled and waved to her. She smiled and waved back. After a while she went back in. A short time later I saw her leave the building. Rushing downstairs I managed to catch up with her and somewhat breathlessly ask if she would have dinner with me. She agreed and we spent a delightful evening together that ended with us sharing her bed. She told me she would like to see me again, but she was not a free agent. She was the mistress of a well-known actor whose name she could not possibly tell me. She suggested, however, that any night her lover would not be visiting I might call round and keep her company. I was very happy to accept her kind invitation and our casual love affair continued as deep winter set in.

One snowy night I had already gone to bed when she telephoned to ask if I would like to keep her warm. Not wishing to appear ungallant, I quickly made my way to her bed. Later, lying together in a state of warm, relaxed, post-coital bliss, we were startled to hear her front door opening. I then heard the unmistakable voice of Peter Finch. He was singing. As we both leaped panicking and guilty from the bed my some-time lover hissed, 'Get out on to the balcony. I'll take him into the kitchen so you can get your clothes and get out of here. Quick!' I made my exit just in time as Finch walked into the bedroom. 'Darling,' he said as he took his mistress into his arms, 'you look lovely standing there with the moonlight behind you.' Despite the fact that I was completely naked on a snow-covered balcony at two-thirty in the morning, I winced for him. 'Come on, Finchie,' I thought as my teeth rattled like jackhammers, 'you can come up with a better line than that!' Hidden by the curtains, I waited as she tried to persuade Finch to go into the kitchen for a drink, but he would have none of it. 'No, no,' he insisted, 'let's go to bed.' I listened in a state of frozen despair as Finch got his way and they tumbled onto the bed.

Finch had clearly been drinking heavily, and in a state of abject torment I realized it was going to take him some while to reach an orgasm, by which time I would surely have petrified on the balcony. Glancing across I saw I had left a fanlight open in my bedroom. This was not the moment for a faint heart. I knew what I had to do. The only way to prevent my untimely and undignified demise was to work out a route and somehow clamber across the front of the building to my own balcony. This far from easy solution to my compromised situation was further complicated by the anti-burglar devices installed by my neighbours. Spikes and barbed wire. Eventually, I managed to climb on to the next balcony. I then made the unfortunate error of glancing in the window as I tiptoed past and saw a couple making love on the bed. At the very moment I looked into the room the woman looked up and saw me sneaking, stark naked, across the balcony. Not unreasonably she began to scream and that sound gave wings to my heels. Like some demented mountain goat I vaulted spikes and barbed wire to land on my own balcony. Trying to make myself as inconspicuous as possible, I pressed myself against the wall just as the doors to the neighbouring balcony were flung open and another naked man appeared. 'What are you talking about? There's no naked man out here,' he announced. The woman's voice insisted she had seen one. The man then turned accusingly, 'Why did you have your eyes open? If you had been enjoying it they would have been shut.' With this he went back inside, slamming the door.

Waiting until the unmistakable sounds of love-making were resumed, I climbed a conveniently positioned drainpipe and managed to haul myself through the fanlight into my own bedroom. With icy fingers I put on layers of clothing before staggering into the kitchen to finish the remains of a bottle of brandy. Frozen to the marrow I then climbed into bed, praying I would eventually warm up. Burrowing into the bedclothes I had just about got comfortable when I heard the buzzer for the front door. My immediate thought was that she had confessed all to Peter Finch. Reluctantly, I dragged myself out of bed and pressed the button on the intercom.

'Is that Tony Booth?' a voice whispered.

'Yes.'

Another whisper, 'This is the police here.'

'Yes.'

'We don't want to alarm you, but we believe there is a burglar in your flat.'

'You're joking!'

'No and what's more he's naked. Are you alone?'

'I bloody hope so!'

'You had better let us in and we'll search the flat.'

I pressed the button to unlock the front door before dashing back into the bedroom and pulling off my extra clothing. Putting on a dressing gown over my pyjamas, I opened the door of my flat to two policemen.

'Don't turn your lights on,' one of them said as they switched on their torches and began peering around. As I was living in a one-bedroom flat their search was quickly completed. 'He's not here. It's all right. Obviously he was after a woman and scarpered when he realized you were a bloke. That means we'll have to search all the other flats – just in case.'

As they were leaving I asked them who had reported the incident. 'An old lady opposite. She's in her seventies,' one of the policemen answered. 'She got up to go to the bathroom and glanced out of the window. She said she saw a naked man climbing into your flat. Not only that, she reckoned there was not just one, but two naked men. Apparently she saw another one on your neighbour's balcony!'

'She must be seeing things,' I assured them. 'Brass monkeys wouldn't risk this cold!'

That was the last night I spent with Peter Finch's mistress. In truth, alcoholic oblivion was increasingly preferable to facing the awful reality of what my life had become. Five-day 'benders' with two days off to recover became my norm and it was not unusual to wake up in a strange city with no idea of how I had got there. All the excitement and promise of my early life as an actor was slipping away and I was not interested in rescuing myself. I became utterly absorbed in my own emotional despair and indifferent to the pain I was inflicting on anyone who came near me. It was at this time that I met a young radio reporter, Annabel Gannon, at a reception. My daughter Lucy, born in April 1967, was the beautiful result of our all too brief relationship. However, by the time Annabel was pregnant I had already met Susan Riley – a fateful encounter that was to be the final act in my self-destructive plot. Annabel disappeared out of my life. From the early eighties I tried, with Cherie's help, to find Annabel and Lucy, but without success. It was thirty-five years before I was to speak to my daughter, when she contacted me through an intermediary. Lucy was now living in Australia, married to Stan and with a young son called Peter. I was on an emotional roller coaster as I picked up the telephone for that first conversation, but this incredibly generous and warm woman, my daughter, made it easy for me and we cried, laughed and talked for a long time. Turning seventy was something of a landmark for me and Lucy becoming part of my life made the year even more memorable.

Making my way to a Chelsea drinking club after lunch with a friend on the Kings Road we passed a block of flats, Nell Gwynne House, where I had lived for a short time. I was hailed from a top-floor window by an acquaintance, Patricia Bell. Having nothing better to do, I happily accepted her invitation to call in for a drink. Amongst the other people in the flat that afternoon was Susie Riley. During the course of general conversation I mentioned I needed a haircut. Patricia suggested I allow Susie to cut my hair in return for dinner. At the time, with no idea of what was in store, I agreed to what seemed a reasonable deal. We had dinner together and later returned to my flat for what I believed was, for both of us, nothing more than an opportunistic coupling. How wrong I was. Leaving for work the next morning, I did not expect her to be in my flat when I returned. However, that evening she was still there, and it was thirteen years before our mutually ruinous relationship was abruptly and finally terminated.

Till Death Us Do Part was so successful that, inevitably, it became a feature film. After shooting for three weeks without a break at Shepperton studios, I was very tired and due to have the next day off. As usual at the end of a day filming, Johnny Speight and I made our way to the bar, but I was too tired either for drinking or company and after only one pint the driver took me back to Highgate, where I had rented a house. When I arrived, Susan was at home and offered to make me something to eat. It was a relief simply to stagger to the couch and collapse in front of the television and as the commercial break started I drifted off into exhausted sleep, coming to as the advertisements finished.

I had barely closed my eyes when I heard my father crying out, 'Help! Help! Help! Nurse! Nurse!' I found myself standing at the foot of my father's hospital bed as he said, 'Thank God you are here. Get the nurse. I can't make a sound. I'm having a heart attack. I'm dying. I need help.'

My father was choking on terrible pain, unable to call out for help. Desperate, but knowing I could not attract the attention of a nurse, I told my father to try and stay calm. 'Give me your pain. If I take your pain that will ease it.'

'It won't work,' he gasped.

'It will work. Believe me. Let me take your pain.' Suddenly, I began to experience a severe stabbing pain in my chest. 'That's right, give me your pain,' I encouraged him, but as the pain increased, becoming unbearable, I began to panic and knew if it continued I would also die. 'I can't take any more,' I sobbed.

'It's alright,' my father shouted and I understood he had managed to make a sound that could be heard on the ward.

Waking with a cry, I sat up on the couch as Susan rushed in from the kitchen to find out what was wrong. I explained my out-of-body experience and told her I would have to telephone the hospital. Calmly, she pointed out we could not telephone every hospital in Liverpool, but more pertinently we had not been told my father was even in hospital. Even so, I was still extremely agitated and concerned, so Susan suggested I telephone my mother. When I could get no reply I tried to telephone my sister. Again no reply. By then I was much calmer and willing to take Susan's explanation that the experience was nothing more than the work of an exhausted mind.

The next morning I awoke to find that Susan, to ensure I had undisturbed sleep, had unplugged the bedside telephone. As I plugged the telephone back in, it rang immediately. It was my sister Audrey, saying she had been trying to contact me all night. My father had been taken to hospital complaining of chest pains. After seeing him settled for the night, Audrey and my mother started down the ward only to hear him cry out. Rushing back to his bedside, they found him in the throes of a massive heart attack, but thankfully the medical staff had been able to save him.

I told my sister I would drive up to Liverpool immediately. I telephoned John Boulting, who was producing the film, and without hesitation he agreed to rearrange the shooting schedule, and of course I must go to my family.

Making my way home to Liverpool I began to think, probably for the first time in my life, about my relationship with my father. Of my parents, it was my mother who was the dominant figure, my father content to let her take this leading role. My mother had inherited the Thompson volubility and the strength of mind and purpose exhibited by most of the women in my family. My father, gentle, quiet, peace-loving, went along with my mother's decisions and I realized that as an adult I probably never had a real conversation with him. No exchange of views, no gentle ribbing, not even a dispute of any kind. Even after I left Gale and set up a home with Julie he made no comment on my actions. But faced with the fear of my father's death I at last understood his strengths and knew how much I loved him. I prayed, all that never-ending journey, for God to allow me the opportunity to tell my father this truth.

I had arranged with Audrey to meet her and my mother and my brother Bob at the hospital and together we walked to my father's bedside. To my amazement my father held out his arms to me and as we embraced he kissed me. It was something he had never done before.

'It did happen then?' I asked.

'Yes, but don't say anything now,' he replied.

When it was time to leave, my father, for the first time in his relationship with my mother, dismissed her and the rest of my family by saying he wanted to speak to me alone. Surprised, they nonetheless did as he asked. As I sat by the bed my father took my hand and told me I had saved his life. He then asked me not to tell anyone what occurred as he was certain no one would believe it, thinking instead he was losing his mind. He went on to say he knew we had never been close, but he needed to tell me he loved me and he had always loved me.

Rejoining the rest of my family we returned to my parents' home, where I was able to spend a short time with Cherie, Lyndsey and Gale. My relationship with Gale remained reasonably civil even when the situation between us was at its most fraught. Now Julie was no longer part of my life Gale was willing to divorce me. More importantly, her life had moved on. She was happy and successful in the travel office where she worked. Both girls now attended Seafield Convent, Cherie showing clear signs of the intellectual potential that would later propel her to the top of her chosen career in the law. It was Lyndsey's misfortune to follow Cherie through school. Equally bright and intelligent, Lyndsey found herself in the shadow cast by her elder sister's achievements, but determinedly carved out her own distinctive route through life. As a young child Lyndsey, with considerable justification, was extremely angry with me. Her continuing anger and frustration at my abandonment are a major factor in the uneasy relationship we now share.

I drove back to London the same evening – I was needed on the set the following afternoon. I returned to Liverpool a few months later for my father's funeral. He died on 6 September 1968. No matter what age one is, it is always a searing experience to lose a parent. Their death leaves a vacuum in your life that nothing can fill; but mixed with my grief was overwhelming relief that, before it was too late, my father and I strengthened a bond of love and understanding that for most of my life seemed so insubstantial.

The sixties drew to a close and another general election loomed. As so often seems to happen, bright hopes and promises had foundered in the mud of squandered opportunity. On the many occasions I met Labour politicians I warned them we faced electoral defeat – but from Wilson down, they were convinced they would win. After six years of a Labour government the Party rank and file were increasingly of the opinion that Wilson's style of leadership had become all public relationship and no public planning. In 1964 the Labour Party presented the electorate with clear-cut political and economic choices. By the end of the decade it was difficult to see what the Labour Party signified and what, if any, were the differences from the Conservatives. What did it stand for when glaring social inequalities remained? How could it be the party of fundamental socialism when no major extensions of public ownership had taken place? How could it be the party of organized labour when so many of the rank and file and trade unionists had become disaffected?

During the 1970 general election campaign I had a conversation with Wilson during which he asked me what had gone wrong. Without hesitation I replied, 'You didn't keep your promises.' I told him the political ground was shifting and if he was not careful we would all go under. And that, indeed, is what occurred: the election was won by the Conservatives, led by Edward Heath.

Six

Lost Time

'The true paradises are paradises we have lost.'

Marcel Proust

The seventies is a decade I struggle to remember, both in the literal sense that I was suffering from the self-absorption and increasing amnesia of the habitual drunk, but also because they were years of disappointment, depression and loneliness. I was still able to cling in some part of my confused brain to a vestige of the political under-standing that informed my beliefs and commitment, and it was prob-ably this that was my only and ultimate salvation as I raged through life alienating friends and comrades. The sixties ideal that it would be possible to find a workable alternative to the excesses of capitalism was already beginning to give way to cynicism. Yet again, capitalism survived by absorbing new ideas and extremes, regurgitating them with a far less radical edge. Johnny Speight, famous for his left-wing politics and the hard-hitting, at least in its early days, *Till Death Us Do Part* now boasted of being a dollar millionaire. The idea behind the British series was sold to the United States and metamorphosed into *All In The Family*. A great deal of money was generated, both from the series and the subsequent merchandise rights.

The theatre also began to experience something of a backlash against the radicalism and inspiration that marked the sixties as theatre managements became more cautious, choosing profit over innovation. Fortunately, it seemed, Kenneth Tynan, the greatest theatre critic of our time, had other plans. When I received a call from him he was about to stage – with the producer Michael White – the satirical revue *Oh! Calcutta!* His enthusiasm was infectious. He told me we would make history and shake the theatrical establishment to its foundations. How could I resist? It was, Tynan argued, the ultimate challenge – not only to be naked and funny, but also naked and serious. I read the script and was persuaded. Clifford Williams, the respected Associate Director of the Royal Shakespeare Company, was to direct the revue, and the six-week rehearsal period prior to opening at the Roundhouse theatre, the former locomotive shed in north London's Chalk Farm, was an extraordinary experience.

The first four weeks were spent doing what the American choreographer described as 'touchy, feely, but no fucking'. A hard time, indeed. During the first week of rehearsal we were put through a punishing regime of dance exercises that left my alcohol-soaked body exhausted. Rehearsals started at ten in the morning, going on until seven or eight in the evening, with only an hour for lunch. A fortunate side effect of all this exercise and resulting tiredness was a reduction in my alcohol consumption. During the second week of rehearsal long robes arrived for the cast. We were instructed to strip down to our underclothes and put on the robes. We then engaged in the so-called bonding sessions that the Americans who had been involved in the production in New York took very seriously. About midweek we removed our underclothes and finally our robes. The cast of five men and five women then had to close their eyes and 'discover things about each other'. During these exercises I was usually paired with the talented and beautiful actress Linda Marlowe. Whilst delighted with this arrangement, I also suffered agonies of embarrassment, as I would, naturally enough, immediately get an erection. I learned later that this was the purpose of the exercise – essentially, familiarity breeding contempt: as we became used to each other, erections would eventually fade. After a few days of this the rest of the cast, without informing me, dropped the closed-eyes part of the exercise and watched each other. Oblivious, I was still trying to conceal my erection from Linda by approaching her from her blind side. By now my enthusiastic penis was beginning to cause consternation as Michael White and Clifford Williams became increasingly anxious about obscenity laws. John Mortimer, QC was summoned to rehearsals and I did not let him down. This difficulty was an issue until the dress rehearsal, when the cool temperatures of the Roundhouse reduced the problem to nothing.

Included in the revue was a sketch about a girls' boarding school requiring six performers and a female understudy. One morning at the end of rehearsal I was called into the office to see Tynan, White and Williams. They had a problem. Each of the women had been tried in the role of headmistress, but the production team were unhappy with all of the interpretations. What they wanted to know from me was, would I take on the role of the headmistress? I was taken aback as there were two gay actors in the cast and I thought they would probably fulfil the task better than I might. Tynan didn't have to tell me it was a great challenge, but he convinced me at least to try. In the rehearsal room the women were waiting. I was incredibly nervous, having absolutely no idea how to play the part. That night, as Susan snored in the bedroom, I sat up trying to think myself into the soul of the headmistress. Finally, given my voice and physique, I decided that lesbianism was the only way. At dress rehearsal I laddered three pairs of tights before managing to put a pair on and as I went on stage, teetering dangerously on high heels, I was greeted with raucous laughter from my male colleagues. Every move, every line of the sketch brought laughter and so, throwing away my lesbian, I played the drag queen. The sketch ended with the cast and crew whistling and cheering their appreciation. I sashayed to the dressing room very pleased with myself.

I had no sooner arrived than Tynan crashed through the door incandescent with fury. I stared in astonishment as he demanded to know what I was doing. He said that, at final rehearsal, my performance as a monstrous lesbian was the best he had ever seen from a man. For the sake of a few cheap laughs I had reduced my performance from something that as a critic he would have applauded, to the level of a cheap drag queen. Hurt, I defended myself, pointing out that at rehearsal my performance had not elicited a single laugh, yet at the dress rehearsal everyone found it funny. Refusing to listen, he was scathing in his criticism. He would rather I play to total silence than destroy his creation. Doing as he wanted, I revived my lesbian character. Unfortunately, the sketch was not a success and played in only five previews.

The evening after the sketch was pulled from the show I was in the bar having my usual couple of drinks when I was approached by a gay man. He told me he had seen every performance so far and wondered why the sketch had been dropped. I explained that, as it had been received in complete silence, the director decided to abandon it. He then wanted to know what happened to the dreadful dyke playing the headmistress. I told him she had been sacked and he replied it was a good thing as she was terrifying. Agreeing with him, I finished my drink and left the bar. Outside I leapt, punching the air like a footballer scoring the winning goal. Five performances and he had not recognized me!

When Tynan first approached me to appear in *Oh! Calcutta!* he and I had many conversations about the peculiar challenges of this particular piece of theatre. Ultimately, my involvement centred on the belief that we would not only defy but also break down entrenched double standards. The nude is an acceptable image in painting and sculpture, but almost always depicted without imperfection. Although theatre is a branch of art, in those days nudity on stage was perceived as unacceptable, partly, I believe, because this would be nudity with all its human frailties, not the idealized form of visual art. Tynan convinced me we could break through the hypocrisy and demonstrate that the structures maintaining social cohesion would remain – allowing the question, 'What was the problem?' to be legitimately posed. It was for me a continuation of the social revolution of the sixties and I was, on that basis, proud to be involved.

Unfortunately, as so often happens, a commitment undertaken for somewhat idealized motives became corrupted. Initially the production struggled to find financial backing, but when it became clear that *Oh! Calcutta!* would be a huge commercial success there was no longer a problem as, amongst others, the Grades and Bernard Delfont offered backing. Tits plus bums were seen to equal large profit and very quickly the management junked any esoteric notions. My intention was to stay with the production for the first month, participating in the initial furore, and then leave. However, mounting debts, principally unpaid tax, persuaded me to remain with the show for a further unhappy twelve months as we moved from the Roundhouse into the West End – my situation somewhat assuaged by the tripling of my original salary.

A Conservative government under Edward Heath was now in power and determined to take the United Kingdom into the Common Market no matter what the political or economic cost. In anticipation of this event, decimalization of currency was introduced in 1971. Suddenly, instead of 240 pennies to the pound, it was a hundred new pence to the pound. The smallest shopping trip took twice as long as we tried to convert the decimal currency back into 'proper' money. We were convinced that traders were making use of the chaos and confusion to push up prices. I have always believed Britain should have joined with the rest of Europe in signing the Treaty of Rome in 1957. The then French Minister for Foreign Affairs, Christian Pineau, made it clear that the intention of the treaty was not to form an exclusive club, but hoped that other countries, particularly Britain, would soon join the initiative. Instead, belatedly recognizing the advantages, we joined under the almost impossible terms dictated by de Gaulle. The Labour Party opposed membership of the Common Market under the terms negotiated by the Heath government. In defiance of the Party line, Roy Jenkins led a revolt during the Commons debate, thus helping to secure British entry into Europe in 1973. The silver lining to that particular cloud, as far as I am concerned, was Roy Jenkins' resignation as deputy leader of the Labour Party. As Ben Pimlott points out in his biography of Harold Wilson, others followed Jenkins providing, with hindsight, an early warning of the SDP defection nine years later. Membership of the Common Market remained a festering issue, and with other economic difficulties mounting the Heath government was soon in trouble. The Israeli war with Egypt in 1973 resulted in disruption of oil supplies. This in turn led to vast increases in the price of oil, creating not only global fuel shortages but also in Britain soaring inflation and the consequent disastrous impact on industry. It was, however, Heath's decision to confront the miners led by the astute Joe Gormley which brought about the three-day working week and finally the collapse of the government, forcing a general election in February 1974.

During this bitterly contested election I first came across Margaret Thatcher, who was to dominate the political landscape for the next decade and a half. Known in the early seventies as 'Maggie Thatcher Milk Snatcher' for her decision to end the provision of free school milk, her constituency, Finchley, was next door to my own, Hampstead. As I frequented a number of public houses in Finchley I was able both before and after hours to campaign against her. Sadly for the future of the country, and despite (or perhaps because of) my street corner rants, Thatcher was returned at the election with an increased majority. It was later clear she had learned the hard lesson of Heath's premiership. Government confrontation with striking miners should be precipitated only in circumstances where it is more assured of victory. That is, in the summer when stockpiles of coal are high.

My drinking and the problems it created meant that the former warm relationship I enjoyed with Wilson was no longer possible. Where once I had been invited to his birthday party I now found it difficult to have the briefest of conversations with him. However, on the rare occasions when I met Wilson during the election campaign I tried to impress upon him the difficulties the Party would encounter in turning out its core vote. Despite the problems faced by the Heath government the media were successful in painting the Labour Party as the party of broken promises and the election ended with a hung parliament, the first since 1929. The Labour majority over the Conservatives was just five seats and Edward Heath pursued every available option in an attempt to remain in power, including offering a deal to the Liberal Party (fourteen seats), then led by the ubiquitous Jeremy Thorpe. Thorpe reluctantly declined the offer and Harold Wilson once again took up residence in 10 Downing Street in spite of rumours, already beginning to circulate, that he was contemplating resignation.

Labour won only thirty-seven per cent of the popular vote – half a million fewer votes than in the 1970 election defeat. The Wilson government took office having gained fewer votes than the Conservatives. Despite this tenuous grip on power, Wilson scorned the offer of a pact with the Liberals, judging correctly that the Liberals would support enough legislation for the Labour Party to function as a government. Within days of coming into office Harold Wilson ended the miners' strike and also the state of emergency declared by Edward Heath. Wilson's new Cabinet included, for the first time in Britain, two women, Shirley Williams and the magnificent Barbara Castle. The election served to strengthen the position of the left of the Labour Party. Tony Benn, Michael Foot and now Barbara Castle were members of the Cabinet that set about repealing Heath's hated Industrial Relations Act and abolishing the Industrial Relations Court.

However, always the shrewd politician, Wilson quickly realized there was little he could do within the political circumstances. He called a further general election in October 1974, ending the shortest parliament since 1681. The results of this election were marginally better for Labour than in February, despite two million fewer people voting. This time the Labour government had an overall majority of three. Government credibility and authority were not only issues in the country, but also amongst party activists and grass roots support.

In a gesture towards the strong political emotion that entry into Europe generated in the country, Labour made a referendum on continuing membership a manifesto commitment. The Labour Party conference in 1974 voted against membership and a special conference in April 1975 upheld that decision. Unbelievably, despite the clear wishes of the members, the leadership unilaterally changed position and recommended a 'Yes' vote, Wilson fearing, it is now claimed, that to do otherwise would split the Party. Yet the Cabinet was far from united. Tony Benn and Barbara Castle opposed the government position. Despite my pro-European feeling, I also still believed the conditions of entry were far too onerous and campaigned vigorously for a 'No' vote. Campaign meetings were noisy and crowded and I was a member of the platform for a final rally in Marylebone town hall. Shortly after I began to speak, Anthony

Greenwood, a government Minister there to support a 'Yes' vote, stormed off the platform, his exit accompanied by boos and catcalls. I was so confident the government would lose the referendum that I invested a not inconsiderable amount with a turf accountant.

In June 1975, however, the government won the referendum with a majority of two to one. Stunned by the outcome, I spoke to many people who were similarly dismayed. Following his support for a 'No' vote in the referendum, Tony Benn was removed from his post as Industry Secretary. Benn's position was not helped by his articulate and intelligent argument for a state-led response to the deepening world recession, winning him no friends or favour from right-wing members of the government. Response from the Left was swift and damaging to Denis Healey's faltering prestige as he was voted off Labour's National Executive Committee.

On a personal level Susan Riley was now a fixture in my life. An attractive bottle blonde, she was at first engaging and amusing, but eventually proved to be my nemesis. Susan's mother, Frances, had been married twice. Her first husband, Susan's father, returned home from the war but shortly afterwards abandoned his family. Her mother then married Sidney Riley and, taking her stepfather's surname, Pamela Cohen became Susan, or Susie, Riley. Sidney Riley is a gentle and tolerant, if reactionary, man and he needed to call on all his tolerance to deal with his wife. Frances suffered with persecution fantasies that led her, amongst other things, to hide food under her bed at night in the belief that her neighbours were trying to poison it. She clearly needed psychiatric help, but neither her husband nor her daughter would acknowledge that her behaviour was in any way bizarre, a judgement maintained to this day by my daughters with Susan – Sarah born in 1967 and Emma in 1970.

The kind-hearted and highly talented actor Dandy Nichols was a constant source of support and advice. Dandy always carried her 'remedies' bag with her onto the set of *Till Death Us Do Part*. From this bag she would dispense cure-alls (hangovers a speciality) to Johnny Speight, Warren Mitchell, our producer Denis Main Wilson and, of course, me. Dandy disliked Warren Mitchell, but even so, when he complained of tiredness she offered to give him one of her remedies to help him through the day. She also offered him something, a 'black bomber', to help him sleep that night. Una Stubbs, who played my wife, and I watched in fascinated amazement as Mitchell raced through rehearsals and then dashed home at the end of the day.

The following morning Mitchell was late for work, something that had never happened before. Just as people were starting to worry he arrived and, dragging himself across the rehearsal room, he collapsed into an armchair. As he croaked his explanation I was in grave danger of choking to death on suppressed laughter. It transpired that Dandy had somehow confused the tablets she had given to Mitchell and, instead of a sleeping tablet, he had taken something that left him rampaging through the house all night. As Mitchell slumped dramatically in the armchair, the others gathered in concern around him. Turning, I caught Dandy's eye and she winked. This was no accident. This was Dandy's brilliant and inventive retaliation against the aggravation Mitchell continually inflicted on all of us. I relished the moment with her. The following Friday, Dandy gave me one of the pills she had 'accidentally' given Warren Mitchell. I understood the effect it had on him as it kept me up for the entire weekend.

Johnny Speight often liked to talk through ideas for his scripts and during late-night drinking sessions at his home we would discuss which sacred cow should be scrutinized and questioned in the next episode. One night, throwing ideas around for a while, we eventually realized that blasphemy was probably the only taboo the series had yet to challenge. I suddenly remembered a story I had heard or read somewhere about Aldous Huxley, whose father was a devout believer. During a debate between the two of them over the existence of God his father insisted God was everywhere. Huxley, a non-believer, or certainly a sceptic, asked if that meant God was in the room with them. His father reasserted that God's presence was everywhere so of course He was in the room with them. Huxley responded by picking up a glass, turning it over on the table and saying 'Got Him!' When Huxley later wrote about the incident his action was condemned as blasphemous by the Catholic Church.

Speight, who had not heard the story before, got very excited by this idea and it was therefore not a great surprise to me when he used it in the next episode. Nor was it much of a surprise to find my character would be the one to deliver the alleged blasphemy. Speight was by now notorious for the late delivery of his scripts. We began rehearsals with the first part of the script whilst waiting for him to deliver the completed version that we knew would contain the 'blasphemy'. The finished script did of course create some consternation amongst the production staff, but Denis Main Wilson decided to allow it. When we arrived at the studio a few days later to film the episode the trade union shop steward, a devout Catholic, objected. Finally, after enduring a lengthy circular argument, I snapped and demanded, 'What is your problem? After all I'm the one who will be uttering this so-called blasphemy.'

The shop steward, now in a state of some agitation, replied, 'What would happen if God appeared and struck you dead?'

'We'd make television history with God making His first ever live appearance, to deliver divine retribution against me.'

My response broke the deadlock as everyone began to laugh. We went on to film the episode without thunderbolts from heaven or any other obvious manifestation of Godly displeasure. In his role as Alf Garnett, Mitchell asserted that God was everywhere. Of course, this was challenged by Mike, who asked if He was in the room. On being told He was, I turned over an empty tea cup and delivered the *coup de grâce*: 'Got Him!'

Alf Garnett's 'You blasphemous Scouse git!' was fortunately lost in a gale of laughter.

It would be dishonest of me not to admit that, in the beginning particularly, there were many good moments working on *Till Death Us Do Part*. It was exciting and innovative and the programme had significant impact on the process of redefining acceptable parameters in British television. For the first time television comedy became a tool for radical, social comment. One of the highlights of my time with *Till Death Us Do Part* came when we appeared at a concert in the Albert Hall in support of medical aid to Vietnam. We were overawed when meeting the great Russian violinist David Oistrakh. In the dressing room a relaxed Oistrakh, attended by tense and watchful KGB operatives, jammed happily with Johnny Dankworth and the other musicians. In many ways Johnny Speight was the victim of his own success. He took British society's innate, thoughtless misogyny and prejudice, parading it before us in a manner that made us laugh with recognition at the same time as it made us squirm with shame. The age of political correctness was born. Speight's writing was often inspired, but having delivered his message it seemed he had nowhere else to go. None of his future work was to demonstrate anything like the same influence or success. *Till Death Us Do Part* ran for seven series, between 1966 and 1968 and again from 1972 to 1975 – a total of fifty-three episodes.

I suppose the moment I finally realized that the programme had lost its cutting edge came in 1972 when *Till Death Us Do Part* was selected to appear on that bastion of bourgeois, middle-of-the-road respectability, the *Royal Variety Performance*. Johnny Speight wrote a very funny fifteen-minute sketch about the family watching the *Variety Performance* and criticizing all the acts. Media concern about possible offensive language in the sketch meant the script had to be submitted two weeks before the show. It became headline news that the sketch would include three 'bloodies'. Clearly the press still assumed or wanted to perpetuate the myth that the royal family were strangers to bad language. At the time I was unemployed and signing on at the social security office in Lisson Grove – a place so popular with the theatrical profession it was called the Actors' Club. My mother announced she wanted to see the show and I asked about complimentary tickets. I was informed the *Royal Variety Performance* did not give out complimentary tickets, but each performer was entitled to buy four tickets at a cost of fifty pounds each. I could not possibly afford two hundred pounds so I asked if they could offer me something a little less expensive. Eventually, after much haggling, it was agreed I could buy two twenty-five-pound tickets for the price of one. Relieved that I did not have to disappoint my mother, I decided not to tell her this meant she and Susan had seats in one of the tiers whilst the relatives of the other performers would be seated in the stalls.

My signing-on day was Monday, the same day as the *Royal Variety Performance*. On the Sunday evening I was contacted by a reporter from the *Daily Mirror* who said he was writing an article on the *Royal Variety Performance*. He told me that Liberace was staying at the Savoy and would be taken to the Palladium in a Rolls-Royce. He then asked about my own transport arrangements.

'I have to be there at midday,' I said. 'I'll catch the bus to St John's Wood and walk to Lisson Grove to sign on. I'll then walk to Marylebone station, take the tube and walk to the theatre from there.'

'You're joking!'

'No.'

'You're signing on?'

'Of course I am. I need the money. I had to get special permission from the dole office to sign on early and do the show.'

'What time are you signing on?'

'Eleven o'clock.'

The next morning as I turned the corner into Lisson Grove I saw a gang of photographers waiting outside the dole office. As soon as they saw me they started taking pictures, causing pandemonium in the office as they followed me inside, still snapping away as I signed on. With my photographic entourage in tow I took the tube to the theatre, arriving at the same time as Liberace – who inadvertently gave the press the picture they wanted as he clambered beaming from his Rolls-Royce. Inside the theatre the dressing room hierarchy was brutal in its simplicity. 'English acts – male' were assigned one dressing room, 'English acts – female' another. There was a separate dressing room for the Americans. Only Liberace and Elton John were given special treatment and they shared the stars' dressing room. Warren Mitchell and I were crammed into a dressing room with the rest of the male performers including Arthur Askey, Dickie Henderson, Ken Dodd, Mike Yarwood and Rod Hull. The line about no room to swing a cat might have been coined for that day.

After the run-through someone arrived in the dressing room with souvenir programmes. That morning my mother, who had come to stay, asked me to get Liberace's autograph for her. Flicking through the programme I saw his photograph and foolishly said, 'Oh my God. I promised my mother I would get Liberace's autograph for her.' Mike Yarwood chimed in, 'Oh yes. I promised my mum too!' And he handed me his programme. Suddenly almost everyone in the dressing room remembered they had promised Liberace's autograph to their mothers, sisters, aunts, cousins. . . . Clutching a pile of programmes, I was despatched down the corridor to the Liberace-Elton John dressing room. I knocked on the door.

'Excuse me, Liberace,' I said 'but I'm in the cast.'

'Come in.'

I opened the door and there he was, lying on a chaise longue wearing a dressing gown decorated with musical motifs and pink tulle at the collar and cuffs. In his hand was a glass of champagne.

Recognizing me he said, 'You're the guy from that show. I watched the rehearsal. I love it. I love it. Come in. Come in.'

'I just wondered if you would mind signing these,' I said proffering the pile of programmes.

'Oh my, you do want a lot of autographs.'

I explained that after mentioning in the dressing room that I had promised my mother his autograph, the others then said they wanted it too.

Nodding with understanding he said, 'So you got the short straw,' and, brushing aside my protestations, he went on, '. . . which is your programme?' When I pointed out they were all the same he said, 'Well, I'll leave yours until last.'

He signed his name on all the programmes until the last one, when he asked my mother's name. 'Vera', I said. He then created the most extraordinary autograph I have ever seen. His name and my mother's were drawn in the shape of a piano with a candelabrum on top. He then wrote underneath, 'You have a very brave son.'

'That's fantastic. Thank you very much,' was all I could think of saying to him, knowing my mother would be absolutely thrilled. I gathered the programmes together and was about to leave when Elton John, who was on another chaise longue, asked 'Doesn't your mother want my autograph?'

'Yes of course,' I said quickly. 'Do you want them all?'

'No. Just your mother's.' He then drew a sketch of himself on the opposite page.

I had scarcely closed their door behind me when heads began appearing from my dressing room. 'Where have you been?' they demanded. 'You were ages.' When I showed them what Liberace had written for my mother there was uproar and they started bawling at me for not getting the same for them. Such is the gratitude of fellow artistes!

The *Till Death* sketch was on in the second half of the show. Warren Mitchell was a stickler for detail and if he was asked to read a newspaper it had to be that day's. We went onto the stage to perform the sketch and as the lights went up Mitchell was sitting at a table reading the back page of the *Evening Standard*. I was sitting opposite him and so could see the front page, which had a photograph of me signing on the dole. After a few minutes, during a conversation between Dandy and Una, Mitchell turned the paper over and I watched as he gripped the paper harder and his knuckles whitened. He began to read the article. His cue came up, but there was silence on the stage. Looking up, he stared around in panic. My personal and professional relationship with Mitchell was by this time at rock-bottom and I fleetingly considered leaving him flailing. But of course I could not do that to another actor and so I said to him, 'You've lost your thread haven't you?'

'Yes. Yes I have lost my thread.'

'Was it something you read in the newspaper?'

'Yes it was. It bloody well was something I read in the newspaper! Disgusting things they put in the paper!' We ad-libbed for a couple of minutes and gradually I got him back to the script.

After the show all the performers waited to be introduced to the royal family. The line-up went all the way up the stairs. We were on the landing next to an American group called the Jackson Five. Standing next to me was the youngest member of the group, Michael Jackson. The Queen Mother started at the bottom, gradually working her way up the stairs. An extremely sociable woman, she spent a lot of time talking to everyone and so by the time she approached us her allotted time for meeting the performers was almost over. The producer, Bernard Delfont, in an attempt to persuade her to speed up, said, 'I'm sorry Your Majesty, but there are still many more artistes to meet.'

'Oh yes, of course,' she said. She shook hands with Michael Jackson and then, turning to me, shook my hand and said, 'Congratulations.' Rendered fearless after consuming the six half-bottles of champagne provided by the management, before she let go of my hand I said, 'No, no ma'am. Congratulations to you!'

She went to move on, but then stopped and turned, 'Pardon?'

'Congratulations on your win on Saturday.' The Queen Mother's horse Inch Arran had raced at Sandown two days earlier. I had been watching the racing on the television and thought her horse had a good chance. I bet twenty pounds and it won at 9–2. Seizing the opportunity, I asked if she intended to run the horse in the Grand National.

'I might,' she replied.

'Well,' I said, 'it's a two-and-a-half-mile horse. I think it should do well in the Grand National.'

The Queen Mother then asked me if I had backed the horse. When I said I had, she enquired what price I had managed to get. When I told her 9–2 she told me she had only got 7–2. Then she remembered that two years previously I had literally bumped into her at the races. A jockey friend of mine had just told me he thought his horse would win and I was rushing to place a bet on it. Spotting an opening in the crowd I dashed forward, almost falling over a sweet old lady. Without really looking at who it was I danced around her apologizing profusely. It was only when she said, 'My you're in a hurry,' I realized I had almost knocked down the Queen Mother. Apologizing again, I explained I had a tip. 'What is it?' she asked and I told her.

So, as we were standing on the steps at the Palladium, she said, 'I remember meeting you at Sandown. You gave me a tip and it won.' Forgetting she was supposed to be in a hurry, the Queen Mother stood for a few minutes chatting about horses until Bernard Delfont, who was by now in a state of nervous exhaustion over the collapse of his carefully planned schedule, leaned across and said, 'Excuse me ma'am. We must get on.'

'Yes, yes,' she said. Then she turned back to me. 'I have to go. But I do like talking about horses. By the way,' she added confidentially, 'I'm not supposed to tell you this because I was advised not to spend any time with you terrible people from the show, but I always watch your programme and I love it!' She moved on, shaking hands, eventually disappearing into the night. We were told by the press officer that immediately after the occasion we should not tell anyone what the royals had said to us, but back in the dressing room people were curious about my conversation with the Queen Mother. When pressed on the subject I attempted to be blasé. 'Just something we have in common,' I replied. As quick as a flash Dickie Henderson said, 'Oh you mean the fact that neither of you carry any bloody money!'

Many years later, with my son-in-law now Prime Minister, I was indirectly to receive more racing information from the royal family. Cherie telephoned me after they returned from the Prime Minister's annual weekend with the Queen at Balmoral. During our conversation she suddenly remembered that during their stay she met the Earl of Carnarvon, the Queen's racing manager. To my amusement Cherie had been surprised when Porchester told her he knew her father was interested in racing. He was kind enough to pass on tips for two horses as they would be absolutely right for me to follow with their approval. Two not so cryptic tips in one paragraph!

It was through my friendship with Dandy Nichols that in 1974 I was offered one of the starring roles in the British film comedy *Confessions of a Window Cleaner*, directed by Val Guest. Dandy showed me the film script one day during rehearsals for *Till Death Us Do Part*. She had been offered the role of Mrs Lea, mother of Timothy Lea, the part played by Robin Askwith. She thought I would be perfect to play, yet again, her son-in-law, this time Sidney Noggett. It was one of the funniest film scripts I have ever read and what I liked most about it was its honesty. Whereas the *Carry On* films encouraged their audiences to snigger like schoolchildren at sexual innuendo, *Confessions of . . .* laughed openly at the ridiculousness of sex, thus, I would argue, reflecting the aims and aspirations of Restoration comedy. I have always believed that if the films had been made in France or Italy, they would have been far more acceptable to a middle-brow audience who would have revered them as 'art'. But, as they were made in Britain they were perceived simply as 'smutty'. The wider public loved *Confessions of a Window Cleaner* and it broke box office records, outgrossing even Mel Brooks's deservedly acclaimed *Blazing Saddles*.

I starred in two further *Confessions* films – *Confessions of a Pop Performer* in 1975 and *Confessions from a Holiday Camp* in 1977, both directed by Norman Cohen, whose work also included *Con-*

fessions of a Driving Instructor and *Stand Up Virgin Soldiers* (1977). My daughters Sarah and Emma also had small roles in *Confessions from a Holiday Camp*. Knowing of my erratic behaviour on the first film, Cohen insisted on a clause in my contract forbidding alcohol consumption whilst on location. However, I was by that point in the decade oblivious to any humiliation. Some years later Pat Phoenix and I were in London and decided to have dinner in a Chinese restaurant. As we entered the restaurant we were greeted by the head waiter, who became very excited when he recognized me. To my mortification and Pat's amusement, he began shouting to the other diners and restaurant staff, '*Confessions of a Window Cleaner* – great picture you naughty, naughty man.' It transpired that the film was hugely successful in Hong Kong. My grandson Euan recently informed me the films have become compulsive viewing for a new generation who watch them on Channel Five.

The mid-seventies were a particularly productive time for me. In 1975 I played the role of a villain in the John Wayne film *Brannigan*. This was at the time when the Watergate scandal was just reaching its peak. A drinking companion of mine had acquired a badge with the legend 'Impeach the Cocksucker' emblazoned upon it. Knowing John Wayne was a prominent Republican, he dared me to wear the badge on the film set. Drunken bravado led me to accept the challenge. Going to work the next day with the badge concealed under my jacket lapel, I arrived to find the set crowded with the usual mob of technicians and people vital to film production. Suddenly, like the Red Sea, the crowd parted and John Wayne lumbered into view. As we were introduced I realized, to my complete surprise, that I liked the man and there was no way I would ever let him see the badge. During breaks in filming Wayne would invite me to his trailer for a drink. The interior resembled the saloon bar of a western and as the 'Duke' entered through the swinging half-doors the barman would pour a large glass of beer and shoot it down the bar for Wayne to grab. We got on well and I was invited to a special 'wrap' party in his hotel. During the party Wayne invited me to stay at his home in Hollywood. He was convinced I would do well in America and when I asked him why, he replied 'because you've got them mad eyes and boy would they go for them mad eyes'. Not many years later, in 1979, John Wayne died. I still have the personalized mug he gave me as a gift at the end of filming.

Despite the films and the television work, a decade of wanton profligacy ended in Carey Street – the bankruptcy court. Unable to afford a barrister, I was forced to defend myself. Unpractised in the ways of law, I had a miserable time at my hearing in front of a judge who made manifest his contempt for theatricals. Declared bankrupt, my reaction to this crisis was, of course, to get drunk.

In the autumn of 1972 my eldest daughter Cherie, turning down Oxford and Cambridge, moved to London to study law at the London School of Economics. The decision to go to university came as a relief to her family as Cherie had, with considerable success, played the role of Thomas a Beckett in a school production of *Murder in the Cathedral*. There had been some anxiety that she would follow 'that damn fool' (me) into acting. Cherie's move to London gave me the opportunity, albeit at irregular intervals, to meet up with her and try to re-establish some kind of relationship. When Cherie graduated with the highest marks of any law student in England and Wales that year, I was incredibly proud of her and looked forward to attending her degree ceremony. Unfortunately, the night before the ceremony I was mugged on Hampstead High Street and had to spend a few days in hospital. Not only did I miss her graduation but also, because of the popularity of *Till Death Us Do Part*, the incident was front-page news, giving some of her more envious fellow graduates ample opportunity to embarrass her.

I could take pride in, but none of the credit for, Cherie's and later her sister Lyndsey's success. I was extremely upset when, prior to and during the 1997 general election campaign, the Labour spinmeisters made much of Cherie's allegedly deprived background. The truth of the matter is that my parents were working-class, but proud, hard-working and respectable people who provided Cherie and Lyndsey with a loving, secure and stable home. Living with my parents as she did, Gale was able to work full-time in the travel department of Lewis's department store in Liverpool. It was only when Lyndsey left home to study law at Cardiff University that Gale also moved out, as she had managed to save enough money to put down a deposit on her own house.

The government was under increasing pressure and in March 1976 Harold Wilson survived a Commons confidence vote by seventeen. Later that month he announced his resignation. Now living in Hampstead, I was a regular drinker in 'The Flask' public house on Flask Walk in Hampstead. 'The Flask' was frequented by actors, writers and artists and, as it was close to the war games station on Haverstock Hill, also by war games personnel. Few people in the pub were prepared to accept Wilson's simple explanation that he looked forward to a quiet retirement with his wife Mary. Rumour and speculation over his shock decision raged, fuelled by increasingly wild stories. Stories of KGB involvement, double-dealing by the British security forces – nothing was too outrageous for our fevered and willing imaginations. These conspiracy theories were explored in Chris Mullin's novel *A Very British Coup*, which I referred to in the Prologue, and for which, incidentally, the excellent actor Ray McAnally won a much deserved British Academy Award in 1989. However, in the end I believe the explanation for Wilson's resignation was the one he offered – he was tired of politics and decided it was reasonable to retire at sixty. Several years after his retirement I met Wilson at a charity fundraiser I attended with Pat Phoenix. We had a brief but friendly conversation and that was the last time I spoke to him.

Wilson's successor as Prime Minister and leader of the Labour Party was Jim Callaghan, a right-wing pragmatist. With his equally right-wing Chancellor of the Exchequer, Denis Healey, Callaghan was to face the gravest economic crisis since 1931. Healey was forced to negotiate financial aid from the International Monetary Fund to prop up the staggering British economy. This aid was offered on terms including a government promise to cut public spending by three billion pounds, which appalled even Anthony Crosland, the Foreign Secretary and very much on the right wing of the Party. Tony Benn's alternative strategy, including import controls and further nationalization, was rejected out of hand by Callaghan and Healey. On 15 December 1978 Healey announced the terms of the IMF agreement to the House of Commons. His announcement was greeted with shocked disbelief by left-wing members of parliament and noisy derision from the Conservative benches led by Heath's successor, Margaret Thatcher. Healey's announcement finished any hope he nursed of winning the leadership of the Labour Party.

The Labour government lost its overall majority following the death of Tony Crosland in early 1977. Secret negotiations with the new Liberal leader, David Steel, to form a Lib–Lab pact became public when the Liberals voted with the government to defeat a Conservative confidence motion. The Liberal Party was still trying to recover from the resignation of Jeremy Thorpe following his trial and acquittal on charges of conspiracy to murder. It was his brilliant defence of Thorpe that first brought George Carman, QC, one of the greatest criminal and libel advocates of the twentieth century, to

125

public notice. Carman was later to mentor my daughter Cherie when she joined his Chambers as a young barrister in 1977. They remained lifelong friends.

Despite the pact with the Liberals the government continued to lurch from one political and public relations disaster to another, culminating in the disastrous 'Winter of Discontent'. Strikes hit the National Health Service and operations were cancelled. Tanker drivers stopped deliveries, creating fuel shortages. Refuse piled up in the streets as local authority workers no longer did their collections and newspapers carried pictures of rats running in the rubbish in Piccadilly Circus. James Callaghan had the dubious distinction of being the first Prime Minister since Ramsay MacDonald to have his government defeated in a Commons confidence motion. Callaghan resigned, calling a general election for 3 May 1979. The Conservatives won the election with a swing of over five per cent, the largest in any election since 1945. Along with many other stricken left-wingers I endured the cringe-inducing experience of watching Margaret Thatcher quoting St Francis of Assisi as she made her triumphant entry into 10 Downing Street. I still consider it one of the more surreal experiences of my life that the woman who later claimed to believe there was no such thing as society, should quote from the words of a man who represents the best of humanity and an active social conscience.

Although the Labour Party was already heading towards electoral rocks when Wilson resigned, Callaghan's strategy as far as I could see did nothing to reverse this process, leading to angry dis-illusionment and rejection by the electorate and consigning the Labour Party to the political wilderness for almost two decades. The accepted wisdom has been to blame Labour's wilderness years on Michael Foot, who followed Callaghan as Party leader in 1980; but quite frankly, following the disastrous leadership of Callaghan, Foot faced an almost impossible task. It was Callaghan who took the Labour Party to the brink of extinction. To loud applause at the 1979 Labour Party conference in Brighton, Tom Litterick said, 'Jim will fix it, they said. Aye, he fixed it all right. He fixed all of us.' (Tom Litterick was MP for Selly Oak, losing his seat following the 1979 general election.) Callaghan's reputation as Prime Minister was not helped when he appointed the inexperienced David Owen to be Foreign Secretary. Shortly afterwards Peter Jay, the economics editor of *The Times*, was made British Ambassador to Washington, one of the most prestigious and sought-after postings in the diplomatic service. Jay was also married to Callaghan's daughter, Margaret.

Early in 1979 I was told an intriguing story about the botched assassination attempt on Marcus Sieff, a member of the Marks and Spencer family, who at the time of the attack was living in St John's Wood. An acquaintance of mine was almost knocked down by (what he later discovered was) the getaway car as it careered wildly round a corner. The rear door of the car flew open and a bag fell from the vehicle as a young man on the back seat tried desperately to pull the door shut again. Shaken and angry, my acquaintance stood in the road shaking his fist and shouting after the rapidly receding car. Then he went to examine the bag, a holdall. Opening it he discovered a handgun that had recently been fired, several obviously faked passports and a bundle containing almost a thousand pounds. Looking around to see if he was observed, he made a decision. Throwing the bag containing the gun and the passports over a hedge, he pocketed the money. He then went to the public house next door to the Royal Artillery Barracks in St John's Wood, where I happened to be, and told me his tale.

Watching the news break on the television I thought it might be possible to make this intriguing story into an interesting novel. During the course of my research I needed information on which weapon is most effective at close quarters. A publican I knew told me that members of the SAS were among his regular customers and that for the price of a few drinks I would be able to get all the information I needed. He agreed to telephone me next time they were in. He called on 17 November 1979 and I hurried over. The two SAS operatives, one a sergeant the other an officer, spoke freely of illegal military activities including murder.

Later we decided to move on to Hampstead to continue our drinking session. I was eager to collect a tape recorder from home in order to record their revelations, which included confirmation of the Conservative government's 'shoot to kill policy' in the north of Ireland. Arriving at my flat on Hampstead Way I found that Susan, who was out when I left, had returned and locked the front door. No amount of knocking and banging on the door would rouse her, so I decided to use an alternative mode of entry. In the rubbish cupboard for the flat were three five-gallon drums containing the paraffin we used for heating. One was empty, one half full, the other untouched. I told the two men I would pile the drums on top of each other and climb through the loft entrance over the front door. As I had used this method on many occasions before I was certain I would quickly and safely get into the flat. They suggested an alternative method of soaking an old shirt from the cupboard in paraffin, wedging it around the front door and setting fire to the door frame. This would create a lot of dense smoke which would be drawn into the flat and within no time at all the occupants would come dashing out. They knew this from their experience in the north of Ireland where it was a favourite method of 'scaring the occupants shitless'. Horrified, I told them my two daughters, Sarah and Emma, were in the flat and on no account should they do anything, but wait for me to open the door.

As I inched my way along the wooden joists in the loft I suddenly heard a rush of air. Turning, I saw to my horror flames and smoke belching into the loft. In my confusion I slipped and put my foot through the ceiling of the girls' room. They awoke screaming and I yelled at them to get out of the flat through the front door – the only means of escape. In the madness born out of mind-numbing panic, I decided not to do any further damage to the bedroom ceiling by jumping through. Instead, I crawled backwards along the joists to the trap door, terrified I would be trapped in the loft. Coughing and spluttering, my eyes streaming in the smoke, I arrived at the trap door to hear the two men laughing. Cursing them, I tried to lower myself back onto the pyramid of drums. Unable to see properly, I slipped and my weight carried me through the lid and into a drum of paraffin which had ignited. Engulfed in flames and screaming in agony, I saw the two SAS men laughing as I managed to pull myself from the drum. Somehow I struggled to my feet, still on fire, as a primal survival instinct propelled me to my neighbour's door. Responding to my frantic hammering the terrified occupant opened the door and staggered backwards as I pushed past him, grabbing a coat to wrap myself in. It was only then that I passed out.

It was five months into a new decade before I saw the sun and breathed fresh air again. It was very sweet. I understood I had been given another chance at life.

Seven

Second Time Around

> 'To conquer fear is the beginning of wisdom ... in the endeavour
> after a worthy manner of life'
>
> **Bertrand Russell,** *Unpopular Essays*

I was suffering forty-five per cent third-degree burns and ten per cent secondary burns to my legs and lower body. Twenty-six visits to the main operating theatre at Queen Alexandra's Burns Unit in Northwood, Middlesex left me weak and vulnerable, but I survived. How or why I was able to gather and sustain the necessary strength of will, I still do not understand. I am simply grateful. The physical agony of my burns was matched by mental agony as I was forced to face the sober reality of my life. Drink allowed me to ignore and evade my responsibilities, but it almost destroyed me and I now faced friendless isolation. *In vino veritas* is without doubt one of the biggest lies associated with drinking. What is true is that a drunk will become increasingly garrulous and outrageous in order to provoke a response. Any response. My misshapen nose clearly demonstrates more than one angry reaction to my level of provocation.

When I regained consciousness in the burns unit I was overwhelmed by the terrible smell of burnt flesh, by my pain and terror, but I knew, unequivocally, that I would never drink alcohol again. Of course, the path of sobriety has not always been an easy one to follow but I have managed it. Incredibly some people, on finding out I no longer drink, try to encourage me with 'Go on, one won't hurt you'. This casual attitude is reinforced by the large number of advertisements for alcohol that are so much a part of our environment. On television, in newspapers and magazines, in cinemas, plastered across hoardings on the sides of roads. Without fail, all these advertisements promise alcohol will lend our lives an extra quality – glamour, machismo, social acceptance – with no mention of its destructive, even lethal, powers. Cigarette packets carry government health warnings and smoking has, quite rightly, become increasingly unacceptable. We smokers are the social pariahs of the age. I fail to understand why alcohol does not carry the same government warning. Ironically, one of the first jobs I was offered in television after my return to work was as a publican in the Granada soap *Albion Market*. On the first morning I walked into the disused pub that was the set, and the smell of stale beer was disgusting. Instead of ordering a drink to try and eliminate the smell I turned and walked straight back out of the door into the fresh air.

Susan rarely came to the hospital and it was my eldest daughter Cherie and her regular Monday night visits that sustained me. One week she told me she was in love with a fellow pupil barrister, Tony Blair. He had asked her to marry him and she had accepted. Cherie offered to postpone her wedding until I was fit enough to attend, but knowing she and Tony wished to marry as soon as possible I urged her not to wait for me. I would be there in spirit. On her next visit Cherie told me she would not be coming the following Monday, she would be away on honeymoon. That long, endless Monday, lying in my hospital room listening to the footsteps and voices of visitors as they passed my door, I realized how institutionalized I had become and how dependent I was on Cherie to relieve my loneliness.

I know most people will learn a few hard lessons on their journey through life. The hardest lesson for me, one I could no longer evade, was the realization and acceptance that I had only myself to blame for my current sorry state. At last I understood that constantly blaming others for my misfortune was emotionally self-indulgent. Ultimately we all have to take responsibility for our own choices and actions. I was determined to seize this second chance and try very hard to turn my life around.

My determination was helped by a considerable stroke of personal luck when Susan found a new partner. Susan made the decision that set us both free from our mutual destruction, inadvertently helping me to anticipate and work towards a more hopeful future. I still, however, needed to become well enough to be transferred from the burns unit to a rehabilitation centre – Farnham Park, near Slough. When a terrible fire in a hostel in east London meant that beds in the burns unit were at a premium, I was moved into a different unit within the hospital. This was a three-bed unit, but throughout the week I was its only occupant. The weekends were a different story as patients were admitted for minor operations such as wisdom tooth extractions. On my first weekend there I had a biochemist and a customs officer for company. The biochemist complained to the customs officer that he felt singled out, if not persecuted, whenever he passed through customs. It had clearly not occurred to him that the fact that he looked, talked and dressed like a hippy might be part of his problem. However, after a little persuasion the customs officer agreed to remove the biochemist from the 'stop list' on customs computers.

After the biochemist went to the operating theatre I had an interesting conversation with the customs officer, whom I shall call Jones. He was at the hospital that weekend working undercover, but his intended target had cancelled his bed at the last moment, rescheduling for the following weekend. His target was Howard Marks, the self-styled cannabis king, who was booked into the hospital for wisdom tooth extraction. Jones told me he was working on a case that involved Marks; knowing Marks's movements, Jones contrived to be admitted at the same time with the intention of persuading Marks to cooperate with his investigation in return for his continued freedom. With my boredom alleviated in spectacular fashion I could barely wait for the next weekend. Howard Marks did not disappoint. He fitted to perfection a fiction writer's description of a man who lived on his wits. Handsome, witty and urbane, in the hour before Jones's arrival I was mesmerized by him. As Jones walked through the door I watched Marks quickly assess the situation and say to Jones, '... do you know me, or should I know you?' I held my breath, waiting to see if this potentially difficult situation would develop any further. The tense moment was broken as Jones farted and like silly school-boys we began to giggle. Within minutes the three of us were laughing and joking like old friends.

When 'Scots' Jones, as Marks had nicknamed him, eventually left to go to the pub, Marks turned to me and commented, the Customs and Excise must think he would be too stoned to notice an undercover agent when he saw one. So the game of 'cat and mouse' between Jones and Marks began with me as the conduit between them. Marks's wisdom tooth extraction was due, he claimed, to having a tracking device implanted in it some years before when he was running a bogus shipment of drugs into Britain. As we talked Marks produced a large, sealed, brown envelope. My burnt feet were still protected by a shield and he lifted my mattress and placed the envelope underneath it. He was using me as safe storage for his secret papers, secure in the knowledge that I would be unable to read them. Marks made me promise that in the event of his accidental death under anaesthetic

I would ensure the envelope was posted. He then left to join Jones in the local pub, but not before offering me a job as a drugs courier. Marks suggested my injuries left me with nothing to lose and also probably placed me beyond suspicion. Thanking him for his offer I declined on the grounds of moral and physical cowardice. Laughing, he wrote down his address and telephone number in case my resolve should crumble at the thought of the large amounts of money to be earned. 'Scots' Jones also gave me his telephone number before he left the hospital. Months later I telephoned both of them and they sent their regards to each other through me.

My next move was to Farnham Park rehabilitation centre. For me this was the next step on the road to regaining my health, but for other people at the centre there was little or no chance of recovery. Their courageous yet hopeless fight against the never-ending pain of severe spinal injuries and their self-deprecating sense of humour were a constant source of inspiration. After a few weeks I was invited to the director's office. Margaret Thatcher's government had pledged to close down 'unnecessary' units such as Farnham Park and the director asked if I would become involved in the campaign to keep it open. The local Member of Parliament was the infamous Ronald Bell, who successfully sued *Private Eye* magazine when it accused him of having sex with his researcher on the floor of the office of another member of parliament – an accusation Bell denied, as although he did engage in sex with a researcher, it was not his own researcher, but that of the member of parliament on whose office floor the deed was committed. Shortly after the director approached me, the unit held an open day attended by Ronald Bell and an old friend and comrade, Joan Lestor, the Labour Member for Slough. I led a delegation urging their support for our campaign. Joan Lestor was delighted to see me, but noticeably shocked by my appearance. During the 1979 general election I helped in her campaign, making an eve of poll speech to a packed meeting in Slough. Despite the Conservative onslaught Joan managed to cling on to her seat by the tiniest of margins. Now she, along with Bell, backed our campaign, which was successful and Farnham Park was spared for another year.

After six weeks at the unit my weight had crept up to eight stone seven pounds, sufficient for me finally to be discharged. Before I left the rehabilitation centre I was given £17, gloves I had to wear to protect my hands and a Job garment – an elasticated body stocking designed to smooth my scars from vivid scarlet, puckered weals into something more socially acceptable. I had to wear it for eighteen months. In Farnham Park I had tried with the help of Tony and Cherie to track down the two SAS men responsible for my injuries. At the time I was still desperate to discover the full truth of what had happened. However, requests for information were met by a wall of silence. The two men told me they had been at Buckingham Palace to receive awards on the day I was injured, but we were informed this was not the case, they were in fact in Germany on that day and their awards had been collected by others. There was no record of the Fire Service being called to Hampstead Way on that night or of the involvement of police from Golders Green station, even though the incident was reported on television and in the newspapers. Furthermore, enquiries at the Army and Navy Club where the officer claimed he was staying revealed that the relevant page from the visitors' book was now missing.

The 'shoot to kill' policy in the north of Ireland was still officially denied by the British government and although I may be wrong in my assumption I now believe the wall of official silence had everything to do with the boastful and injudicious claims the SAS men made on this issue. Of course, they could not have anticipated my fall into burning paraffin, but they demonstrated a severe lack of initiative if not human compassion by doing absolutely nothing to rescue me. My enquiries resulted in a letter being sent to me at Farnham Park. The letter was postmarked Hereford and contained a newspaper cutting – a report on the death of two young girls, electrocuted in their bath. The letter also contained a detailed plan of my flat on Hampstead Way with the bathroom clearly highlighted. My daughters Sarah and Emma were still young girls and of course I understood the implicit threat of the letter. I immediately abandoned my quest.

My sister Audrey arrived to collect me the day I left Farnham Park. I had lost so much weight that the clothes she brought for me to wear belonged to my daughter Lyndsey. The felt boots for my feet given to me by the rehabilitation unit – size sixteen for my left foot, fourteen for my right – plus the Job garment disguised the fact that the jeans were too short. The friends I made during my stay at the unit gathered on the steps, delighted to see an inmate escape. I cried as we waved goodbye. I did not return to Hampstead, but went home to Liverpool. Audrey had arranged a small welcome-home tea party and I sat in her living room whilst she and her friends discussed the intimate details of my appearance, talking mainly in the past tense. Of course, she acted out of love and concern for me, but it was a fairly bizarre experience. The following day Audrey drove me to my mother's home and a tearful reunion. My mother was now suffering from the early stages of Alzheimer's disease and I was obviously physically frail. It is strange the tricks life can play on you – neither my mother nor I would have imagined, even ten years earlier, that we would once again be living together under the same roof, both of us in our different ways fragile. I was also afraid. Afraid of the future, afraid most of all that I would never act again.

The first step was to regain my strength and fitness and to do this I needed to put on weight. A simple enough aim, but I could not cook as my hands were still encased in protective gloves and my mother now relied on the meals-on-wheels service. For the first few days I ate what my mother left. Another potential source of hot food was the local fish and chip shop, a return journey of around two hundred yards. However, I could only walk thirty yards at a time without resting. By the time I arrived home from my first attempt I was clutching a parcel of cold, congealed fish and chips. A radical reassessment of strategy was called for. Despite all the difficulties I learned to cook whilst wearing gloves.

One evening my mother and I sat watching *Coronation Street*, her favourite programme. In one of her more lucid moments she recognized Pat Phoenix on the screen and suggested I contact her. The next day I telephoned Pat at Granada studios and we arranged to meet. The intervening years since our first, youthful fling had been difficult ones for both of us, but all that history fell away as Pat and I recognized mutual need and respect. Once again we became lovers but, more importantly, this time also deeply committed partners. My decision to leave my mother's house and move into Pat's home, Sunny Place Cottage, was made considerably easier when my brother Bob decided to move in with our mother after the breakdown of his marriage. Pat made it very easy for me to settle into her home. One of our first visitors was Tom Pendry, the local Member of Parliament for Stalybridge and Hyde, also a former drinking companion of mine. Pendry and I met several years earlier when we were both involved in a fracas with Norman St John-Stevas in a bar in Hampstead. Pendry insists I behaved provocatively towards St John-Stevas until his friends intervened on his behalf, and as Pendry came to my aid I wandered off into the night leaving him to fight them all. Pat knew Tom Pendry as she was a lifelong supporter of the Labour Party, but we could not guess then just how important politics was again to become in our lives.

Cherie and Tony were living in a terraced house in Hackney that was constantly burgled, reducing them at one point, after their bed was stolen, to sleeping bags on the floor. Alongside her blossoming career as a barrister Cherie was also giving up some of her spare time to work in a free legal advice centre in Hackney. She told me a story of two local villains who came to her complaining of police harassment. She assured them she would take up the matter with the local police. Soon after the two men left the advice centre Cherie received a telephone call from Barry Cox, a London Weekend Television executive and also Tony and Cherie's neighbour. Cox told Cherie to come home immediately as there were intruders in her house. Dashing home, she arrived to find the two men to whom she had just given legal advice being escorted away by the police. On seeing Cherie one of the intruders said, 'Hold on, that's my brief.' Barry Cox managed, struggling valiantly, to restrain the incandescent Mrs Blair.

One day in 1982 I received a telephone call from Cherie. She told me that Tony wanted to enter politics and as I had been involved with the Labour Party for so many years she asked for my help. I was thrilled to hear that our family tradition of political activity and commitment begun by my grandfather Thompson was about to be picked up by a new generation. Tom Pendry suggested I give his telephone number to my son-in-law. Over lunch at the Gay Hussar restaurant in Soho (long a haunt of Michael Foot) Pendry advised Tony to put himself forward as the Labour Party candidate in the upcoming by-election in the safe Conservative seat of Beaconsfield. The by-election was created by the death of Ronald Bell – the same Ronald Bell I met when he and Joan Lestor visited Farnham Park. Although Beaconsfield was unwinnable for Labour the by-election would receive television coverage and bring Tony Blair to the attention of other constituency parties as well as Michael Foot, then Labour Party leader.

Tony easily secured selection as the Labour candidate and on our way home from a short break in Cornwall Pat and I helped to canvass the only Labour ward in Beaconsfield. A crowd of people had gathered on the small housing estate, more intent on meeting Pat than listening to Tony, but the visit served its purpose. Photographs of Tony Blair appeared in the national newspapers. During the campaign Tony attended a wedding at his old college, St John's, Oxford. Later at the reception a fellow guest asked what he was now doing. When Tony told him he was standing in the Beaconsfield by-election the immediate response was, 'Don't worry, you'll walk it.' Tony informed him he was not the Conservative candidate, then to be told, 'Well, the Liberals should save their deposit.' A disdainful sniff and hasty departure was the response to the news that Tony was in fact the Labour Party candidate. Michael Foot campaigned in Beaconsfield. Foot was impressed enough by Tony later to describe him to me as future Cabinet material. As expected Tony was soundly beaten, coming third in the poll with a vote of 3,886 and losing his deposit.

A few months later Michael Foot and I were both victims of one of those horrendous rail journeys that are a speciality of British railways. I was travelling from Manchester to London to meet Pat with the intention of accompanying her to *Cats*, the Andrew Lloyd Webber musical. I did not make it. Instead of two and a half hours the journey took almost six and Foot invited me to join him in his compartment. During our conversation I asked him if he was aware, as a Privy Counsellor, of British government assassination squads operating against suspected Republican sympathizers in the north of Ireland. Naturally shocked and at first unwilling to believe what I told him, Foot became more convinced as I explained how I had come by the information. I described the fire in which I was injured and the stories the two SAS men had related. He promised to find out what he could, but disappointingly and inevitably, he too was met by a wall of official silence.

Despite Tory glee at their general election triumph in 1979, within two years Margaret Thatcher was the most unpopular Prime Minister in living memory. Her New Right agenda, informed by what I believe to be the flawed ideas of Friedrich von Hayek and Milton Friedman, attempted to dismantle all that was best in post-war Britain. With the economy in deep recession and unemployment soaring, there were violent protests on the streets of Toxteth and Brixton. Yet with the conviction of the zealot Thatcher insisted in her speech to the Conservative Party conference in 1981, 'You turn if you want to, the lady's not for turning.' Whilst this hardline stance was greeted by rapturous applause the Conservative government still needed a miracle, but God was clearly far too clever to show His hand.

I doubt whether many of the British public had even heard of the disputed territory of the Falkland Islands until the government withdrew its military and naval presence, virtually inviting Argentina, which vigorously contested British ownership of this territory, to launch a military invasion on 2 April 1982. Thatcher had her miracle – a winnable war to distract from the calamitous domestic situation. Much to my dismay, I once again found myself at odds with the Labour leadership as Michael Foot at first supported the government's military offensive in the Falklands. At the time I was presenting a weekly late-night radio show for the BBC in Manchester and I used the programme to argue against this military adventure. Following the sinking as it sailed out of disputed waters of the Argentinian cruiser the *General Belgrano*, with the resulting loss of more than three hundred lives, I was 'rested' by the BBC, despite the pleadings of the station manager. The Falklands 'triumph' saw the Conservative poll ratings rise from a low of twenty-three per cent to forty-six and a half per cent and presented the Conservatives with a blood-stained election triumph.

The Falklands campaign recast Thatcher in the mould of a strong and decisive leader just at the time the right and left of the Labour Party embarked on bitter, internecine warfare. Following the 1979 general election, Callaghan remained as leader of the Labour Party, mainly I believe because the Party was too stunned to remove him. For some time there had been a rumbling debate on the left about the need further to democratize the selection of Labour candidates and, more crucially, the election of the Party leader. Seizing the opportunity to move against Callaghan at the 1980 Party conference, the left wing forced through the mandatory reselection of members of parliament. The campaign to elect the leader by electoral college rather than by the Parliamentary Party was deferred to a special conference. Callaghan resigned in an attempt to pre-empt the decision of the special conference and allow his preferred candidate, Denis Healey, to succeed him as Party leader. However, his strategy failed, and Michael Foot came through the middle to win the leadership.

On 24 January 1981 the special Party conference at Wembley voted to move to an electoral college system for leadership elections. Just as the left wing were able to celebrate this significant democratic advance, several prominent right-wingers – Roy Jenkins, David Owen, Shirley Williams and Bill Rodgers – announced the launch of their Council for Social Democracy. Although initially styling themselves as a pressure group within the Labour Party, they revealed their true intention in March when twelve members of this 'pressure group' resigned the Party whip. Later the same month the Social Democratic Party was formed. Civil war was finally declared in the Labour Party in April 1981 when Tony Benn decided to challenge Denis Healey for the post of deputy leader. It seemed that the traditional ability of the Labour Party to encompass a wide spectrum of views from the centre left to the hard left, even when disagreeing wildly, was now not just lost, but destroyed by anger and bitterness.

For me a passionate commitment to the Labour cause has always been a prerequisite for membership of the Labour Party. It remains my absolute belief that those political fly-by-nights (also known as 'the Gang of Four') were utterly indifferent to the damage their actions might cause the Party. Their commitment lay wherever a successful career might be, even if their actions contributed to the implosion of the Labour Party. They were the rats running from the ship they believed was sinking. Although history now exposes their flawed political analysis, the initial momentum of the SDP was fuelled by their victory in a by-election in Warrington, traditionally a Labour stronghold. When, some time later, Shirley Williams announced she was to stand as the SDP candidate in the Crosby by-election I urged Cherie to put her name forward for the Labour nomination. She entered the selection process at a late stage, but despite that only lost selection by one vote. Williams went on to win the by-election, spectacularly overturning a Conservative majority of 18,000. It was, however, a pyrrhic victory.

Cherie was selected by one of the Thanet constituencies as their candidate to fight the 1983 general election. I asked Tony Benn to speak in support of her at a rally in Margate. The meeting was scheduled to begin at eight o'clock and when we arrived the town hall was packed. A loudspeaker relay system was set up in the square outside for those who could not get into the town hall. Benn was at his most brilliant and persuasive and I felt sorry for my daughter as she followed him. However, she spoke with precision and panache, finishing to a standing ovation that almost, but not quite, matched Benn's. I was interested and very satisfied to note that Roy Jenkins also spoke that night in another hall in the same constituency, to less than fifty people.

Our attention now focused on finding a winnable seat for Tony. The constituency Cherie was fighting was, despite the valiant efforts of her campaign manager (her sister Lyndsey) and a weak incumbent Conservative MP, unwinnable. The general election campaign was barely under way when the sitting Labour MP for Sedgefield, a fairly safe Labour seat, announced his resignation. Immediately the constituency Party in Sedgefield was inundated by hopeful applicants. Tony Blair was determined to secure the nomination and used his masterly communication skills to great effect. With the support of John Burton,[1] a constituency officer in Sedgefield whom Tony met on

[1] John Burton became not only Tony Blair's election agent, but also a close and trusted friend.

his first visit to the constituency, Tony fought off the challenge from trade unionists and several members of parliament seeking safer seats, coming through the middle to secure selection. During the selection process Tony promised Party activists that Pat and I would help in his election campaign. Pat was still working in *Coronation Street*, but we managed to spend a weekend canvassing in the constituency.

The Labour Party faced almost insurmountable odds in the 1983 general election campaign. Despite Thatcher's Think Tank report advocating significant reduction of the Welfare State, it seemed that the only issue facing canvassers on doorsteps was the Falklands 'success'. The right-wing press somehow contrived to present Thatcher as a modern-day Boadicea and the Labour Party as electoral disaster. The result of the election demonstrated how far the public were taken in by this propaganda – the Conservatives won a landslide victory, taking 397 seats, increasing their overall majority to 144. It was not only the media that was delighted to see Tony Benn lose his marginal parliamentary seat in Bristol South East. I was shocked by Neil Kinnock's apparent delight as he whispered the news to Michael Foot. Worse, the Labour Party faced the very real prospect of losing its position as the official Opposition, forced to battle for second place with the Liberal/SDP alliance. On a personal level, political hope was kept alive when Tony Blair won the Sedgefield seat.[2] He promised to buy a house in the constituency, but as financially hard-pressed young barristers it was a difficult commitment to fulfil. Tony and Cherie eventually bought a house in Trimdon, but could not afford to furnish it. Pat, generous as ever, helped them, sending everything from bed linen to furniture. As the overcrowded Sunny Place Cottage was gradually cleared Pat cheerfully seized the opportunity to embark on an orgy of refurbishment.

Michael Foot resigned as Labour Party leader soon after the near-annihilation of the 1983 poll. His successor, Neil Kinnock, won the leadership by a comfortable majority and Roy Hattersley became deputy leader. In 1983 Hattersley was the representative of the right wing in this 'dream team' combination. I do not believe I am the only person in the Labour Party who is now not only surprised, but also somewhat confused, to find that in the modern Party Hattersley is now regarded as a left-winger. I am uncertain where that leaves me

[2] Tony Blair polled 21,401 votes, giving him an 8,000 majority over his nearest rival. In 1997 his vote increased to 33,526, leaving the other candidates trailing by more than 25,000 votes.

on the political spectrum. Kinnock's great task was to persuade Party members and supporters that all was not lost – that there was a way back from the brink, and that Labour would live to fight another day. At the 1983 Labour Party conference he eloquently urged the need for unity and strength of purpose if the Party was ever to defeat the Conservatives: 'They are the enemy; they must be defeated and we must defeat them together ... if we give greater attention to arguments between ourselves than to our enmity against them, we will not do it. If we give more attention to impressing each other than convincing the people we have to convince, we will not do it.'

My son-in-law was amongst those swept up in the passion of Kinnock's commitment and enthusiasm. When the former MP and then media mogul Robert Maxwell moved on the Mirror Group of newspapers Tony Blair made a speech in the House of Commons opposing the proposed takeover. Tony quoted from the legal judgment made in a recent court action involving Maxwell in which the judge declared Maxwell an unfit person to run a public company. Tony was immediately called into the Whips' Office to face the bullying Labour Chief Whip, Michael Cocks. Cocks, furious at Tony's outspoken attack on Maxwell, demanded to know on whose authority Tony had spoken. Tony's response was that he did not know he needed permission to speak out against the activities of a known crook. Cocks pointed out that Maxwell had donated twenty thousand pounds to the Labour Party. An unbowed and unrepentant Tony then asked the crucial question about donations to the Party and the necessity of and freedom to continue asking questions about the business activities of the donor. Michael Cocks was described in his *Times* obituary as falling out of favour when Neil Kinnock took over as Labour leader: 'Younger MPs were said to resent the old-fashioned discipline which he still sought to impose via the Whips' Office.' Unable to intimidate this young MP, Cocks ordered Tony to appear in the Leader's Office at eleven o'clock the next morning.

Tony telephoned me later that evening, convinced his parliamentary career would be over the next day. I laughed and told him in these situations Parliament was something like the armed services. The commander faced two options – promotion or demotion. My money was on promotion, as Kinnock's front-bench team needed new and younger faces. Tony said he would try and telephone as soon as possible after his interview with Kinnock. When he called, he was giggling. 'What did he give you?' I asked. 'City scandals,' Tony replied, 'this could run and run.' A few weeks later I visited Tony in the House of Commons. Whilst in the lavatory I was confronted by the scowling and capacious Michael Cocks, who warned me that my son-in-law should watch his back. Scowling back, I informed him that Tony already understood that.

Tony shared an office with Gordon Brown, another bright new entry from the 1983 election. Tony thought highly of Brown, but possibly not as highly as Brown thought of himself. Tony shared a good workplace relationship with Brown, but whilst Tony would go home each evening, Brown stayed in the House networking; the relationship was not a particularly social one.

Cherie and Tony, growing tired of the constant burglaries at their Hackney home, moved to a house close to Arsenal's Highbury Stadium. On 19 January 1984 our family's first grandchild Euan was born. Tom Pendry made sure the event was noted in Hansard, when he congratulated Tony in the House of Commons.

In March 1984 the miners were called out on strike by their leader, Arthur Scargill. Although like many in the Labour Party I supported the miners in their struggle against proposed pit closures, I felt they had been lured into a political trap. Thatcher and her compliant satraps, determined to avenge the humiliation of Heath's government at the hands of the miners led by Joe Gormley, organized themselves with military precision. The huge stockpiles of coal were common knowledge and with summer only weeks away I believed Scargill's strategy to be rash and misguided. Despite these misgivings, which I took every opportunity to voice, once the strike started I gave all the support I could to the miners. It became clear very quickly that this was a struggle the government was going to win. During the strike I was interviewed by TVam. While in the hospitality suite waiting for my turn, in walked Neil Kinnock, who was also to be interviewed. As we watched the television news a report came on about the miners' strike. Sadly shaking my head I commented to Kinnock that in my opinion the miners were lions led by a bloody donkey. When he was called in front of the cameras Kinnock repeated my phrase (omitting the 'bloody') and as he left I called out, 'Nice one, Neil.' Smiling, he replied 'Thanks Tony.'

Pat had thought seriously for some years about leaving *Coronation Street*. She was becoming increasingly unhappy with the direction the writers were taking and what was happening to her own part – the storylines were getting thinner and increasingly unlikely. She had the self-honesty and personal strength to face the brutal truth of the situation in a way the producers would not. What could they realistically do with the show's sex symbol, who had passed her fifty-fifth birthday? Pat also believed the programme had failed to adapt and reflect the radical social changes taking place in British society. Its corner shop was not run, as everywhere else, by an Asian couple. There was rarely a non-Caucasian in the show and there was certainly no attempt to deal with the changing role of women or issues of unemployment. *Coronation Street* appeared trapped in a parallel universe of 1950s working-class mores, and the production team unable or unwilling to do anything about it.

During the spring of 1984 Pat made the decision to leave the programme. I could only admire her courage and strength of purpose, but I was concerned that throwing up professional security at her age was a huge risk. I believed this was a decision that should have been made much earlier when she was being offered some of the best parts available in films and theatre. I knew from bitter experience that being out in the cold was not fun and I worried that so long an association with one character would make new roles, particularly on television, more difficult to find. As soon as Pat's decision was made public the press went crazy. The line between reality and fantasy was not just fudged, it appeared lost as we were besieged at the cottage by reporters and television crews. A fictional character was leaving a fictional street and yet Pat could not go anywhere without someone rushing up to her and begging her not to leave. The management at Granada Television were convinced her decision was the result of my disruptive influence, but they were wrong. The truth is, Pat held strong personal and political opinions and did not need me to inform them. During the miners' strike she and I were touring the country in Agatha Christie's *Spider's Web* and whenever we were near a mining community we would go and lend our support and encouragement. It was also very useful to have Pat in the car as her presence guaranteed easy passage through police roadblocks – the police were more interested in getting her autograph than in questioning us. Ultimately, and with a dreadful inevitability, the government's thorough pre-planning proved too much and Thatcher relished putting the miners to the sword.

The 1984 Labour Party conference was critical of Neil Kinnock's position during the miners' strike. However, his leader's speech to the conference was a triumph. Appeals for party unity had as yet gone unheeded and Kinnock needed to stamp his authority firmly on party structure and organization, making it clear that we still not only viewed ourselves as a party of government, but also most importantly we were a party capable of government. Kinnock confronted and faced down the Militant faction led by Derek Hatton, then deputy leader of Liverpool City Council. In a speech described by the *Guardian* as 'the bravest and most important speech made by a Labour leader in over a generation', Kinnock castigated Militant for their political and economic mismanagement of the city of Liverpool:

> I'll tell you what happens with impossible promises. You start with far-fetched resolutions. They are pickled into a rigid dogma, a code and you go through the years sticking to that, out-dated, misplaced, irrelevant to the real needs and you end up in the grotesque chaos of a Labour council – a Labour council – hiring taxis to scuttle around a city handing out redundancy notices to its own workers. I am telling you, no matter how entertaining, how fulfilling to short-term egos – I'm telling you and you'll listen – you can't play politics with people's jobs and with people's services or with their homes.

During his speech Kinnock was heckled by supporters of Militant and after joining in with the heckling Hatton walked out of the conference hall. Most of the audience applauded Kinnock. Neil Kinnock went on to complete his rout of the hard left in a speech the following day attacking the miners' leader, Arthur Scargill. Like the rest of the Labour Party Kinnock supported the miners' campaign to prevent pit closures, but he was angered by Scargill's political naivety and foolhardiness. Kinnock believed Scargill's call for strike action was less about pit closures and the future of the mining industry and more about trying to destabilize the government. Kinnock forcefully shredded the leadership quality and ability of the miners' leader, making Scargill look, in the words of Beatrice Webb, like 'an inspired idiot drunk with words'. With hindsight this conference and Kinnock's forceful and brave leadership were a decisive moment for the Labour Party on the stony path back to government.

In October 1985 *The Times* described Neil Kinnock's political position as 'Gaitskellism from left of centre' and I found myself on the horns of a dilemma. I had never been an admirer of Gaitskell, but like most of the Labour Party I understood the need for unity. I first faced this political conundrum in 1984 when Tony Benn, having lost his seat at the 1983 general election, was selected as the Labour candidate to fight a by-election in Chesterfield. I knew Kinnock viewed Benn as part of the problem the Labour Party faced in once again becoming a party of government. However, Tony Benn was selected by the constituency party in Chesterfield and I am also his long-time friend and admirer. Chesterfield was a seat Labour needed to hold, so despite being attacked in the press for our canvassing and support of the Labour Party candidate, Pat and I worked in Benn's campaign. With very little help from the official Labour Party machine, Tony Benn was returned to Parliament.

In 1985 the Labour Party created a Campaign and Communications Directorate with the aim of improving its media and public image. Peter Mandelson, the grandson of Herbert Morrison, was appointed director. Mandelson immediately set about transforming Labour's 'cloth cap and ferret' image. He quickly demonstrated his then unerring ability to seize the moment, enhancing his reputation by claiming a good bit of the credit when the Labour Party emblem changed from the red flag to the red rose. In reality what happened was that at the end of a rally in the Midlands dozens of red roses were sent up to the platform to Neil and Glenys Kinnock, who decided to share the roses with their audience. The media picked up this idea and not only was Labour's red rose image born, but the Mandelson myth was also under way.

Eight
And More Politics...

'... and yet God's will be done,
I knew a phoenix in my youth...'

W. B. Yeats, 'The Phoenix'

With Pat's love and support I was recovering emotionally as well as physically from my burns and she encouraged me to feel that my life could and did have renewed meaning and purpose. I believed, with perhaps some justification, that the torment of my burns and my recovery against all recognized odds had taught me the meaning of pain. In reality, I was yet to discover in a most brutal fashion what true suffering was really all about. The overwhelming sense of loss I experienced when Julie Allan left me was as nothing compared to the ten-month period between 1986 and 1987 when I endured the most horrible and demanding of emotional ordeals as first my wife, then my sister and finally my mother died. The three most influential women in my life, each of them loving, strong-minded, open and courageous, who in their different ways shaped and reshaped my life – and now they were gone forever.

My brother Robert continued to live with our mother for several years after I had moved out to join Pat. My mother became increasingly frail with Alzheimer's disease and when eventually Robert met his future wife, Olwen, it was clear my mother would need full-time care in a nursing home. At the time I was working a long summer season in Bournemouth with Pat, so Robert and my sister Audrey made all the arrangements, including packing up and selling my mother's house. During my mother's time in the nursing home Cherie and Tony not only visited her regularly, but also took her away on holiday. She came on several holidays with Pat and me, too. On one occasion we decided to take my mother to Yugoslavia. This involved an overnight stay in a hotel near Gatwick airport, as the flight to Yugoslavia was an early one. Going into my mother's bedroom in the morning I found her sitting on her bed dressed and ready to go. 'Well,' she said to me, 'I have enjoyed my holiday. Are we going home now?' Though it was funny and the recollection of it still makes me smile, it was also heartbreaking. It is difficult to witness the disintegration of a parent in such a way – especially one as vibrant and challenging as my mother. When, after a few years in the nursing home my mother had a heart attack, she was moved to Fazakerley Hospital. She was unaware of the deaths of both Pat and Audrey, and despite coming close to death several times my mother would rally. We decided to keep the deaths of both Pat and Audrey from her, but I realized she was waiting to see her daughter. Eventually my cousin, Father Paul Thompson, unaware of the family pact, told her of Audrey's death. A few days later my mother died. I stayed with her until around three o'clock that morning, when the nurse advised me to go home and rest. Fortunately, the hospital was able to contact my other cousin, Father John Thompson, who was with her at the end. My mother often despaired of me and I know there were times during my adult life when she did not like me, but I never doubted her love for a moment. Her escape from the demands of hard reality – money was always tight in our household – was our local library. She was a voracious reader and the pleasure of reading was one of her greatest gifts to me, one I still share today. Although my mother enjoyed a romantic novel her interests and reading tastes were many and varied and she would often pass on books to me if she felt the issues raised were important.

My sister Audrey was an auburn-haired warrior and we fought like cat and dog through our childhood. I was jealous of the love and affection my father clearly felt and demonstrated towards my sister, while she in turn believed my mother favoured me. As I was three years older than Audrey it was one of my duties to escort her to school. The local bullies seized the opportunity to mock and taunt me as I walked along the road in the company of my six-year-old sister. They were, however, careful to keep some way ahead of me so that when I could finally take no more and began to chase them, they were always too far ahead. Their luck could not last. When one of their number slipped and fell I pounced on him, releasing all those months of pent-up frustration, humiliation and anger. As he yelled for help the gang returned, led by his older brother. Curled up on the ground, I was in the early stages of receiving a good kicking when suddenly a screaming, raging banshee came out of nowhere. It was Audrey and in no time at all my attackers were put to flight with her in hot pursuit. Calling her back, I lay on the gravel path in our local park alternately laughing with embarrassment and crying with pain. As Audrey lay dying from breast cancer in the same hospital in Manchester that had treated Pat, we remembered this story and for the very last time we were able to laugh and cry together. Both Cherie and Tony read the lessons at Audrey's funeral, as they had done only a few months earlier at Pat's. After my sister's funeral, Tony and I went for a walk together. His quiet, unassuming compassion and understanding for my grief helped to comfort me as I struggled to make sense of my numbing loss.

Pat Phoenix and I lived together for six years before lung cancer finally claimed her life. Those six years were both exhausting and exhilarating as Pat was a highly intelligent, articulate woman who was also extraordinarily generous with her time, money and possessions. Soon after Pat and I made the decision to live together she suggested that Sarah and Emma, who were still in London with their mother Susan Riley, should come and live with us at Sunny Place Cottage. Relieved and delighted at Pat's offer, I desperately wanted my two youngest daughters to share my new life away from the mayhem of the recent past. I understood, even though I was the one who went through the agony of burning, that the incident was deeply traumatic for Sarah and Emma as two terrified witnesses to the whole event. My rediscovered sobriety and resulting self-awareness meant I also wanted to try to make up for the drunken neglect that had been the dominant feature of their childhood. However, redemption was not going to be that easy as neither Sarah nor Emma wanted to leave London or their friends and schools. Although disappointed, I had to accept their decision, but they did make frequent visits to the cottage to enjoy being outrageously spoiled by Pat, who offered them much love as well as presents.

It was also during the years I shared with Pat that my daughters Jenia and Bronwen came back into my life. I had been denied any contact with them once their mother Julie removed them to America, but Jenia now made the decision to find me. By then she was studying at university in California and she travelled to Britain and stayed with Pat and me. I was and remain deeply thankful that Jenia was able to make that decision. I am also still tearfully amazed when I recall the loving generosity of Pat who, despite the persistent level of media obsession with her life, was able to create a home, a safe and warm space, for us all to be. Once Pat and I were living together in Sunny Place Cottage the press became preoccupied with the question of marriage. We found the experience faintly ridiculous as we were both by then in our fifties. In 1982 we spent eight days sailing up the Mississippi on a riverboat and discussed the feasibility of marrying on board, but unfortunately the captain did not have the authority. We did get engaged on Pat's sixtieth birthday but, far from damping down curiosity, this only increased speculation.

When it came, Pat's illness was a devastating blow for all of us. For a long time Pat chose to keep me from the knowledge of just how seriously ill she was. So, I thought nothing of accepting an offer from John Newman and Daphne Palmer, the management that had presented our three summer seasons, to take another Agatha Christie play on a twenty-six-week tour of the country. It makes me miserable even now to recall that it was only towards the end of the tour that I realized something might be wrong. I know I was kept in ignorance, but I cannot help but wonder if it is also true that I really did not want to see what was in front of me – Pat's vibrant energy was ebbing away. Famous for her outbursts as Elsie Tanner on screen, she was equally famous for the outbursts in her private life. She had a wild, exciting Irish temperament that would shoot like a lightning flash through any situation she found unacceptable – once passed it was gone forever. But I began to realize the lightning was no longer gone in a flash. Instead it was leaving behind a dull, lingering ache. At first I thought perhaps it was because she had lost the security of *Coronation Street* and faced a less certain future. Although she was now earning more money than she had ever done in her life, she still did not know where the next job was coming from, and when we finished the tour we would both be unemployed. When I confronted her she told me a half-truth. She admitted to being ill, but not the extent and magnitude of the problem. When I finally discovered the truth I was at first angry that she had not been honest with me, but at the same time overwhelmed by the love that would inform such a decision.

In the last few days before she died, Pat and I decided we wanted to be married. Cherie worked tirelessly and efficiently to remove the legal obstacles and my wonderful cousins Father John Thompson and Father Paul Thompson married us by special licence in the hospital. I struggle now to recall specific details of our wedding day, although I desperately want to remember every tiny one. Once I understood that Pat was dying I did not want to sleep or leave her side. How could I when every fleet-footed moment was so precious? The walls of Pat's hospital room encompassed our entire universe and I was unaware of irrelevancies such as meals or sleep or even if it was night or day. For that reason I cannot recall the time of our

Koo Stark took this photograph in 1986
backstage at a fundraiser organised by
Bill Kenwright for Pat's cancer charity
following her death earlier that year.

There were no prouder parents than Gale and I on the day Cherie was appointed a Queen's Counsel.

This man should never be given power!

Tears and pride from the Blair-Booth clan following Tony Blair's first speech to conference as leader of the Labour party, 1996.

With a jubilant Sarah and Emma just after Tony Blair was declared the new leader of the Labour party.

Rodney Bickerstaffe, Annette Crosbie and me outside Buckingham Palace supporting the 'Pensioners Deserve Better' campaign.

Leo Blair and me on election night May 1997.

The soon-to-be prime minister and his wife leaving the count after retaining his Sedgefield seat.

With Steph, June 2000.

My daughter Lucy with her husband Stan and my grandson Peter.

At the wedding reception following my marriage to Steph, 2 October 1998. The photograph includes my youngest stepson Will, my daughter Jo, and in the foreground, my great-nephew Nick.

In the saddle for *The Duke*. An award-winning film written and directed by the talented John McArdle.

As narrator in the *Rocky Horror Show*, Southampton December 1999.

Jim Cartwright and me in his play, *Prize Night*, Royal Exchange Theatre, Manchester.

Sophie Dahl, Tony Dorrs and me in the *Revenger's Tragedy*, directed by Alex Cox. In the film Sophie Dahl played my wife – Mick Jagger eat your heart out!

Trying to organise a family group photograph at my 70th birthday party. Only my daughter Bronwen appears ready for the shot.

June 2000. A face that has lived life to the full – and then some!

marriage, but I can recall how heartbreakingly beautiful Pat looked. Typically, although she was far too ill to get out of bed, her hair was done, her make-up was immaculate and she wore a new nightgown. Ever my glamorous star. I clung to the belief that somehow my desperate passion and need would transfer life to her. If I held her tight enough, if I kissed her enough, if I told her I loved her enough, then this nightmare would fade like mist in the morning sun. Surely something as beautiful, tender and honest as our wedding would produce the vital magic to keep her with me? But it was not to be. Pat died in the early hours of 17 September 1986.

In the months that followed I experienced an almost unbearable loneliness. I no longer knew the purpose of my life. I had fought to recover from my burns and I had found happiness and a kind of peace with Pat. Now all of that was gone, shattered. The rock-solid and dependable presence of my mother and sister was also gone. I was bereft. Cherie and Tony invited me to spend Christmas with them, but I did not feel able to undertake the journey. Instead an old actor friend of mine, Brian Mathieson, travelled to the cottage to stay with me. His company was a kindly relief. In the new year I faced the challenge of trying to wind up Pat's business affairs. To my horror I discovered she had been defrauded by some of the people she had trusted the most, one of whom sent me a bill for over eight hundred pounds for attending Pat's funeral. Others clamoured for mementoes and possessions. At her funeral, two women Pat and I believed to be among her closest friends told me they knew I would now be lonely. They both suggested I should call them, no matter the time and they would immediately come to the cottage to comfort me. I was stunned by such cruel insensitivity, but having spoken to others who have experienced similar loss, such predatory behaviour is not an uncommon feature of a funeral wake.

Later that year Julie Goodyear started to telephone me. Years before Pat had been on her way into Lewis's department store in Manchester when she was approached by Goodyear, who told Pat she was a single parent and desperate to break into theatre work. Moved by her situation, Pat found a job for Goodyear as assistant stage manager at the Oldham Repertory Company. After Pat's death her long-time housekeeper, Kitty Smith, decided to retire. I was lucky enough to replace her with Vi and Bert Farrow, who moved into the cottage to look after me. Julie Goodyear still continued to telephone my home several times a day to complain of her loneliness. Realizing the situation was becoming increasingly difficult for me, Vi Farrow intervened making it clear to Goodyear that her attentions were insensitive and unwelcome.

In the early spring of 1987 my daughters Sarah, then twenty, and Emma, seventeen, visited me. Rummaging around in the accumulated mail they found an invitation from Granada Television to speak, in place of Bill Roache, the Coronation Street actor, at a meeting organized by the Campaign for Press and Broadcasting Freedom.[1] Sarah and Emma insisted I attend and it was there that Nancy Jaeger first entered my life. She was the person who had organized the meeting. Later, after dinner, Nancy asked if I would give her a lift home – it transpired she lived not far from me. Unaware of the fateful course on which I embarked, I agreed. I was lonely and flattered by the attentions of this much younger woman. There were brief moments when I did doubt the sense of what was happening, but I failed to listen to internal warning bells. I wanted desperately to believe she loved me. Of course, with the wisdom of hindsight I can now understand I was much too needy. My grief created in me a profound sense of disconnection – part of the world, but somehow not in it.

When a general election was called for 11 June 1987 it was the old desire and taste for political campaign that persuaded me to leave the cottage and once again join the fray. Neil Kinnock's moving speech to the Welsh Labour Party conference on 15 May 1987, when he spoke of being the first Kinnock in a thousand generations to attend university, was a powerful motivator. In reality the Labour Party could not expect to win this general election. The process of reorganization within the Party and the rehabilitation of the public perception of what Labour had to offer still had some way to go. The Conservatives continued to frighten the voter with the spectre of the 'Winter of Discontent' and the power of the trade unions. More shockingly, during the last week of the campaign the Thatcher government was still able to make use of the 'red scare' to convince the electorate that a Labour government would leave the country undefended against a Soviet invasion. Clearly the Labour Party faced a long, hard path back to government.

Despite all the progress the Party was making I believed the leadership had yet to recognize and take advantage of the considerable artistic talent within the Labour ranks. When I met Bryan Gould in early 1987 he was then Labour's campaign coordinator. I found

---

[1] The Campaign for Press Freedom was set up in 1979. In 1982 'Broadcasting' was added to its title. Funded initially by media trade unions, the CPBF now enjoys much wider support. Its stated aim is to campaign for a more diverse, democratic and accountable media.

him a charming and clever operator who also saw the potential in exploiting Arts for Labour. I had lobbied Kinnock strenuously on this issue, but it was Gould who was convinced enough to contact Colin Welland, the Oscar-winning writer of *Chariots of Fire* and then an enthusiastic supporter of Arts for Labour. Welland agreed to write a party political broadcast for the Labour Party and he persuaded Hugh Hudson to direct it. The end result made a huge contribution to the ongoing process of improving the public image of the Labour Party, becoming popularly and affectionately known as *Kinnock – the Movie*. Still not fully aware of the self-promoting abilities of Peter Mandelson, I was astonished by the adroitness he displayed in associating himself with the development and success of this broadcast.

I worked hard during the 1987 general election campaign and with my writer friend Ron Rose travelled all over the country. The arrangement between us was a simple one. He did the drinking for both of us and I drove. Campaigning in the north-east constituencies, Ron Rose and I based ourselves at Tony and Cherie's house in Trimdon. One evening Tony asked me to attend a prize night for a ladies' darts team in Durham after first driving him over to another constituency. Arriving at the venue I thought my role would be to present a prize to the winner and then do some canvassing. I made a serious error of judgement. As I presented the first prize to the woman who was a runner-up, she kissed me, committing me to exchanging kisses with the other winners. And runners-up. And members of the many teams. There were a huge number of prizes, and bruised lips and chapped cheeks were the order of the night as some of the more sturdy darts players embraced me firmly, lifting me off my feet and, urged on by their rowdy team-mates, engaged me in some serious mouth-to-mouth contact. Meeting Tony later I managed to growl 'Thanks a bundle,' to him and the giggling, inebriated Ron Rose. Showing absolutely no sympathy for my travails, Tony complained to Ron about the unfairness of a situation where the son-in-law needs to worry about what his father-in-law is getting up to.

Back at home I followed my usual Saturday morning routine of a visit to Glossop. I like a wander around the market followed by a visit to my turf accountant. This way I hear most of the local gossip and hopefully pick up and also share some good racing tips. That particular morning I arrived at the market to find it invaded by the media. I really hate it when my more pleasurable routines are disturbed; and being in no way a particular fan of the British press I was not pleased to find my Saturday disturbed in this way. It transpired that David Owen was in town campaigning for the Alliance. I like to believe, when the occasion demands, that I can be a reasonable man, but my loathing for Owen knows no bounds. I lay in wait with a megaphone kindly supplied by a member of the Glossop Labour Party. As he strode on to the market I began to heckle him. Knowing the terrain and the stall-holders, I was able to track Owen along the rows of market stalls urging people not to listen to him. As others soon joined in the heckling, it was not long before the heroic Dr Owen beat a retreat. The same evening my daughter Jenia telephoned me from America to tell me the incident featured in CNN's coverage of the British election. About a year later I was at Heathrow airport when I bumped into David Steel, the leader of the Liberal Party. Steel's greeting was enthusiastic as he gleefully informed me Owen's discomfiture was one of the best moments in an otherwise disastrous general election campaign by the Alliance. No love lost there, then.

On polling day I toured the marginal seats in the north-east helping to get the Labour Party vote out and hopefully boosting morale. I arrived in Mansfield at around five o'clock in the afternoon to find the local Party headquarters already packing up for the day. Angrily, I pointed out that with Labour facing an enormous electoral task such an apathetic or casual attitude was completely unacceptable. Alternately bullying and chivvying, I drove the remaining Party workers out on to the streets to catch voters on their way home from work. Whilst my assertiveness did not make me particularly popular Alan Meale managed to hold the seat for Labour, albeit winning by fewer than sixty votes. Later, my son-in-law asked why I helped Meale with his campaign given Meale's unpleasant verbal attacks on Tony when they both sought nomination for the Sedgefield seat. I explained to Tony that my support was not personal, but political. I wanted to see a Labour victory. On the rare occasions when I now meet Alan Meale he reminds me of the narrowness of his victory in 1987 and generously attributes it to the last-minute exertions on polling day. Leaving Mansfield, I drove over to Chesterfield to show support for Tony Benn before racing back over the Derbyshire Peaks to cast my vote in my own constituency of Stalybridge and Hyde.

As the general election results began to come in it was obvious that once again the Labour Party was staring at defeat. Although cold reason still dictated our electoral weakness against the Conservatives, our main concern was to beat the Alliance or face political oblivion. The Conservatives lost twenty-one seats, but still hung on to 376. Satisfaction was derived from the failure of the Alliance to establish itself as the official opposition. All their grand schemes and promises (ultimately, naught but castles in the air) resulted in twenty-two seats. Tony Blair increased his majority in Sedgefield at this election and once Parliament had re-assembled the triumvirate of Cherie, Anji Hunter (a friend of Tony's from childhood) and myself urged Tony to stand for election to the Shadow Cabinet. It was clear that Neil Kinnock would now have to look to replacing some of the old guard. Interestingly, in the light of subsequent events, Gordon Brown, perhaps already viewing Tony as a potential rival, urged caution. Brown, of course, had his own ambitions. Both men were elected to the Shadow Cabinet, Tony becoming Shadow Energy Secretary.

During Tony's brief time at Energy, I was watching a television documentary about the American space agency NASA. The programme discussed the problems faced by NASA in operating their telescope in Phoenix, Arizona because of light pollution from street lighting in the city. Research into this problem demonstrated that two-thirds of the street lighting was wasted as it threw light into the sky and only one third was actually used to light the streets. After a series of trials the NASA scientists had invented a system of lighting that saved precious energy by focusing the light on to the streets, cutting energy bills for the city of Phoenix and allowing the scientists to observe the night sky unimpeded. I recorded the programme and passed the tape to Tony who at the time was embroiled in the battle over government plans to sell the electricity industry, for a give-away price, to its cronies in business. I pointed out to Tony that the documentary demonstrated not only environmentally sound practice, but also how to slash the profits of the electricity companies. I also firmly believe the night sky is one of nature's very best shows and we deserve the opportunity to view it in all its splendour. Whilst Tony and I giggled at the prospect of headlines reading 'Blair Plans to Blackout Britain', I still think this is an idea worth serious consideration.

Tony and Cherie were now the parents of three small children, and whilst Tony is certainly an ambitious and talented politician he is also a loving and committed father and husband. Despite the terrible model of fatherhood and marriage I represented for Cherie and Lyndsey, they were lucky to have the shining example of my parents' devotion. Both of them were discerning enough to love men of emotional strength and integrity and make good lasting marriages. Whilst Tony was engaged in the steep learning curve of politics, Cherie's law career was also going from strength to strength. She made the move from criminal to employment law and her intelligence and obvious talent were recognized when she was offered the chance of a place in history by becoming the youngest female QC in the country. She turned down the offer because her youngest child Kathryn, then eighteen months old, was too young to attend the ceremony. Cherie waited another six years before taking up the offer. The political downside to Tony's commitment to his young family meant he was unable and probably unwilling to participate in the parliamentary games of late-night drinking and plotting.

Gordon Brown, however, was aligning his career with that of the newly appointed Shadow Chancellor, John Smith. Tony Blair, of course, remained resolutely loyal to Neil Kinnock. Soon after Tony was elected to the Shadow Cabinet Nick Brown,[2] who had supported Tony in his campaign, changed his allegiance to Gordon Brown with whom he felt more comfortable. It was already clear that Gordon Brown perceived Tony to be a major political rival, not least because Tony served successfully in a variety of Shadow government posts. Gordon Brown, good though he may claim to be with numbers, has kept his interests both narrow and focused specifically on the Treasury. Though in my opinion he lacks many leadership qualities, one of his more glaring flaws is his lack of wide experience in government departments. One of the Shadow posts held by Tony was Shadow Chief Secretary to the Treasury during Roy Hattersley's tenure as Shadow Chancellor. On several occasions Tony was required to take the place of Hattersley at parliamentary committee meetings. At one of these meetings Tony was probing the economic policies of the then Conservative Chancellor, Nigel Lawson, when another committee member, Dennis Skinner, interrupted. Skinner was unaware of Tony's strategy and his ill-timed and crass intervention allowed the relieved Lawson to escape further questioning. Outside the committee room Tony made his displeasure obvious, grabbing Skinner by his jacket lapels as he pushed him up against the wall. Skinner's response was to shout, 'No violence! No violence!' as Tony made it very clear what he would personally do to Skinner if he ever interfered in such a manner again. Later, when he told me of the incident, Tony said there were surreal moments during which it was possible to believe Skinner was a Tory 'sleeper' given the number of times his ill-considered interventions had in the past allowed Conservatives to escape difficult questions.

Although I had once again become involved and excited by politics I

[2] Nick Brown was appointed Chief Whip in 1997, a role that made him a key figure in the camp of Gordon Brown.

still had to face the challenge of the theatre. Fear is a great inhibitor, but somehow I found the determination and courage to return to acting. Pat and I played regular summer seasons – invariably an Agatha Christie play. My first job after leaving hospital was in 1982 when I was the co-lead with Pat in *The Unexpected Guest* at the Devonshire Park Theatre in Eastbourne. To our great satisfaction the production was a huge success, the management delighted with the press notices and the queues at the box office. Cushioned not only by Pat's concern that I should succeed, but also by her complete professionalism and integrity, I stepped back out onto a stage. An added bonus to this particular run was that my daughters Sarah and Emma chose to come to stay with us for a few weeks during their summer holiday from school. They enjoyed themselves so much their summer visits became a regular part of our annual routine. Pat and I worked well together. We were *simpatico*. Coming to the end of a long tour of *Spider's Web*, another Agatha Christie play, we were still trying out ideas for a particularly difficult scene even with only two performances left. I laughed at her obsessive behaviour whilst at the same time loving her for it. She never gave less than her best. Every performance counted.

During the summer of 1985 Pat and I took part in an afternoon television chat show as mystery guests. The other guests, Marjorie Orr and Russell Grant, were astrologers whose skills, and that of a computer, would be tested by guessing Pat's and my profession from the minimal information of the date, time and place of our birth. The computer was a miserable failure and Russell Grant was hardly better, but Marjorie Orr, particularly in my case, was astonishingly accurate. She was adamant that I had been hospitalized twice with serious health problems. Whilst arguably she might have heard about my time in the burns unit it was extremely unlikely she could have known that as a child I had suffered from diphtheria. Chatting in the green room after the show, Orr told me she had completed my astrological chart for the year. She predicted I would be called to audition for a role in a new television soap opera. She also predicted I would not expect to be offered the part, but I would be wrong and it would be offered to me on 17 December. Needless to say I was somewhat sceptical. In December, after several months out of work, I was called to an interview at Granada Television for a new soap opera, *Albion Market*. The meeting did not go particularly well and I left Granada deeply pessimistic. On 17 December, however, I received a telephone call informing me the part was mine. Stunned, I rummaged through the desk drawers to find the chart Marjorie Orr had given me. How could she have known? As far as I could see the only obvious error was her assertion that I was the father of eight daughters; in fact at that time it was seven. My marriage to Nancy Jaeger was still to come.

Nancy Jaeger and I were married in the summer of 1988 at her parents' home on Vancouver Island, Canada without any members of my family present. It was only after our marriage that it became clear just how right-wing she is. Of course marriage is about much more than political allegiances. I believe a certain level of disagreement can be both entertaining and enlightening. However, between Nancy and me it amounted to much more than the odd dispute whilst watching *Newsnight* or *Question Time*. I came to realize that we occupied very different spaces in terms of the social and moral understanding which must underpin political belief.

On 25 December 1989 my youngest daughter Joanna was born. I telephoned Cherie who was spending the holiday in Sedgefield and she was delighted by my news. Lyndsey brought her first child, my bright and delightful granddaughter Lucy, born in October of the same year, to visit. After graduating from the University of Cardiff, Lyndsey had taken time out to travel extensively. On her return to London she was interviewed successfully for a job at Herbert Smith, the City of London lawyer. It was at Herbert Smith that she met her future husband, Chris Taverner. By the time Lucy was born Lyndsey had moved on from Herbert Smith to work as the lawyer for Hackney Council before quitting the law to train as a homeopath. Inspired by the birth of Joanna, I looked forward to the new decade with great hope and expectation. My optimism was short-lived. Nancy soon wanted to return to work. I was only too happy to take over the role of Joanna's primary carer; I wanted to spend as much time as possible with her. This I could do, as I was then on the books of an agent in Manchester who was not particularly motivated to find work for me. It was not until 1994, when the wonderfully efficient John Markham became my agent, that my job prospects and levels of employment increased substantially.

There was an awful inevitability to the collapse of my marriage to Nancy, but I was able to find considerable solace not only in caring for Joanna, but also in Labour politics. Tony Blair was promoted to Shadow Employment Secretary early in 1990. This was a highly sensitive area involving industrial relations and trade union law. Tony held countless meetings with trade union leaders and was meticulous in his attention to the difficulties and obstacles to be overcome. Charles Clarke, now Member of Parliament for Norwich South, said of Tony's approach: 'He showed in the whole process an ability to decide where he was going.

He would set a course and move towards the target clearly, manoeuvring around the various obstacles, walking around the chair rather than tripping over it. Blair both knew where he was going and how to get there by displaying a mixture of intelligence and opportunism.'

Ironically, Tony had actually wanted the Transport brief as he believed it to be a serious and pressing issue, but Neil Kinnock gave it to John Prescott. At the first meeting of the new Shadow Cabinet Tony arrived a little late. The only available chair was one nearest the door. This became Tony's chosen spot. I was concerned about his public profile as whenever the television cameras were allowed into a meeting it was difficult to see Tony. However, the strategy paid off, as he was able to observe the modus operandi of the entire Shadow Cabinet and learn from the experience.

Just as it began to seem that the Tory propaganda of Thatcher's invincibility might contain some truth along came the poll tax, the issue that had much to do with finally bringing about the ejection of Margaret Thatcher as Prime Minister and leader of the Conservative Party. With her autocratic tendencies by now completely dominating not only the Cabinet but also her own world-view, she refused to listen to dissenting voices, even claiming the tax would be a popular move. There was a massive public demonstration in London on the day before the poll tax was introduced and very quickly unhappiness with this unjust taxation spread, igniting nationwide protest and demonstrations. People in the most unlikely places took to the streets to express their anger. My future wife, Stephenie, was at the time living in the small Dartmoor town of Tavistock, a place not renowned for political ferment, but even in Tavistock there was a demonstration by several hundred people.

The pressure on Thatcher's premiership increased with her public mauling in the House of Commons by the Deputy Prime Minister, Geoffrey Howe, who resigned from the government in protest over Thatcher's negative attitude to Europe. Howe's skilful annihilation of Thatcher's leadership qualities was all the more spectacular given that this was the man famously likened to a dead sheep by Denis Healey. Michael Heseltine, seizing his moment, launched a leadership challenge. Who would ever forget the sight of Margaret Thatcher's shocked face as she emerged from the British Embassy in Paris, where she had gone for a European summit meeting? She had obviously expected an outright win on the first ballot. Her tearful farewells as she finally left Downing Street forever left me unmoved. I loathed the woman and everything she represented. I believe her policies were fundamentally destructive and ultimately catastrophic. Clear examples of that can be seen in the current legacy of a historically underfunded National Health Service and in a bankrupt and too often fatal rail system.

By the time of the 1992 general election Gordon Brown was firmly in the political camp of his fellow Scot, the Shadow Chancellor John Smith. Tony Blair argued for many months before the election that Smith's plan to produce a Shadow budget would be a critical mistake allowing, as it did, the Tories to rubbish it. He was ignored and Smith and Brown went on to walk straight into the trap laid by the Conservatives' astute political tactician, Chris Patten. Smith and Brown were not the only members of the Labour Party to feel the sharpness of the Patten wit and intellect. Peter Mandelson was an earlier victim as, unsure of his remit, he was wrong-footed more than once on ITV's *This Week* programme broadcast on the eve of the Labour Party conference. I have always admired Chris Patten, who was appointed by John Major to run the Conservative campaign during the 1992 general election. Unable adequately to defend his own seat in Bath against the Liberal Democrats, Chris Patten's loyalty was rewarded when he was made the last Governor of Hong Kong. Besides protecting himself from any challenge, I believe Major unintentionally helped the Labour Party by sending Patten to Hong Kong. Whilst I am certain Labour would have won the 1997 election, come what may, I also believe a leader with the obvious qualities of Patten might have saved the Tories from a total rout.

The 1992 general election should by all reasonable expectation have been won by the Labour Party. The probity of the Conservative government and some of its Ministers was beginning to be questioned and the electorate had clearly manifested its displeasure at the introduction of the Community Charge, as the poll tax had become. However, the media and political skill of Chris Patten stole any advantage from the Labour Party organization as it failed to take any real advantage of these fault lines. Popular memory would now have us believe that the ill-advised Sheffield rally organized by the Labour Party near the end of the election campaign was the reason we lost. I have always been unwilling to accept that reasoning. The campaign was certainly not helped by the foolish comments of John Smith and Gordon Brown on Labour taxation policy. They gifted the Tories the 'double whammy' propaganda and helped them back into power. How could two consummate politicians of the recognized skill of Smith and Brown have made such a dreadful mistake?

Nine

The Son (in-law) Rises

'I'll be leader ... Come with me, and see what we can find'
Harry Castling and C. W. Murphy

Labour's general election defeat in 1992 was devastating. I really believed that this time the Labour Party had done enough to satisfy the electors and prove it was once more a party of government. Yet certainly in the last week before polling day all the high hopes and enthusiasm characteristic of the early days of the campaign began to slip away. Thirteen years after the last Labour government the Conservatives, despite all their manifest faults, could still frighten the voters with the prospect of a Labour government – trade union policies, taxation policies – all the old bogeymen were paraded. The country chose John Major, a grey man in a suit as their Prime Minister. The alternative was Neil Kinnock, a brave visionary with a genuine fire in his belly for reform. Kinnock had learned the lessons of the Labour Party's mistakes and in my opinion would have been a great prime minister. I watched Kinnock interviewed on television as the election results came in and it was clear once again that Labour had lost. He spoke of his strong sense of disappointment and his belief that the country deserved better. Kinnock had wanted to resign after the 1987 general election defeat, but his wife Glenys persuaded him against it. This time he insisted, provoking a leadership contest.

My gloom was not lifted by the inevitable victory of John Smith. My support went to Bryan Gould, but John Smith and Gordon Brown had clearly worked hard on their strategy to secure a substantial vote in any leadership contest even before the general election defeat. Gould never had a realistic hope of winning the leadership of the Labour Party. The results of the leadership contest were announced at a special conference in Blackpool – a resounding victory for Smith. Shortly afterwards I was sitting in the reception area of the Grand

Hotel. Bryan Gould came in and was forced to run a gauntlet of silent backs as no one turned to acknowledge his presence. I had just ordered tea for Tony Blair and myself, and rising from the table I took Gould by the arm and invited him to join us. As we chatted I tried to cheer him up with the reminder that our party was founded by and on dissent and that he was part of that great tradition. I was genuinely saddened when, sometime later, Bryan Gould decided to quit British politics and return to his native New Zealand.

John Smith appointed Gordon Brown as Shadow Chancellor and Tony Blair Shadow Home Secretary. Tony was quickly disillusioned by the Smith–Brown axis. He felt, as one commentator described it, 'they were sleep-walking into oblivion'. On the subject of oblivion, it was around this time that the gross fraudster Robert Maxwell took his final leap, jumping or pushed from his boat. I remember a train journey to London when I sat opposite the chief crime reporter from the *Sunday People* – a newspaper then owned by Maxwell – and he told me how Maxwell particularly liked to humiliate those in the public eye and especially anyone in a position of authority. I have heard the story of Alastair Campbell's contretemps with the political editor of the *Guardian*, Michael White, when White made a less than flattering comment about Robert Maxwell and the circumstances surrounding his death. I would think Campbell was one of the few people to mourn for Maxwell. I do not believe that too many of those whose pension fund was raided by Robert Maxwell grieved too much.

During the time Tony Blair was Shadow Home Secretary I was also striving in a totally futile role as an opposition spokesperson on the council of Equity. I travelled to London every other month to attend the meetings and was a regular guest either at Cherie's home in Richmond Crescent, Islington or at Lyndsey's home around the corner in Richmond Avenue. This arrangement suited me well as it meant I was also able to spend time with my grandchildren, whose number eventually expanded to five with the birth of Lyndsey's son James. At Cherie's home I witnessed at first hand the level of my son-in-law's frustration with the pusillanimous strategy deployed by the Labour leadership. Their plan for Opposition was to do nothing, believing that it was only necessary for the degenerate Conservative administration to be the author of its own downfall. Tony Blair argued that the Opposition had a duty to oppose and the electorate had a right to know what Labour stood for and that we should not expect to take power simply on the grounds of not being the Tories. On more than one occasion when Tony's frustration boiled over he threatened to resign and return to the Bar.

His persistent questioning of Smith's strategy soon began to make him unpopular with the leader. At the Labour Party conference in 1993 I was backstage chatting with Tony and Cherie. I watched as an aide informed Smith and Gordon Brown that Jeremy Paxman wanted to do a live *Newsnight* interview with either one of them. Live interviews are very tricky, requiring quick thinking and an iron nerve. Neither Smith nor Brown wanted to do the interview so they beckoned Tony over and informed him he would do it. Tony argued to no avail that his remit was the Home Office and not the Treasury. Dismissing any protest, John Smith insisted Tony should do the interview. That night, watching the programme I was yet again impressed by my son-in-law, who handled the interview with considerable aplomb, drawing on his earlier experience as Shadow First Secretary to the Treasury.

Ironically, Tony Blair was ultimately to benefit from the preference of John Smith and Gordon Brown not to participate in interviews where they did not have prior knowledge of the questions. Tony Blair was the senior Shadow Minister deployed to deal not only with the media, but also to speak at regional Labour Party meetings. His remit covered subjects as diverse as arms to Iraq to the notorious brown envelopes which became such a feature of Conservative Party life. Unwittingly, Tony became the 'face' of the Labour Party.

The health of John Smith had been a cause for concern since his first heart attack in 1988. Having spent time in a rehabilitation centre where a number of the patients were recovering from strokes, I understood that Smith would find it difficult to stand up to the highly stressful rigours and demands of leadership of the Labour Party and then hopefully as leader of the government. As a former drinker I understood only too well the repercussions of using heavy exercise as an antidote for a hangover. Even after his first heart attack John Smith continued to enjoy malt whisky; combined with his love of climbing the Scottish Monroes, it was inevitably a risky cocktail. I believed that by 1997 Smith would be looking to resign as Party leader on the grounds of ill-health. At Richmond Crescent I was involved in conversations with close family and friends on the possibility of Tony eventually becoming leader, but none of us wanted or could have anticipated the suddenness of John Smith's death. Tony was clearly deeply affected by the unexpected news. The look of shock and genuine sorrow on his face when the news was given to him on live television remains fixed in my mind. On the same news bulletin Denis Healey, whilst expressing his regret at Smith's death, reminded viewers that life must go on and Blair was the obvious new leader.

Whilst the death of a decent human being such as John Smith diminishes us all, I believe Smith was a political plodder whose perceived virtue of innate caution masked a lack of flair and innovation. The battle for leadership of the Labour Party was between Gordon Brown who believed that the mantle would pass to him, and Tony Blair who knew he would have to fight for it. Brown went up to his constituency in Scotland even before John Smith's funeral. As soon as the funeral was over, battle commenced. Tony informed Brown by telephone of his decision to stand as a candidate in the leadership contest. Brown remained in his Edinburgh fastness. His campaign manager, Nick Brown, relayed an endless stream of bad news to him in the form of polls indicating Tony would win. Gordon Brown suggested to Tony he should fly to Edinburgh for a meeting. Tony turned down this suggestion. Brown, now unhappily aware of the reality of the unfolding situation, returned to London and the now (in)famous meeting in an Islington restaurant where he capitulated. What was Brown so afraid of? I believe he should have stood. I also believe he would, inevitably, have lost by a huge margin and any thought he might have had of being the rightful leader would have been utterly and finally squashed.

Peter Mandelson's star had waned somewhat under John Smith's leadership of the Labour Party. Mandelson was initially desperately uncertain whether his allegiance should be offered to Brown or Blair. He is not a team player nor is he particularly popular amongst his Labour Party colleagues and I believe this was partly why his supporting role in the leadership contest was disguised by the code name Bobby. Peter Kilfoyle and Mo Mowlam, both Labour Members of Parliament, were running Tony's leadership campaign and had been loyal supporters from the beginning. Both of them had their own reasons for having reservations about Mandelson. Kilfoyle, an old-style socialist whose roots are Liverpool working-class, represents the antithesis of Mandelson who sees himself in the vanguard of New Labour thinking and strategy. Mo Mowlam's instinctive reservations about Mandelson were proved correct by the whispering campaign that surrounded her departure as Northern Ireland Minister and Mandelson's subsequent installation in that post. I would certainly have been very unhappy to hear Tony was making use of the skills of Peter Mandelson. I do not like Mandelson and nothing he has ever done or said has convinced me otherwise.

Once Brown withdrew from the leadership race, Ken Follett tried to put together a rival bid. He first approached Robin Cook, who declined, and Jack Cunningham was then targeted. This suggestion was drowned in a tidal wave of derision. Cunningham is the Member of Parliament for Copeland. The nuclear power plant at Sellafield is in this constituency. A substantial proportion of Labour Party membership has always opposed the nuclear programme and Jack Cunningham's support for Sellafield does not win him popularity. Margaret Beckett, John Smith's deputy, was standing for leader, but more names were needed on the ticket to make it a contest. I was amongst those who suggested that John Prescott should be persuaded to take part. During the 1992 general election campaign I had spoken at meetings with Prescott and trade union leaders such as Jimmy Knapp and Lew Adams from the rail unions and Bill Morris from the Transport and General Workers' Union. Now, the union leaders suggested Prescott should concentrate on winning the deputy leadership contest, thus providing a balanced ticket with Tony Blair as leader. For Margaret Beckett it was a double whammy. Not only did she fail to secure the leadership, she also lost the vote as deputy.

It was during the leadership contest that Tony accidentally developed his very personal campaigning style. At a packed meeting in Southport he suddenly cut short his prepared speech and removing his jacket rolled up his shirt sleeves and sat down on the edge of the stage. He then had a conversation with his audience, giving them the opportunity to talk directly to him. I had accompanied Tony to this meeting and the reaction of the audience was a defining moment for me. It proved how good Tony was in that kind of situation. The audience warmed to him and he was direct and honest in his response. Later, in the car driving to Liverpool, I encouraged him to adopt this approach more often.

The results of the contest were announced at a special conference. Afterwards Tony, Cherie, her mother Gale and I gathered in the doorway sheltering from a light drizzle. As the leader's limousine drew up we were joined by Margaret Beckett and her husband Leo. Getting out of the car, the driver indicated that Tony and Cherie should climb in. Tony opened the car door and insisted Margaret Beckett and her husband take it. Accepting the offer they drove off, leaving the newly elected and youngest ever leader of the Labour Party to try and hail a passing taxi in weather that had now turned to heavy rain. When he was eventually successful we all piled into the cab with an elated but soaking Tony Blair.

On a visit to Richmond Crescent in the summer of 1994 I talked to Tony and Cherie about the need for a press secretary. Tony needed his version of Bernard Ingham, who had been Margaret Thatcher's extremely effective Press Secretary. I suggested the most obvious choice was Alastair Campbell, who was making a name for himself as a political pundit both in the newspapers (*Daily Mirror*) and on television. I also suggested Jackie Ashley. Her father is Jack Ashley, the former Labour Member of Parliament for Stoke. She is also married to Andrew Marr, the BBC's political editor. With her experience of the media and also as a television news reporter, she would have made a good second choice if Campbell had turned down Tony's offer. Campbell was spending the summer holidays with his family in the south of France and as Tony and Cherie were also holidaying there it seemed to me they might just bump into each other. The secure and loyal political presence of Jonathan Powell[1] and Anji Hunter around Tony was reinforced when Alastair Campbell joined the team. When Margaret Thatcher was premier she made it a rule that only those who fitted the criteria of being 'one of us' would be appointed as government spokespersons. After a Labour victory one of the first actions of the Prime Minister's press secretary would be to replace all the Thatcher-appointed spokespersons in each Ministry. I do not suppose for one moment this presented any kind of problem for Alastair Campbell.

The exhilaration and excitement of my family's progress in politics was paralleled by the final collapse of my marriage to Nancy Jaeger. We now lived in the pretty Cheshire village of Broadbottom, having sold Sunny Place Cottage, but although we continued to occupy the same house it was clear by the end of 1994 that the relationship was over. Nancy finally left me taking our daughter Joanna with her at the beginning of December 1995. I was ill with a bout of influenza, bedridden with a high temperature, and unaware that she had left. As I struggled back and forth from bed to bathroom to kitchen and back again, I suppose I may have been vaguely conscious that something was up, but if so I was too ill to bother. Only after several days in bed and beginning to feel better, I got up late one evening to make myself a hot drink. Whilst I was in the kitchen the phone rang in the sitting room. I walked in and sat down next to the telephone, placing my drink where I expected a small table to be. To my surprise the cup simply fell to the floor and I groped around trying to switch on the table lamp to find out what had happened. The table lamp was not there either. Dragging myself up from the couch, I crossed the room and switched on the overhead light. My jaw dropped in disbelief as I stared at the almost empty room. As if also shaken by

[1] Jonathan Powell is Tony Blair's Chief of Staff. Given his background as a member of the diplomatic corps and the fact that his older brother Charles served Thatcher, he would not appear to be an obvious supporter and trusted intimate of a Labour Prime Minister. However, in Powell's case appearances are deceptive and I have always liked him.

the shocking discovery, the telephone stopped ringing. As I moved from room to room switching on the lights it was a similar story. For the most part I was unconcerned by this; however I was upset when I realized that some of the things no longer there had originally belonged to Pat. My sense of humour had returned by the time I got back to the kitchen. I began to giggle – Nancy had left behind two mugs, two knives, forks and spoons: two of everything.

The worst thing, the very worst thing, was the knowledge that while all of these material things could be replaced – the role of Joanna in my life could not. Joanna and I had spent much of her first five years in each other's company. I consider myself very lucky to have enjoyed a special relationship with her for that time, but the absence of my youngest daughter continues to leave a considerable hole in my life.

At the same time as my marriage was enduring its terminal throes I was also faced with the prospect of further serious health problems. Initially suspecting I was suffering from cancer of the colon, my doctors eventually discovered that the problem was in fact a twisted colon – an unfortunate and unpleasant side effect of my burns. Once my medical situation was resolved I began to feel, despite the enormous difficulties of my divorce from Nancy, that my life could only get better. Alone in my house I was able to enjoy a sense of peace so long absent from my life. Family and friends urged me to get out more, but I was content in my chosen solitude. I spent a lot of my time reading and telephoning old friends, both political and theatrical. More reassuringly, people I had not spoken to in years telephoned me to renew contact.

In August 1996 my life once again changed dramatically after an introduction in the garden of a neighbour, Marian Halfpenny. Marian, who was a source of enormous support during this difficult time, invited some friends over for a drink. Looking out of my bedroom window on to the scene in her garden my heart skipped a beat as I saw for the first time the woman who is now my wife. Rushing downstairs and out into the garden, I did not stop to look in the mirror at the sight I would present. As I was introduced to Stephenie Buckley I was lost and found in the same instant. My moment of lust, love and adoration was immediately spoiled when I learned, to my complete disappointment, that Stephenie was leaving for a camping holiday in France with her children the next morning. Panicking, I raised every fatuous reason I could think of to dissuade her. The more I persisted the more she resisted and my only comfort was in persuading Stephenie to have lunch with me on her return.

The ten days of her holiday were an eternity, but I have been in the fortunate position of keeping Steph with me ever since.

I am an avid and devoted watcher of television news bulletins. One of the great fears of my life is that the revolution will begin without me, so I like to keep track of events as they unfold. I was watching the BBC news one lunchtime in June 1995 when the newsreader said that we were going directly to Downing Street for an important announcement by the Prime Minister, John Major. Major, standing in the garden of Number 10, announced 'I am resigning,' and then paused. I leapt out of my armchair, punching the air and yelled at our startled and fleeing cat, 'There's going to be an election!' But Major then went on, '. . . as leader of the Conservative Party'. My immediate reaction was to curse the smirking, prim Major, but this initial response was replaced in seconds with a smile as I realized Major's tactic would only backfire. It was not going to placate the electorate, who wanted to see a general election not a leadership election. Major's mendacious strategy would hopefully add another fifty seats to Labour's eventual election victory. Little did I realize then that Major and his dissolute government would cling to power to the bitter end of their five-year term of office, subjecting a disgruntled and disillusioned electorate to a further twenty-two months of Tory rule.

Tony Blair's elevation to the leadership brought a fresh injection of not only youthful energy and vigour, but also a clear-eyed determination to carry forward the reform of the Labour Party constitution and structure begun by Neil Kinnock. The Labour Party conference at Blackpool in 1994 was the first one after Tony became leader. I decided I wanted to get a good view of Tony during his speech, making it easier to assess his performance, and I watched him from a vantage point at the back of the balcony rather than sitting in the front row with the rest of the family. This keynote speech to the conference is crucial in maintaining the leader's continuing status and esteem within the Party. Tony not only had to carry his audience with him, he had to enthuse and encourage them in the long haul to the next general election. He succeeded in this aim with flying colours, even managing to slip into the general euphoria his decision to revise Clause Four of the Labour Party constitution.[2] What a difference some thirty years can make.

[2] 'To secure for the workers by hand or by brain the full fruits of their industry and the most equitable distribution thereof that may be possible upon the basis of the common ownership of the means of production, distribution and exchange, and the best obtainable system of popular administration and control of each industry or service.'

When Hugh Gaitskell tried to do the same thing the resulting furore almost tore the Labour Party apart. Even so, Tony's announcement sent shock waves through the conference, which later in the week voted by a narrow majority to reaffirm the principle of Clause Four. The issue would be decided at a special conference in April 1995 in the Methodist Central Hall, Westminster. The new statement of purpose was backed by all sections of the Labour Party and Tony Blair declared:

Today a new Labour Party is being born. Our task now is nothing less than the rebirth of our nation. A new Britain. National renewal. Economic renewal so that wealth may be in the hands of the many and not the few. Democratic renewal. Labour in office, the people in power. A social renewal, so the evils of poverty and squalor are banished for good. New Labour.

At the time, the argument in support of revising Clause Four claimed the debate was simply around a form of words. I was not entirely convinced by this line of reasoning. Whilst recognizing the clear need for reform of the Labour Party – the fiascos of the 1979 and 1983 general elections certainly concentrated the mind – I do not believe tradition is always a bad thing. The old Clause Four called for public ownership and the 1945 Labour government acted on this principle to the considerable benefit of the nation. I thought it was absolute madness when the post-1979 Conservative governments sold the nationalized industries and utilities to the private sector. I have always believed there is a very strong case for renationalization. The severe economic and social problems privatization has generated, particularly the privatization of the rail system, unequivocally demonstrate the inherent flaws and iniquities of the capitalist system.

Tony was not alone in facing the challenge of a major speech at the 1994 Blackpool conference. Cherie had found the transformation into a public person, in her role as wife of the leader of the Party, fairly nerve-racking. But she was determined and she was growing in confidence and stature. On the evening of the same day that Tony made his first speech to conference as leader, Cherie had been asked to speak at a fringe meeting in support of Aung Sang Suu Kyi: Cherie was to read one of the arrested Burmese leader's speeches. Tony was closeted with his advisers as Cherie and I tried to find somewhere in their hotel suite where I could help her rehearse her speech. We quickly realized that the only available space was the bathroom. I listened as Cherie went through her speech. Hearing voices, Tony put his head around the bathroom door and I beckoned him in. We sat side by side on the edge of the bath and watched Cherie make an impassioned delivery. After a few minutes Alastair Campbell appeared and joined Tony and me on the side of the bath. We presented, I would think, a formidable practice audience for Cherie and her speech was certainly well received that evening. My eldest daughter has, I believe, displayed an amazing serenity in the face of the enormous pressures of public life. Her political ambitions, her career ambitions, her income, her marriage, even her taste in clothes have all come under intense media scrutiny and throughout it all she has somehow retained her equanimity. Obviously not a skill she inherited from me.

Tony Blair not only had to win over the hearts and minds of the grassroots membership of the Labour Party, he also faced another problem inherent in the job of leader – an elected Cabinet. Whilst Tony still believed Gordon Brown was the best person for the post of Shadow Chancellor, he was also wise enough to realize that one of his own people, Alun Michael, should also be on the Treasury team.[3] Of course, Brown was not pleased by this development, but could do nothing about it. Even then the myth of Gordon Brown's 'stolen' leadership was being widely promulgated, but I have always thought there was a fundamental flaw in this story. If he believes, and as his supporters maintain, that the Labour Party wants him as leader, my question to him would be: why then did he not stand against Tony Blair in the leadership contest? Is it because Brown ultimately lacks political courage? It seems to me that an open and clear contest is not something he appears able to countenance.

Frustration levels at the way the Conservatives clung grimly to power were high everywhere. Somehow, the Tory-supporting newspapers managed to generate the idea that John Major, although a somewhat dull and grey figure, was in fact a decent, cricket-loving, regular kind of guy. Someone who was capable of clinging to government as he did had to be more than a little devious and cunning. I remember being at Cherie's house one afternoon when Tony came storming in. He was raging at Major's attitude over a cross-party agreement on Northern Ireland. 'The bastard,' he yelled as he tore off his tie and stormed upstairs. I looked at Cherie and

[3] Alun Michael, the MP for Cardiff South and Penarth, was a junior Home Office Minister in the new Labour administration. After scandal forced the resignation of Ron Davies, Michael was appointed Secretary of State for Wales, eventually becoming Leader of the Welsh Assembly. He faced tremendous resentment in this latter role and eventually resigned just before a vote of confidence would have forced him out.

smiled. Comment was unnecessary. She giggled as she followed Tony upstairs.

During 1994 my writer friend Ron Rose persuaded an old friend of his, the successful London agent John Markham, to see me. It was a considerable relief when John Markham not only agreed to put me on his books, but also I began to get much more work. He telephoned me one day to ask if I would be interested in taking over from Nicholas Parsons in the role of narrator in *The Rocky Horror Show*, then running in London. As I had not seen the show John arranged tickets for me and my daughters Sarah and Emma to see it at the Duke of York's Theatre in St Martin's Lane. It was a hot summer's night and I remember at the interval having to fight my way through the bar to stand at an open window. Joining me, Sarah said, 'You're not thinking of doing this are you Dad?' Both Sarah and Emma looked completely shocked when I told them that, on the contrary, I was excited by the prospect of a nightly tussle with the groundlings. For me, it was also the start of a long and happy association with the show and a lasting friendship with its creative producer, Chris Malcolm. *Rocky Horror* is a unique theatrical experience and, as the much-abused narrator, I was able over a period of time to engage in some highly interesting exchanges with the volatile *Rocky* audience. It is usual for the audience of *The Rocky Horror Show* to dress up in similar costume and make-up to that worn on stage. I remember once when the show was in Swansea I was greeted with warm enthusiasm by stallholders on the local market. They were doing brisk trade in basques and other assorted underwear to people with tickets for *Rocky Horror*. During that same tour Cherie, Lyndsey, Sarah and Emma came to Basingstoke one evening to see me in the show, although I should point out they did not dress up.

Through the expertise of John Markham I was also offered a role in the award-winning film *Priest*, written by Jimmy McGovern and directed by the talented Antonia Bird. Initially, there was not really a part in the film for me, but Jimmy McGovern and Antonia Bird combined several smaller parts to create my role of the bigoted, right-wing, sexist Catholic, giving me the opportunity to reveal the dark side of Catholicism. In the film my grandson Euan makes a fleeting appearance as my son. Euan spent most of his time on the film set playing poker with the crew. Eventually I was approached by the gaffer, who begged me to prevent Euan from taking part in the card games as the crew were losing too much money to him and it was beginning to affect their morale. A few days later a somewhat chastened Euan returned to London escorted by Andy Roberts, the brilliant guitarist who also composed the score for *Priest*, and one of the actors from the company. He was, however, not quite as chastened as I believed. I later learned that he spent the journey playing poker with his companions and they too had lost money to him.

Not soon enough, Major called a general election, but even in this final act his petty-mindedness was obvious. The campaign period was six weeks – a clear attempt to bore the electorate and make it harder to maintain the momentum of the campaign. To the delight of Millbank I was offered a role in a film, *Owd Bob*, which would take me to the Isle of Man for much of the election period. Coincidentally, one of the producers on the film was Julie Allan, the mother of my daughters Jenia and Bronwen, although it was not until some final pieces of editing needed to be completed in London that I met her again. Memory does not allow people to grow old. I remembered Julie as a young woman and of course she had aged, as we all do. But more than that, it was a strange experience because given all that had happened between us I expected to feel more than I did. After the editing was completed Julie and I left the building together. We parted on the street amiably enough, but with no hug, no kiss and as I watched Julie walk away I realized it really was all a very long time ago.

I was disappointed to miss most of the excitement of the election campaign and the Isle of Man in April is not the most appealing of locations. It rains a lot. It is also very cold. But none of this could detract from my feeling of certainty that at last the Labour Party would form a government, and a government with a substantial majority. But Tony refused to take anything for granted and he and Cherie travelled the country campaigning tirelessly. On the morning of Friday 2 May 1997 nothing, absolutely nothing could spoil my joy as I watched my daughter and son-in-law move on a tidal wave of popular support towards 10 Downing Street.

Ten

Times are Changing

'Expectations are the most perilous form of dream.'

Elizabeth Bowen, *The Death of the Heart*

'Things Can Only Get Better' by D:Ream provided the anthem for the 1997 Labour Party campaign and that belief, that things would get better, sustained a sense of euphoria which still had people recalling, for months afterwards, their favourite election night moment. It was an historic night for the Labour Party. It was also a momentous and emotional night for my family. Never in my wildest dreams could I have imagined this. And, after eighteen years of Conservative rule, it was also satisfying to watch as that party paid the price for its overweening greed and arrogance. Did you see David Mellor lose his seat? And Neil Hamilton? Were you still up to experience the rush of gorgeous, gleeful triumph when Stephen Twigg ousted Portillo in Enfield Southgate? This was a landslide victory. At Tony Blair's birthday party a few days later on 6 May, I remember everyone was very excited by the victory and the knowledge that at last the Labour Party had been given the opportunity to make a real difference. The excitement was tempered by a sober and thoughtful recognition of the implications of such a large parliamentary majority – and the subsequent burden of expectation placed on the shoulders of this new government.

But, lying almost forgotten in the euphoria, was the manifesto pledge to continue with the Conservative spending plans for the first two years of government. I failed to understand why such a commitment was ever made. I believed it was a pledge that would leave the government a hostage to fortune, particularly when it very quickly became clear that the Treasury would have far more money than was initially thought. These unexpected funds should have been put to immediate and good use, demonstrating good faith to an electorate desperate for both symbolic and positive action. This would have been one manifesto pledge few would have been upset to see broken.

After my return from filming on the Isle of Man I made my first visit to Downing Street since the 1960s. My previous experience of Downing Street was as a guest confined to the public rooms, but now I saw 'backstage'. In many ways it reminds me of the theatre. Front of house, in this case the reception rooms, are grand and designed to impress visitors. However, it is a different story backstage. There, although large, there is not the same pressure to impress and the emphasis is on comfort. This distinct lack of grandeur means that by degrees my grandchildren have been able to turn 11 Downing Street into something that resembles a home with all the detritus and paraphernalia that children naturally accumulate and leave around the place. Sitting down to dinner with my family there was the usual energetic exchange of views around the kitchen table. I seized the moment and began to explain to Tony why I thought the government should change its mind on spending plans. I urged him to go on television and announce to the nation his intention to break his manifesto pledge on public spending – that there was more money for health and education than initially anticipated. Far from being distressed, the electorate would be impressed with his honesty. Warming to my theme I felt I was just reaching my most eloquent when Jonathan Powell appeared, as if by magic, requesting an urgent meeting with Tony. Tony left the table and I did not see him again until breakfast the following morning. Over the toaster I tried to resume our conversation from the previous evening. Once again, Powell appeared in the doorway to summon Tony, still eating his toast, to yet another urgent consultation.

Perhaps it is no more than coincidence, but I have noticed on subsequent visits to Downing Street that whenever I begin to talk politics with Tony, Powell or another aide will materialize with an urgent request for Tony's attention. Unfortunately for my daughter and grandchildren, this often means they are left with the unwanted opportunity to hear the final stages of my polemic. However, whilst Tony escapes from me, he is often cornered by his children who will bring issues they feel are important to his attention. I believe his family are a true bonus to Tony in his role as Prime Minister. Being a father to young children who come home every night from school is his connection to 'real life' – something that perhaps can be lost in the otherwise circumscribed prime ministerial world.

On a visit to London some time before the election I stayed with Tony and Cherie at their home in Islington. It was around the time the bosses of the former nationalized industries awarded themselves not only massive pay rises, but also substantial bonuses. Like many other members of the British public I was incensed and disgusted by their gluttony. Over supper I discussed the matter with Tony and Cherie, who agreed it was appalling, and Tony said he would talk to Gordon Brown about it. On the train home to Manchester I pondered over the problem, but decided the best strategy would be to wait and hear Brown's response. Returning to Richmond Crescent a few weeks later I asked Cherie what had happened and she informed me that the Shadow Chancellor thought it best to wait and see. Though not really surprised by this news, I was still irritated and responded with 'Typical bloody Gordon!' As the election loomed I decided to discuss with Tony and Cherie an idea of mine. 'Who', I asked, 'are the most hated and despised people in Britain at the moment?' Without waiting for their response I went on, 'the greedy bastards who run the privatized utilities'. I suggested one of the first things the incoming Labour government should do was to have a one-off tax of the former public utilities and claw back some of the money that rightfully belonged to the British people. I believed this plan had a number of advantages. First, coming as it would out of left field, it would be a surprise, but more importantly it would have the full backing of a significant proportion of the electorate. Cherie was an enthusiastic supporter of the idea. Tony quite rightly was a little more cautious, but eventually my daughter and I convinced him of the merits of the plan. This 'windfall tax' was an enormously popular strategy. It bloodied the noses of the privatized utilities and demonstrated to an enthusiastic public that Labour really did want to roll back some of the iniquities inflicted by eighteen years of Tory rule.

The 1997 Labour Party conference was held in Blackpool and, despite leaving hospital following surgery only the week before, this was one conference I was determined not to miss. My daughter Sarah came to stay with me for a few days and on the Tuesday we went together to the Winter Gardens to listen to Tony Blair's first speech to the conference as Prime Minister. Despite my later, possibly inevitable, disagreements with government policy, at that moment I thought my heart would burst with pride. More than anything I wished my parents had still been alive to witness Tony and Cherie on the platform together at the end of his speech. Naturally, my parents loved all of their grandchildren, but Cherie occupied a special place. Not only was Cherie their first grandchild, but also they had particularly doted on her from the time she was a baby and they took care of her when Gale and I were away from home on tour.

The following evening I attended an Arts for Labour event and I persuaded Steph to go with me. There was a massive security presence in Blackpool and as I wanted to take Steph for dinner at the conference hotel later in the evening I asked Fiona Miller, who organizes Cherie's office, to arrange a security pass for her. I was still not well enough to drive and so Steph and I set off that evening in her car. We spent a frustrating period driving around looking for a parking space close to the church that was serving as one of the conference offices. Eventually, spotting a side street, I told Steph to park the car – it would be all right as I had my disabled parking badge with me. At this early stage in our relationship, not knowing any better, she happily took my word for it and we went to join the queue in the church office. After a wait we reached the front of the line to be told we were in the wrong one and needed to join another, albeit smaller, queue. By then desperate for a cigarette, I left Steph to collect her pass whilst I went outside to smoke. Standing near the entrance I smoked and gossiped with other nicotine outcasts and then decided to wander round the corner to check the car. What I saw almost made me choke. The police and military were in the process of setting up a cordon around Steph's car in order to do a controlled explosion. My strangled scream was cut off by Steph's arrival and her obvious displeasure at the scene that met her eyes.

Tackling the problem with what is best described as polite assertiveness, she persuaded the security forces not to blow up her car. Fortunately, the police recognized me and revelling in my obvious discomfort they took great pleasure in making me the butt of more than one comment and joke. However, worse was to come, as having rescued her car Steph was particularly incisive and articulate in her condemnation of my parking advice. Despite that we went on to enjoy a pleasant evening; and driving home later we saw two shooting stars streak across the sky. As their paths crossed they formed, for a moment, a giant kiss. Happily superstitious soul that I am, I decided to interpret this sighting as a hopeful symbol for the future – personally and politically.

My wife possesses that specifically female skill of selective deafness, but it took me some time to realize this. I was delighted when she appeared happy for me to ramble at great length on the many subjects on which I have an opinion, unaware that she had switched off and was only nodding or saying 'yes' and 'no' occasionally to keep me happy. It was a skill she had learned when bringing up four strapping, talkative and intelligent boys, *all* of whom wanted *all* her attention at any one time. The other habit she has that I failed to notice for some time is that she always falls asleep in the car. A combination of my talking and being a car passenger acts like Mogadon (a sleeping tablet) for her. Driving home one summer evening in 1998 I asked Steph to marry me. Whilst I expected her to ponder my suggestion for a few moments I did not expect the total silence that followed. Thinking perhaps that she could not hear me, I repeated my proposal. Again silence. By now completely disconcerted, I turned to look at her. She had obviously just woken up, but by the look on her face she had registered at some level that I had said something that required a response.

Suppressing a giggle I said, 'Well?'

'I didn't quite catch what you said', she extemporized.

'I thought it would be nice to get married on my birthday', I repeated.

'Oh yes. That might be nice,' she replied before closing her eyes and going back to sleep.

Both Steph and I wanted as many members of our family as possible to be at our wedding, but as Tony and Cherie were going to be in China on an official visit on 9 October (my birthday), Cherie asked us to change our plans and marry on 2 October. This was the Friday of the Labour Party conference, again held in Blackpool. As our wedding was to be in Liverpool, Cherie and Tony were able to leave the conference when it ended at Friday lunchtime and travel to Liverpool later that afternoon. But before the wedding there was the conference and Steph and I went over to Blackpool on Tuesday morning in time for Tony's speech in the afternoon.

I was delighted and also touched that so many people – politicians, trade unionists and comrades – came over to offer their congratulations on my impending nuptials. As we queued after lunch to get into the Winter Gardens, Charlie Falconer joined us in the line and brought us up to date with the latest conference gossip before hurrying off to the media enclosure. Steph and I made our way upstairs as I wanted to look at the floor of the hall from a vantage point. We had decided to take up the offer of Lew Adams and his union colleagues to sit with them during the leader's speech rather than join the rest of my family on the front row. This time I wanted to sit in the middle of the audience and get a genuine feel of the reaction to Tony's speech. Turning to go back downstairs, I spotted Tony and Cherie with their entourage making their way backstage. I called out, wishing Tony luck, and despite being about to make a major speech he stopped and came over for a brief moment. This was the speech during which Tony praised Mo Mowlam, the Northern Ireland Minister, and she received a standing ovation from the conference. The warmth and appreciation for her was sincere and well deserved.

It is in no small part due to the efforts of Peter Kilfoyle, the Labour Member of Parliament for Liverpool Walton, that Steph and I had such a memorable wedding day. Not only did Peter ensure our privacy on the day – no one but invited guests could enter the church – he also contacted the Devonshire House Hotel on Edge Lane and they arranged every detail of a marvellous day for us. The night before the wedding we stayed at the hotel and we were married there the next day with a few friends and family members present. My friend the actor John McArdle was our best man and Steph's oldest son Tom was our other witness. Later in the afternoon we went to my cousin John Thompson's church, St Francis de Sale in Walton, where we were joined by more friends and family including my daughters Lyndsey, Sarah and Emma who travelled up from London. My youngest daughter Joanna was a very pretty bridesmaid. Of course the rules of the Catholic Church meant we could not have a religious service, but my cousin and his wonderful secretaries Bobbie and Eileen organized readings for all our children and there was music and certainly much laughter. Afterwards we returned to the hotel for a reception. Tony and Cherie could stay only a short time as they were anxious to return to Chequers and their children before leaving again in a few days for China. It was a beautiful and happy wedding, so much so that when the time came for Tony and Cherie to leave, their security personnel expressed their disappointment – they wanted to stay longer!

I was spending more time in Liverpool than I had done for some years. In 1997 I played Jack in Jimmy Murphy's play *Brothers of the Brush*, directed by Robert Delamere at the Everyman Theatre. The play is powerful, hard-hitting and emotionally draining. I was delighted to be offered the part. The first half ends with an ugly and violent episode and after several performances we achieved a rare moment of magic that only occurs in live theatrical performance. Along with the other actors I left the stage to stony silence and we had almost reached our dressing room before there was a reaction from the shocked audience. Suddenly, we heard thunderous applause and, turning to the others, I said, 'Fantastic. Now comes the hard part. We have to do that every night.' Of course it is not humanly possible to create that level of tension and response every night. Audiences differ, as do performances, but we did our best and the play received good notices.

In the summer of 1998 I was back in Liverpool again to work in a short film, *The Duke*, written and directed by John McArdle. The film is semi-autobiographical and explores the relationship between a young boy and his doting grandfather. At the end of the film I was required to dress up as John Wayne to save the boy from the school bully. As a small boy I often dreamed of becoming a cowboy; now finally, somewhat late in the day, I was given the opportunity to pretend. Not only that – I got to be John Wayne for a few hours. It was great. The final showdown involved riding a horse, something I had not done since I was burned. The Merseyside police loaned the oldest, the most placid and quite the biggest horse I have ever seen, but he and I got on very well together. A few months later, when I attended a home game at Anfield, he was on duty and he recognized me. Fortunately, I had some of his favourite mints in my pocket and this giant gelding and I spent several minutes exchanging friendly nuzzling. *The Duke* was filmed in a few days over the August bank holiday and it is a little gem of a film. I was thrilled for John when he won the director's prize at the Naples film festival.

I had not worked for the BBC for a long time, not since the days of *Till Death Us Do Part*. I am certain this was due to my drunken and increasingly erratic behaviour through the seventies. When, in early 1999, BBC Wales offered me a role in the series *Jack of Hearts* I hoped I was finally forgiven. Steph and I planned to go on holiday at the end of January, but would be back in time for me to start filming. As we drove home at the end of our holiday we stopped for something to eat and Steph's mobile telephone began to ring. It was my agent, John Markham. There was a slight mix-up over dates and I was required in Cardiff early the next morning. Dashing home to pick up my scripts, I grabbed a few hours' sleep before driving down to Wales. I spent the best part of six weeks there and loved every minute. The production team were friendly and supportive and my role as a man obsessed with gaining 'justice' for his murdered son was interesting – a 'meaty' part.

One day we were shooting a scene that involved me trying to gain entry to my ex-daughter-in-law's home. On 'action' I was at first to attempt the front door and when that failed to try and force my way through the sitting room window. During rehearsal it had proved somewhat difficult to make this window rattle and during the first take, urged on by the director, I grabbed the upper part of the sash window and again tried to shake it. The window remained sturdily silent. Before the second take Tim Llyn (the director) and I discovered what appeared to be a convenient hand grip on the window frame and take two was ready to go. This time I strode purposefully down the path to the house, kicked and banged at the front door and then turned my attention to the window. Grabbing the frame, I pulled hard. To my utter consternation I began to stagger backwards. The entire window frame had come away in my hands. The only coherent thought to pass through my horrified brain was that on no account must I drop it. But this was a Victorian sash window frame and it was extremely heavy. Somehow I maintained my grip on it until the prop men could rush to my aid and we were able gently to lower it to the ground. Turning, I saw the crew helpless with laughter as the actress who was playing my intended victim stared at the empty window space with a look of complete, blank astonishment on her face. Worse, this was not a purpose-built set, but someone's home loaned to the BBC for the series. Carefully, the props refitted the window back into the space whence it came. Then the entire unit fled the scene. I asked if the window would be secure and was told it would be fine – as long as no one ever slammed the front door. The clear moral of this story is, never loan your house to a film crew, no matter how glamorous it may seem!

During filming I stayed in a hotel that was next door to the site where the beautiful new millennium stadium was being built, and as a rugby fan I watched its progress keenly. It was also an interesting time politically to be in Wales as the election for the Assembly got under way. Time after time I was told by members of the film crew and by people stopping me in the street of the deep resentment in Wales of the attempts by Tony Blair to manipulate the outcome of the election so that Alun Michael would become Leader of the Assembly. Rhodri Morgan was the popular choice and I could not understand why Tony was so against him. When I spoke to Cherie I tried to warn her of the strength of feeling against Alun Michael, who was perceived as a Blairite puppet who did not reflect the wishes and aspirations of the Welsh people. Too late, I think, the government recognized that a backlash was gaining momentum and although Michael did become Leader, the Welsh Labour Party eventually got their way when he resigned and Rhodri Morgan took over. Unfortunately, the government handled the situation badly and only really succeeded I believe in denting its reputation and credibility in Wales.

One of the questions I am regularly asked during interviews with the press, particularly since Tony became Prime Minister, is 'Are you not worried about embarrassing your son-in-law?' As my political views are just that – my thoughts on the political situation – and in no way reflect my feelings about my family I never cease to find myself bemused by the question. Throughout my life I have held strong political opinions and that is unlikely to change before I draw my last breath. I find extraordinary the assumption that I would be required to lose my own political voice as my son-in-law found his. To be fair, Tony has never once suggested otherwise – not to me anyway.

I believe a large parliamentary majority can lead, and at times has led, to the stifling of debate and dissension, both vital for maintaining a vibrant and healthy democracy. The political honeymoon for the new government was particularly extended and it was some time before problems began to manifest themselves. I started to become unhappy as the consequences of maintaining the Tory spending plans were gradually revealed, particularly the plans for reforming the Welfare State. I do not think there are many people who would not agree that reform was long overdue. Systems put in place in 1945 could no longer cope fifty years later, but I was shocked by the insensitive and inept behaviour displayed by the government over some aspects of proposed changes. I was invited to a party in Downing Street on 10 December, the same evening the House of Commons voted to end payment of Single Parent Benefit. I turned the invitation down. The idea of partying whilst some of the poorest people in Britain had benefit taken away from them was too much for me, no matter how much the government trumpeted its intended alternative. But it is with the issue of the state pension that I have become most involved.

In the early 1980s the Thatcher government broke the link between the state pension and average earnings and since then not only has the value of the pension steadily eroded, but the status of pensioners has declined along with their income. With many other people I believed that a Labour government would be committed to eradicating such gross social and economic inequality. I have never been a fan of Gordon Brown. His brooding, obsessive character is tiresome, but I find his attempts to suggest that he harbours left-wing sympathies offensive, and never more so than when in the 1999 Budget he increased the state pension by a mere seventy-five pence. At a stroke he offended more than eleven million voters. Not exactly a master stroke of political strategy and intuitive understanding. The National Pensioners' Convention, then under the leadership of Jack Jones, had been campaigning for some time for the restoration of the link between average earnings and the state pension. This Budget decision by the staggeringly insensitive Chancellor of the Exchequer gave an enormous boost to the NPC campaign as incensed and offended pensioners and their relatives looked to collective action. I hate injustice. I hate to see decent people treated with contempt and indifference. There is no dignity in poverty and I was furious and disbelieving that a Labour government would behave with such indecency.

Jack Jones urged me to become involved in the pensioners' campaign and in November 2001 I was asked to speak at a pensioners' rally organized by the NPC at the Methodist Hall in Westminster. I was proud to share a platform with amongst others Barbara Castle, Jack Jones and Rodney Bickerstaffe, all seasoned and doughty fighters for social justice. During the morning I dashed around giving radio and press interviews and I was reminded that age does leave its mark. Whilst the mind is as active and keen as ever, energy levels are not always what they once were – but it was a tremendous rally with people travelling from all over Britain to take part. Keir Hardie once said 'Parliament does not respond to argument. It responds to pressure.' After speeches at the Methodist Hall we took our campaign right into the Palace of Westminster as pensioners lobbied their constituency representatives. Called upon to give my speech again, I wondered if I was the first actor to address a mass meeting within the Palace. Vanity made me hope so, but the one thing I was sure of was that following our demonstration the government could have been in no doubt of the strength of feeling generated by the pensions issue.

In a speech to the 1993 Labour Party conference Gordon Brown said he wished to 'achieve what in fifty years of the welfare state has never been achieved. The end of means-testing for elderly people.' If the link had not been broken the state pension would now be at least twenty pounds a week more, effectively allowing pensioners to share in the growing prosperity of the country and removing any necessity for the socially divisive and deeply humiliating process of means-testing. Part of the government argument against restoring the link with earnings has been that pensions are a universal benefit; thus all pensioners, including Mrs Thatcher, would enjoy the increase. However, I would wager Mrs Thatcher enjoys an annual level of income that is taxable. Any increase would be drawn back into the Exchequer, as it would for all pensioners over a certain level of income. This government argument becomes even more nonsensical when we consider the winter fuel allowance. This is two hundred pounds tax free, paid to all pensioners including Mrs Thatcher. I do not think this is 'targeting the most needy', the government defence of the Minimum Income Guarantee, but in reality no more than means-testing under another name.

For many people struggling to bring up a family on a low income saving for retirement is just not an option. Like the notice outside a church in Liverpool that read 'Jesus Saves', and underneath someone had written 'Not on my wages he doesn't', the reality for many people is that contributing to National Insurance provides the only prospect of income on retirement. This point was made again and again to me after I returned home from the rally. Suddenly, the issue of pensioner poverty was high on the political agenda and people would stop me in the street to congratulate me and urge me to continue my support for the campaign. It was not only pensioners who wanted to talk to me, but younger people who saw their parents and grandparents struggle to make ends meet on an income well below the national minimum wage. The introduction of the minimum wage is something the Labour government is rightly proud of. However, if the government recognizes the need for a minimum income, why does it resolutely refuse to recognize the need for a minimum pension, one that guarantees a decent standard of living?

Shortly after the Westminster rally I was approached by the affable and imaginative Mike MacCormack who makes the documentary series *Counterblast* for BBC 2. He asked if I would be interested in making a documentary on the pensions issue. This was a wonderful opportunity both to maintain the momentum of the campaign and explain the issues to a wider audience. I accepted Mac's offer with alacrity. We spent several weeks discussing various ideas, determined to achieve maximum impact. This was followed by a hectic shooting schedule of just one week with everyone involved working frantically, but good-humouredly, to finish on time. The documentary, *Old Rage*, was broadcast in February 2001 and a half hour's on-line debate followed. There was a flood of e-mails, far more than could possibly be answered in half an hour, and over the next few weeks the National Pensioners' Convention received hundreds of enquiries about membership. I was continually surprised by how many people saw the documentary. Some weeks later I was at Downing Street when I bumped into Anji Hunter, who congratulated me on it. Tony was just coming into the room at that point and on hearing her turned on his heel muttering, 'Not you as well!'

After the documentary was shown I received many invitations to address pensioners' meetings. I tried to do as many as possible, particularly as an election was imminent, and I wanted to impress on people the importance of using their vote and demonstrating the power and size of the pensioner constituency. I also thoroughly enjoyed these meetings and the opportunity to talk to people about the issues. For one meeting, at Redcar, Steph and I travelled to the north-east together. The rally began after lunch and as I took my seat on the platform I was somewhat surprised to see the Conservative Member of Parliament, Alan Duncan, walk through the hall and even more surprised when he sat down in the front row next to my wife. The chairman had barely finished his opening remarks before Duncan's young assistant leapt to his feet, demanding the meeting allow Duncan to address it. The chairman pointed out that this was not a political rally but a pensioners' rally, and asked the young man to sit down and be quiet. Alan Wright, the local BBC radio presenter, made a funny and telling speech and then it was my turn. I did my usual barn-storming urging the pensioners not only to organize and fight, but also to vote in the forthcoming election. I was followed by the leader of the local council who happened to be a Labour politician.

Throughout this and the question and answer session that followed Duncan remained in his seat, but finally, unable to contain himself further, he got to his feet and asked again for the opportunity to speak. Quite reasonably he pointed out that a Labour politician had given his point of view. In a whispered aside the chairman asked me how I felt about this request and at that point I could see no reason not to agree. Taking the microphone on the floor of the hall, the first thing Duncan did was to make an extremely rude comment about my eldest daughter's marriage. My wife has been a positive influence, finally persuading me at this late stage in my life that acting on a rush of blood to the head is rarely advisable. Getting even rather than mad is ultimately a much more satisfying and intelligent strategy. However, on this occasion anger got the better of me and, rising to my feet, I demanded from the platform that Duncan apologize. The meeting was in uproar as outraged pensioners also demanded that Duncan apologize. When the chairman finally restored order he reprimanded Duncan and made it clear he would have three minutes to speak and not a second more. How could a senior Tory figure throw away an opportunity to outline and explain policy to potential voters, preferring instead to try and score cheap, personal points? Steph later told me that Duncan and his companions assumed she was my minder from Millbank and throughout the meeting talked in loud whispers of the need for the Labour Party to keep me on a tight leash. Steph did not bother to disabuse them of their mistake, preferring instead to let them revel in their silliness. A short time later an alternative version of the 'Duncan incident' appeared in *The Daily Telegraph*. This version claimed I had leapt from the platform to assault Duncan physically. Sadly the days when I might have considered such a feat are over, but it was still flattering to have that story told, wrong though it was.

In 1999 I was invited to address the *Tribune* rally at the Labour Party conference, to be held that year in Bournemouth. The invitation was extended over an earlier *Tribune* dinner at the Gay Hussar restaurant in Soho. Travelling down to London I arrived at Euston station and spotted Alex Ferguson, the legendary and gifted manager of Manchester United football club, standing alone on the concourse waiting for his driver. 1999 was the year United won the triple crown, but at this point they had secured only the premiership title and Ferguson was on his way to meet up with his team, who were to play in the FA Cup the next day. I was startled by the extraordinary effect he had on my usually calm and rational wife. She was so thrilled to meet him she could only stand there dumbstruck, beaming in admiration. Steph's reaction was all the more surprising as she is not even really interested in football. She did manage to pull herself together enough to ask for his autograph for her youngest son, William, a keen Manchester United fan. I am of course a devoted Liverpool fan, but even so I have huge admiration for Ferguson.

Later that evening I enjoyed dinner at the Gay Hussar with, amongst others, Steve Bell, the *Guardian* cartoonist, Mark Seddon, the editor of *Tribune* and Michael Foot. At one point during the dinner Michael asked Steph how she coped living with me. Laughing she replied that on the whole it was fine, but she often found herself in more trouble than ever before in her life. Guilty by association! Michael was delighted to hear this and said he could quite easily believe it was true. So much for the loyalty of friends and partners! Michael was on good form and conversation ranged across many issues and I was delighted when Mark Seddon asked me to speak at the *Tribune* rally. I decided to use the opportunity to express my point of view on the abolition of the House of Lords. It is my opinion that there is absolutely no justification for inherited privilege; nor do I have any sympathy for the arguments in favour of retaining the monarch as head of state. The establishment of a republic cannot come quickly enough for me.

The constitutional changes devolving power away from London by allowing Scotland a parliament and Wales an assembly were brave and radical moves by the new government. Like many others I was hopeful that this same radicalism would lead to the final abolition of hereditary power and the creation of a fully elected second chamber. I was not only angry, therefore, but also deeply disappointed at the tinkering rather than full-blooded change that the government tried to pass off as reform of the House of Lords. I believe in many ways the current situation is now worse than the one before and I find myself in the extraordinary and uncomfortable position of almost being nostalgic for the old system. The large parliamentary majority enjoyed by the Labour government has meant little effective opposition in the House of Commons. With the Lords full of hereditary peers there was at least some spasmodic opposition to the government. With the Second House made up mainly of government appointees, unknown or obscure individuals with seemingly nothing to gain from asking questions or forcing debate, its teeth are completely drawn. I am at a loss to understand either its purpose or justification.

Women are poorly represented in the House of Commons. There are many reasons for this, but the more obvious are male-dominated structures and traditions that take little account of life outside the House – simple things like commitments to family and children. If the government seized the opportunity for genuine and radical reform it could also seize the opportunity to create afresh an institution that reflected the reality of modern life and thus actively encourage more women into the political system. Then finally perhaps this country might begin to move towards a truly democratic and egalitarian representative system. Coming as I do from a family dominated by strong-minded and intelligent women, I feel that the absence of women from politics and leading roles in society generally is a huge waste of talent and potential.

Sally Aprahamian is a gifted director and I was fortunate enough to work with her in the television series *Extremely Dangerous*. Sean Bean played the lead and our mutual passion for football meant we always had a lot to talk about. My great friends Glyn Owen and Ron Donachie also had parts, so the long hours of waiting around that are so much a part of the process of filming became a good deal more bearable. Glyn's character dies and there was a scene where he was laid out in an open coffin whilst his daughter and another character talk over his body. The young actress playing his daughter experienced some difficulty with the scene and several takes were needed. By lunchtime success was still elusive and it was decided to have a break and try again later. Clearly, as Glyn's character was dead he was required to do no more than lie very still and make no noise. With this in mind, Glyn decided it was perfectly safe to have a couple of pints with his lunch. Returning to the set he climbed back into the coffin and the other two actors went through their lines. It is a dreadful experience as an actor when you cannot get the lines right. Panic makes it even more difficult. However, a lunch break seemed to ease nerves all round and after only a few takes the actress was moving fluently through the scene. Tension mounted and people held their breath, hoping this time she would make it. Suddenly Glyn, who had fallen asleep, began to snore completely ruining the take as everyone, cast and crew, fell about laughing. Eventually, the scene was completed with the dead lying quietly and the living remembering their lines.

By now I had recovered my health and happiness. I was revelling in new and exciting job offers and for the first time in years, really since Pat died, I felt confident and positive about my future. Steph helped me to achieve a sense of serenity I did not realize I might possess and which I know came as a surprise to many people. Perhaps it is our very different characters that make our relationship work, but whatever it is I am grateful to her for turning my life around.

About five miles into the journey down the motorway to Bournemouth to speak at the *Tribune* rally the mobile telephone began to ring. It was my agent and he urged Steph to make me head back home as I was called for an interview at the Royal Exchange theatre in Manchester. I had never worked there before and insisted on driving another few miles whilst I pondered the chance of a successful interview. Finally, Steph's logic prevailed – if I did not go to the interview the chance of success would be nil. Turning the car round we headed back to Manchester and I went straight to the interview, giving me no time to be nervous. I was offered a part in Jim Cartwright's new play – so new he had not at that point finished writing it – which was to go into production in the next few weeks. The play, *Prize Night*, was directed by Greg Hersov who at times must have felt his sanity severely threatened by the strain of rehearsing the unruly cast. The cast were one of the best groups of people I have ever worked with. Funny, friendly and supportive, we have continued to see each other socially after the play ended. Our most recent *Prize Night* outing was to the wedding of Jenny James, who went on to play Gina the barmaid in *Coronation Street*. Jenny was offered the role of Gina after a producer from Granada Television saw her performance in *Prize Night*. It is a terrific play, a unique theatrical experience for all those involved in it.

Jim Cartwright told me he had written a part specially for me and at the first read-through I turned the pages to my first scene. It was almost a blank page. Neatly typed at the top was 'Tony's Karaoke Scene'. I was assured there was no reason to worry, the scene was still under construction. With only days to go before the previews I had a meeting with Greg and Jim. Greg and I fully expected Jim to produce a script, but instead he suggested we improvise most of the scene. My reaction was a mixture of panic and excitement and I am not at all certain which of those was the dominant emotion. The professionally generous and lovely actress Sue Twist played the role of my wife and we had a good time with the improvisation. Sue and I never played the same scene twice and the technical staff would gather at the back of the theatre each evening to watch what we would do. A few months later Sue won the best actress category at the *Manchester Evening News* theatre awards for her performance as a different character in the play.

During the run of the play I shared a dressing room with Alan Gear, all twenty-three stone of him. My ribs would ache from laughing at his constant barrage of jokes and wisecracks. Alan and I developed a routine on matinée days, taking it in turn to go out between performances and bring back sandwiches and assorted goodies whilst the other rested. I mentioned to Alan that on the following week's matinée day I would achieve twenty years of sobriety – a significant personal milestone. Generously, on the anniversary afternoon although it was my turn to go shopping Alan insisted I rested. Within a few minutes of Alan leaving I received a call from the stage door saying I had a visitor. Unwillingly, I went to meet my visitor only to be told she was waiting in the canteen. Increasingly grumpy about the inconsiderate person who would disturb my rest, I stomped into the canteen. I found the entire company, my wife and close friends assembled for a surprise celebration party Alan had arranged. Completely overwhelmed by the warmth of my reception, I cried.

This was not to be my only emotional experience during the run of *Prize Night*. One evening before the performance a telephone call came through from Gale. She wanted to tell me some family news before I was besieged by reporters. Cherie was pregnant. Cherie had not told me sooner as she was concerned for Steph and how she might feel. Only a few weeks earlier Steph had needed a hysterectomy, a great worry for all of us. I was stunned by Gale's news, but also thrilled. The next day I telephoned Gale at her home in Oxford to find out all about it. I had some difficulty hearing what she was saying and after several minutes I asked what was wrong with her voice – why was she talking so quietly? 'Because I'm sitting on the floor hiding from the press and I don't want them to hear me,' she replied. 'Why don't you just pull the curtains?' I said. 'Well if I do that they will see me and know for certain I'm here.'

It turned out that, on hearing my voice on her answering machine, Gale had crawled on her hands and knees to the telephone to speak to me. I could not help laughing at the image this conjured, but poor Gale was having a difficult time. During our conversation I asked the inevitable question – how did the pregnancy happen? Gale laughed and told me that when Cherie broke the news to her, she had asked the same question. 'Oh mother, how do you think it happened? The usual way of course!' was our daughter's mildly exasperated response.

Although obviously very tired Cherie coped well with her pregnancy. There is a history of late pregnancies in our family. I remember when I was a teenager my mother's sister-in-law, my aunt Alice, became pregnant at an age when she was old enough to believe at first she was experiencing the 'change of life'. The reality of her condition was a source of great embarrassment to my aunt – people would know she was still enjoying sex in her forties – and she tried for some time to keep it a secret. Thankfully, social attitudes are now more relaxed and enlightened. There was much speculation in the newspapers about the baby's name. Early on in Cherie's pregnancy I talked to Frank Brown, a close friend of mine, and told him I thought Cherie and Tony would choose 'Leo' if the baby was a boy. Frank and I discussed at length the possibility of placing a bet on the basis of my hunch. Although at that time I did not have inside information we regretfully concluded that if I was right no one would believe us. Even if Frank placed the bet it might still be traced back to me and we decided it might possibly be construed as insider trading.

When Cherie went into labour Gale telephoned me from Downing Street to tell me. Luckily for Cherie it was not a particularly long labour, but during that afternoon and evening it seemed to last an eternity as I hovered around the telephone waiting for Gale's calls keeping me updated on progress. When Gale called me shortly after midnight on 20 May to say we had a new grandson I experienced a rush of happiness and relief that everything had gone well. Turning off the telephone, which was already beginning to hop with calls from the press, I finally went to bed. The next morning we got up to find a press encampment just outside our back door. The media interest in the birth of Leo was extraordinary. Staying out of sight I telephoned Fiona Miller, Cherie's assistant, and asked how they wanted me to deal with the press. Between us Fiona and I constructed a statement and I then went outside to read it to the assembled media. The year 2000 turned out to be a more than usually eventful one for my family. My daughter Sarah married in June, with her sisters Emma and Joanna among the bridesmaids. Sarah then contributed to my growing number of grandchildren when she gave birth to her daughter Alexandra later that autumn.

It has been my great good fortune to enjoy a warm and close relationship with my stepsons. An added bonus is finally being able to discuss at endless length and on a daily basis, football. For this pleasure I have been prepared to overlook their keen and inexplicable support for Manchester United and their resolute determination not to see the joy of being a Liverpool fan. In the spring of 2000 my stepson Sam was writing a project for his History A-level on the effects of the debate on nuclear weaponry within the Labour Party. His hypothesis was that from the end of the Second World War this issue was incredibly divisive, with the Party polarized by the debate. His hypothesis went on to suggest that the nuclear issue was still unresolved within the Party – it was simply no longer discussed. Remembering my old comrade and friend Tony Benn was Secretary of State for Energy during the seventies, I arranged to take Sam over to his Chesterfield constituency to meet him and discuss the project. Greeting us warmly and immediately arranging mugs of tea all round, Tony then spent more than an hour talking to Sam, answering his questions, outlining and explaining his standpoint on the nuclear debate. He talked about his time in the Cabinet and the compromises and arguments that had taken place. It was a typically generous action and I for one will miss Tony Benn's presence on the political stage. His retirement from politics, although inevitable, leaves a vacuum; and whether you agree with him or not, his point of view is always interesting and certainly worth listening to.

By the end of the year all talk was of a general election the following May, but it was already clear that, barring mishaps of a truly cosmic nature, Labour was on course to win an historic full second term. Yet despite this Labour voters from very different backgrounds told me of their frustration that the government had failed to live up to the high hopes and expectations generated in May 1997. Perhaps too many of us had dared to dream an impossible dream and could only, in the light of cold reality, be doomed to disappointment or, worse, cynicism. Whatever, it seemed to me it would be more in hope than expectation that many would still vote Labour if they voted at all. Unfortunately that appeared to be the position too many people found themselves in on election day as the lack of real political opposition removed choice. It was a good day for Labour, but I am far from certain it was a good day for democracy.

Epilogue

7 June 2001

> I have fought the good fight
> I have stayed the course
> And I have kept the faith

2 Timothy

Sitting at home in Broadbottom waiting for the election results to start coming in, I had time to reflect on the differences from that night in May 1997. As then, Cherie invited me to go to Trimdon for Tony's count, but I decided not to go – the experience would have been something of an anticlimax after the joy and exhilaration of the 1997 triumph. By almost unanimous consent the general election of June 2001 was the most boring in living memory. Everyone blamed everyone else for a record low turnout, but it was clear for whatever reason that voter apathy won the day. There was an incredible difference in atmosphere and intent between 1 May 1997 and 7 June 2001. Although the surge of excitement and self-confidence that swept through the country following Labour's first election victory was clearly unrepeatable, it seemed almost as if something was lost along the way to the 2001 election. There was a sense of dejected inevitability to the minimal interest levels during the campaign and the ensuing low turnout at the polling stations. The devastating outbreak of foot and mouth disease put back the election from May to June and perhaps some momentum was lost. During a conversation with Cherie the plight of the farmers came up and I told her that in my opinion it would only be reasonable to delay the general election. Whilst I do not have a natural sympathy with farmers, and particularly the National Farmers' Union, on a train journey home from London I was shocked to see field after empty field. It was almost as if the countryside was in mourning. It would have taken an incredible insensitivity not to recognize this.

My absence filming in the Isle of Man during the 1997 general election campaign was, I recognized, a considerable relief to Millbank, concerned that I may have a negative impact on potential Labour voters. That is I might, in tabloid parlance, behave like a 'loose cannon'. This time, however, Cherie asked for my help some months before the election was called and the start of the campaign saw me back in Crosby, where it all began. On my birthday in October 2001 I reached my biblical entitlement of three score years and ten, an age that at times I did not expect, in all honesty, to achieve. Waiting in the Labour Party committee rooms just down the road from my old family home in Ferndale Road, I thought about the long, complex and often stony road that brought me back to this place. Life can be a strange business – as someone once said, life is what happens to you whilst you are busy making other plans. So much has happened to me. Heartache, pain, laughter, tears and despite everything much joy and love. During the long and agonizing days when I lay in a hospital bed recovering from my burns I came to understand that life can still offer choices even at the darkest of moments: even when we believe ourselves robbed of everything. My life was in ashes, but my ability to give and receive much love remained intact and my socialist conscience still burned fiercely. I had a choice: to continue with and ultimately succumb to the bitterness and self-induced destruction of drunkenness or to grab on to and make the most of this new chance of life I was offered. Alcohol provides no answers, no solutions. Of course, I still make mistakes, still get things wrong – life is like that. But I love my family and I am eternally grateful still to be here with all of them.

But even the plans of a superannuated daydreamer like me would not have thought of this one. Standing waiting for Cherie with her old schoolfriend and Leo's godmother Kath, we chatted about their school days and the hopes and dreams of their adolescence, giggling at the thought that Cherie clearly got far more than she would have bargained for. As usual Cherie was running late, but her genuine delight at seeing Kath and me made the waiting crowd burst into spontaneous applause. One of the things I love about my eldest daughter is that she has remained, despite all the pressures and temptations, a genuinely nice person who connects with the people around her. Inevitably for a short while after she moved into Downing Street she became a little grand. Being referred to as 'the Duchess of Downing Street' by the rest of the family meant it was a phase she grew out of very quickly and she was soon back to her true self again.

Part of Cherie's mission in Crosby was to meet young women, potential first-time voters, and persuade them of the importance of using their vote. Walking into the pub where Cherie was to meet the group of women, Kath told me it had been one of their favourite watering holes as young women. Certainly Cherie was clearly very comfortable in her surroundings. As she chatted to the group I watched as they reacted warmly and positively to her. I said to someone standing near me, 'What a campaigner she is.' He responded, 'What a chip off the old block!' Laughing, I stumbled backwards and into the formidable frame of a female Special Branch officer. The officer was not pleased, but then neither was I as I bruised myself on her barely concealed weaponry. Later, when we returned to the hotel where Cherie and Tony were based in Liverpool, I was astounded at the number of armed officers both inside and outside the hotel. I am constantly fearful for my daughter and her family and whilst on the one hand I am relieved to see the level of protection they are given, on the other hand that protection is a reminder of the dangers of modern political leadership. It is also, I think, a sad reflection on and indictment of modern life that such protection is necessary.

Walking out of the lift on the floor where Tony and Cherie were temporarily encamped, Kath and I stepped aside to let the Swedish Prime Minister and his party pass. Going into the suite we found Tony seizing the opportunity to grab a quick nap, but opening his eyes he smiled a greeting. We all sat around drinking tea and swapping family gossip for about half an hour before Tony and Cherie had to get changed for a television debate on the set of the Channel Four soap opera *Brookside*. As Kath and I were leaving Tony asked me if I knew the current storyline on *Brookside*. Unfortunately, I could not help as it is not a programme I watch. I am more of a *Coronation Street* fan myself.

The following weekend I went to help with the campaign in the Bury constituency of David Chator. At the constituency office I sat drinking a mug of tea and talking to the candidate, but Steph, who was with me, disappeared. Eventually deciding to look for her, I found her helping to tie ribbons to campaign balloons and being told off by other helpers for not making the ribbon quite long enough. Those balloons were to prove a particular trial to Steph that day. Setting off down the street to the market it was a dry but breezy day and we were all in high, good spirits. A Labour Party stall set up on the street near the market was already busy handing out leaflets and badges when we arrived. The plan was that David Chator would work his way through the market talking to people, encouraging them to vote for him on 7 June and I would accompany him. Various other Labour Party workers would also come along with us to hand out leaflets, stickers and bin sacks with the legend 'It's Time to Bin the Tories' emblazoned across them. Steph was presented with an enormous bunch of balloons and asked to give them out. Although David Chator was elected for the first time in 1997 he has clearly worked hard in his first term and was popular with his constituents. Every few yards people were stopping him to shake his hand and wish him well.

Glancing over to Steph I could see that the balloons were attracting the attention of the younger members of the constituency and despite the difficulties created by the breeze Steph appeared to be dealing with the situation. Concentrating on my own task, it was some time before I saw her again. It was only when someone suggested to me that my wife might be in some need of assistance that I located the red balloons and made my way towards them. It was the insistence on long ribbons that was the essential cause of the problem. That and the breeze. As I arrived there was a small boy standing next to Steph tugging on the bottom of her coat.

'Hey missus can I 'ave one of them balloons?'

To my astonishment a voice made echoey from being stuck inside a bunch of balloons replied, 'Yes of course you can. Just as soon as I can get the ribbons from round my neck and give you one.'

Another tug on the coat. 'OK, but can I 'ave one for my little sister as well?'

Parting the balloons I discovered my flustered wife, her face more red than the balloons she was holding. The difficulty of holding so many balloons in a breeze meant that a few had become entwined around her neck and, trying to pull them away, she had only made matters worse. As I started to rescue her, the little boy again piped up, 'Can you two 'urry up? Me mum's shouting me.' Releasing Steph I handed two balloons to the little boy who ran off to join his mother. I looked at Steph and burst out laughing, but at that moment my disgruntled wife could not see what was so funny. Just then the little boy returned. 'Me mum says can I 'ave two more balloons? I've let go of the others.' Steph started to laugh and we both walked with the boy back to his mother and presented her with two balloons – and a leaflet and stickers and a bin sack. We also extracted a promise that she would vote for David Chator. She reckoned it was the least she could do after Steph's experience. Another Labour vote secured!

Leaving Bury market later that morning we travelled to a different part of the constituency, Ramsbottom. Members of the local party met David, Steph and me and once again we were given leaflets and stickers to distribute. This time, however, Steph chose to eschew the balloons. Once again a Saturday market was in full swing, but the strategy was a little different – slightly more low-key – as Ramsbottom is not natural Labour territory. Still, our reception was on the whole positive, but things 'hotted up' somewhat when the local Conservatives also arrived to canvass the market. I was interested, from an anthropological perspective, to observe their strategy. Whilst the Labour Party workers circulated around, stopping people and chatting, taking the campaign to the electorate, the Conservatives took a position in the centre of the market and handed leaflets to people as they passed, waiting for potential voters to approach them. I could not decide if this was because they were too grand or too nervous to approach people; or if they knew the game was already up and were just going through the motions; or perhaps the Conservatives have simply lost the knack of effective campaigning.

On that point, the leadership election that followed the Conservative general election defeat appeared to be no more than an exercise in wanton self-destruction that makes the near-implosion of the Labour Party in the early eighties look like a friendly exchange of views. The Tories now clearly need their Neil Kinnock, but unfortunately for them they do not have anyone in their party who remotely approaches Kinnock's level of vision, drive and inclusive ambition for his party. Any idea that the right-wing Kenneth Clarke or the even more right-wing and odious Iain Duncan Smith might bring unity to the Party, or that with either of them as leader the Tories would once again be acceptable to the electorate, is utterly ludicrous. This country has moved on since the days of Margaret Thatcher and it is increasingly clear that Thatcher is to the Conservatives what the Winter of Discontent was to the Labour Party. She is a major factor in all that makes them unelectable. I believe it will take someone of greater moral and political courage than that possessed by either Clarke or Duncan Smith finally to exorcize Thatcher's ghost and grasp the enormous challenge of reform and modernization of the Tory Party. But on that sunny Saturday morning in Ramsbottom I do not think any of us, no matter what our political persuasion, could have envisaged the size of the coming Labour landslide.

It was almost lunchtime and after several hours of canvassing I was famished. There was a baker's stall on the market with some pork pies tantalizingly displayed. Succumbing to the demands of my stomach, I bought a pie and began to eat it with relieved enjoyment. Out of nowhere two elderly women appeared and began loudly to berate me for eating on the street. At first I thought it was some kind of joke by the other Party workers so I offered the women a bite of my pie. Clinging to each other for support in their disgust their remonstrations became even louder as I offered them a Labour Party leaflet. By now thoroughly irritated by their rudeness, I suggested to them that I could make a note of their names as possible Labour voters. The horror of this possibility almost made them terminate their tirade, but these women were clearly made of sterner stuff and after several deep gasps of air they returned to the attack. Surprisingly, they obviously felt they had every right to behave in this way and were also, not so surprisingly, clearly enjoying the attention they were drawing to themselves. Shoving the last of the pork pie into my mouth and moving closer to them I said, 'I suppose a kiss is out of the question then?' My pie-filled mouth and wolfish leer had the desired effect and sent the pair scuttling over to the Conservative Party workers still grouped together in the middle of the market. I watched as, with pale faces and shaking hands, the two women pointed out the demon in their midst. I had clearly lived up (or would it be down?) to all their expectations. Whatever, David Chator increased his majority at the election.

Happily oblivious to all this campaigning, my youngest grandson Leo celebrated his first birthday on 20 May. I travelled down to London with Steph and my youngest stepson William on the weekend of his birthday. With Cherie we attended a Labour Party rally for pensioners on the Saturday afternoon. The popular actor Richard Wilson was also there to lend his support to the Labour campaign and we were greeted enthusiastically by the large audience. After spending time shaking hands and chatting to people I left the rally with my family and we accompanied Cherie back to Downing Street. We spent the night there before going on to Chequers the next day for Leo's birthday party.

Leo really is the most happy and placid little boy. Bright as a button, he is doted on by his older brothers and sister. Euan took great delight in buying a very noisy birthday gift for his baby brother – a guitar so Leo could practise with his father. It was interesting to see how many of the older children also enjoyed making a racket with the toy guitar! There is a swimming pool at Chequers and lots of Leo's friends from the swimming club he attends were invited to his party. Cherie is a strong swimmer and as a child she successfully took part in many competitions; Leo is also clearly very happy in the water. After the swim there was a proper birthday tea with crumpets, jelly and cake. Standing watching the children enjoying themselves I chatted to one of the servicemen who staff Chequers and he told me how much they enjoy having the children there. It was a delightful change from the normal routine.

On Monday morning it was back to the campaign trail for Tony. Cherie went with him as often as her court appearances would allow, but believing the general election would be in May, she had scheduled a case expected to last many weeks for June when she thought the election would be over. The scale of the farming crisis was completely unanticipated by everyone. The pace and number of my campaign commitments has now begun to slow down, but I still get the same buzz I have always had during a general election. As much as I fear lack of opposition to an over-strong government, I feel apathy is equally the enemy of democracy. I urged people to use their vote, and particularly when I spoke to pensioner groups both before and during the election I argued it was important to demonstrate to the government the strength of pensioner power and unity. Pensioners are a significant proportion of the electorate. They are also the age group more likely to vote. Turning out en masse would underline these factors and help to maintain the pressure on the government over the state pension.

Tony Benn was not the only long-serving Member of Parliament to retire at this election. My own constituency MP, Tom Pendry, also stood down. Tom and I have not always seen eye to eye over the years, but despite our occasional differences he has helped me with more than one difficult situation. He was also a hard-working and committed constituency MP. More significantly for my family, it was Tom Pendry whom Tony Blair first approached for advice when he decided he would like to run for Parliament and Tom was pleased to help. Pendry announced his decision to retire in plenty of time to enable a full selection procedure to be implemented, thus avoiding the controversial and extremely unpopular practice by Millbank of 'parachuting' a candidate into the seat. There was no shortage of applicants for this very safe Labour seat and two candidates in particular stood out: James Purnell, who eventually won the nomination, and Jane Milton, a very bright and able young woman who came second in the vote.

Early on in his campaign Purnell secured the backing and support of Roy Oldham, the influential and seemingly irremovable leader of Tameside council, without whose support the nomination could not be won. Oldham and I share a deep mutual antipathy, if not hatred, and this left Purnell in something of a quandary. At the time he was working in Downing Street and it was therefore likely that Tony and

Cherie would ask me if he had visited. Eventually, Purnell arrived at my home one Sunday afternoon, having been driven over by Oldham, who remained in his car out of sight around the corner. Unaware of this I was prepared to chat for some time until, finally noticing Purnell's discomfort, I asked what was wrong. After explaining he left, although to be fair he did visit a number of times prior to the selection meeting. After that we did not see him again until late afternoon on polling day and that was completely unexpected.

Steph and I were visiting our friend Beth who lives on the main road through Broadbottom. I went outside to have a cigarette and Beth's son Matthew, a good friend of my stepson Sam, came outside with me to talk. We looked up in surprise as a passing car suddenly squealed to a halt, executed a life-threatening U-turn and stopped in front of us. Out climbed James Purnell. This was the first time I had seen him during the election campaign and lost no time in pointing this out. Steph, coming out of the house to see what all the noise was about, spotted James and said, 'Oh you're too late now. I thought you weren't bothered so I've just been down and voted Liberal Democrat.' Purnell's face was a picture of shock until he realized she was joking and he immediately began to claim he had of course tried to visit us, but we were always out when he called. Tom Pendry made a point of visiting me at least a couple of times during an election campaign and it was effort like this throughout the constituency that ensured him a large personal vote. Although James Purnell was elected to Parliament the Labour majority in this seat was several thousand votes down from 1997. It seems the political loneliness and disappointment of the Labour Party's wilderness years are, for some, already a distant memory.

Purnell told us that Anji Hunter had just telephoned him to say some of his constituency workers should now be sent over to Oldham, where Phil Woolas was fighting to retain his seat. Labour Party helpers there were concerned the electorate was not turning out to vote, despite the fact that the National Front Party was mounting a strong challenge. Only a few weeks earlier Oldham had been the scene of race riots provoked by the National Front. Any idea that this vile organization might gain any political capital or credibility was utterly repugnant and Steph and I decided we would also go and help in the constituency. I do not think I have ever been to Oldham when it was not cold and this June evening was no exception. We arrived at the Party election office, shivering. Within a few minutes we were back on the street clutching a list of those people who when canvassed declared an intention to vote Labour, but who, according to returns from the polling station, had not yet voted. Our task was to call at their homes and ask them to vote.

Late afternoon or early evening is not a particularly good time to be calling on people. Either they have just got in from work and are tired and wanting to make dinner or, if you want to make yourself really unpopular, you call just when people are settling in front of the television to watch their favourite soap opera. We avoided most of these pitfalls because most people were not at home – or not answering the door. Of those I did speak to most had already voted, but it was worth the effort when I persuaded twenty or more people to come out and vote. At one house a young, attractive woman opened the door just enough to be able to peer round. I asked if she was a Labour supporter and when she nodded assent I then asked if she had voted. She told me she was planning to visit the polling station shortly, but I would have to wait. She was getting dressed and did not have any knickers on. She was wearing only a blouse and that was the reason she could not open the door any further. I began to laugh, but seeing my wife approaching I muttered something about there being nothing wrong with my timing and beat a hasty retreat down the garden path. As we finished our list I saw the young woman, now fully clothed, and she waved and called out that she was on her way to vote. Canvassing certainly has its moments.

Back at the campaign headquarters the mood was determinedly upbeat and optimistic, but there was still a frantic, last-minute effort to get out the last of the vote. People were rushing in and out checking returns from the polling stations around the constituency and happily there was a continuous stream of reinforcements arriving to help. Relieved to be warm again, and rewarded with a mug of tea for my efforts, I chatted to other workers. Almost inevitably, the conversation turned to the subject of John Prescott, who earlier in the campaign had punched a demonstrator who had thrown an egg at him from uncomfortably close quarters. I do not think anyone blamed Prescott for retaliating – rather, there was much sympathy for him and agreement that his action was probably the single most exciting incident in the whole campaign. It was then I remembered that it was in this constituency in 1997 that Prescott and I almost came to blows. Clearly, he finds election campaigning a little stressful.

Arriving home Steph and I changed into pyjamas and dressing gowns and settled down in front of the television to watch the election results come in. Before half past ten the exit polls were predicting another landslide for Labour and meltdown for the Conservatives. Despite the predictions it was still essential for a political junkie like me to stay up until the early hours of the morning and see for myself as events unfolded. I watched Tony and Cherie at the count in Trimdon. This time Tony waited for the results as Prime Minister. At the count in 1997 it was all to come – then, he had still to wait a few more hours for John Major to concede defeat. By midnight the television commentators were talking up the smallest crisis or event, desperate to generate some excitement. When the election results were declared in Hartlepool I think many people experienced their election night moment. Peter Mandelson's acknowledgement of his re-election was described in several newspapers the following day as the Gloria Gaynor of Hartlepool singing 'I Will Survive'. At one point Steph was so embarrassed for him she actually got up to leave the room before realizing that we could turn over or switch off the television. But I watched his entire performance in a state of horrified fascination. Like a rabbit snared by the headlights of a car, I could not tear my eyes away. On a purely human level I did feel a degree of sympathy for this man. Politically, I felt only grim satisfaction. Mandelson was utterly ruthless in his political ambition and he was finally paying the price for all the resentment he accrued over the years. I believe his speech finally demonstrated that, while he had won the battle to retain his seat, he had lost the war to acquire any political credibility.

By three o'clock on the morning of Friday 8 June the waiting was over. Labour had won an historic full second term. For most of my lifetime, apart from the golden periods of 1945 and again in the sixties, the Labour Party has struggled to convince the voting public it is a credible party of power. The Conservatives have assumed the mantle of government almost as their given right, and after the misery of the 1979 general election and the internecine warfare that followed it was hard to believe at times that Labour would ever again be a political force. The bitter disappointment of losing the 1992 general election reinforced those anxieties and even in 1997, when it was clear we would win, there was still a campaign to be fought. Labour still had to win an election and form a government. In 2001 it was no contest. The assumption that the Conservatives were the natural party of government was no longer applicable. This is the goal I have spent my entire political life fighting for, but at moments during this campaign I was left wondering what the fight was about. What's left?

Something that has remained unchanged over my life is my enduring close sympathy with and commitment to the Labour Party, but I recognized very clearly during Tony's first term as Prime Minister that after a lifetime of political engagement with the Party I no longer felt part of what was happening. Rather like the moment one realizes one is getting old when policemen start to look like schoolboys, I looked around at the make-up of the new government and realized I knew very few of them. The old guard with whom I went into battle were gone, but I remained optimistic that the social and moral values that have always underpinned the Labour Party would be carried forward with determination and integrity by this next generation. I would have to admit in all honesty that in some ways I have been disappointed.

Politically a big difference between Tony Blair and myself is that, for the most part, he will seek consensus whereas, even my closest friends would admit, consensus is not part of my lexicon. Looking back over my experience of political activism it struck me that for most of it I have been engaged in confrontation; but then my lifetime has seen enormous social and political change. Without the courage and tenacity of political giants like Nye Bevan, Clement Attlee, Michael Foot, Barbara Castle and Tony Benn those changes would not have happened. We should not forget just how radical the introduction of the National Health Service and the Welfare State were. They symbolized a seismic shift in our attitudes to and understanding of social justice. Tony Blair inherited a situation where many of the key aims of the Labour Party have been achieved, but that does not mean there is nothing more to do. Perhaps I am in danger of becoming a cliché, complaining about the strategies and innovations of those coming after, but in my defence I do accept the need for the continuous development and evolution of the Party to embrace modern realities. Having said that, the reality of poverty does not change, the reality of deprivation and inequality does not change and it is my steadfast and heartfelt belief that the Labour Party was founded to address these grim problems.

I find the current dash for the middle ground deeply frustrating. It is my experience that the middle ground holds no space for the poor, deprived and dispossessed. Instead it is the stamping ground for the educated, professional, liberal classes, allowing them to make empathetic noises and gestures whilst utterly failing to grasp the reality of life on the margins. Campaigning with the National Pensioners' Convention has served to underline and reinforce this conviction. Whilst I was making the documentary *Old Rage* I was angered by the iniquities of pensioner poverty and moved by the dignity demonstrated again and again in the face of petty, everyday humiliations. One woman told me her ambition was to be able to walk into a shop and buy herself a new coat – not one from a charity shop, but a brand new, never-worn coat. After a lifetime of work and raising children her reward from the government was retirement lived out on the edge of poverty. Fundamental to democracy is the acknowledgement that we cannot all agree with each other, and realistically the only way forward is to find the common ground that will suit the greatest number of people. However, that said, I refuse to accept that a situation which condemns millions of pensioners to poverty or the humiliation of means-testing serves the interests of any decent people. I am angry with and remain determined to challenge the government's ongoing refusal to deal in a socially fair and economically just manner with the issue of pensions.

Analysis of the political implications of the 2001 election will obviously continue for some time. The low turnout clearly demonstrates substantial voter disengagement with the political process. If this is simply the result of satisfaction with the status quo, then the government can pat itself on the back. If however, as I believe, it is the result of a far deeper problem of cynicism then the government cannot afford complacency even with the enormous parliamentary majority it now enjoys. A government elected on less than fifty per cent of the vote cannot claim to have an overwhelming mandate. But the right-wing manifesto of the Conservatives was rejected. The issues they chose to concentrate on – particularly immigration – did not on the whole reflect the preoccupations and anxieties of the electorate. The performance of the National Front in the two Oldham constituencies was newsworthy not because they posed any significant threat but because they were a blip – an indication of a particular problem and situation. What is clear is that the issues that did engage the electorate during the campaign were predominantly health and education. I believe this is a very positive indication that as a population we have moved on from the self-centred absorption of the Thatcher years and are now beginning to focus on issues that affect us as a community. When the Labour Party was formed over a hundred years ago the fundamental cornerstone of its ambition was political, social and economic equality for all from the cradle to the grave. It is clear from this last general election campaign that the public still looks to the Labour Party to deliver on these traditional values. This is what is left to fight for. I will continue to fight the fight until we reach the promised land.

Index

Index

Index